LEAN AND GREEN COOKBOOK 2021

Harness the full power of "Fueling Hacks Meals"
with 400+ Super Fast, Super Easy, and Enjoyable
Recipes to Lose Weight

by

SARAH ALICIA JONES

To my dear and passionate readers, seekers of novelty, taste, and better health. May you use these new recipes to reach your desired body weight goal and put new energy into being the change you want to see in this extraordinary life.

Contents

Introduction

Lean and green diet is the same as green diet, except it makes use of lean protein sources in place of the high fat ones.

In general, lean protein sources include skinless poultry, fish (e.g. cod and haddock), lean cuts of meat, eggs and vegetable proteins such as lentils and beans.

Some may assume that the lean diet is better for everyone when it comes to losing weight and improving health than a conventional low-fat diet, but the evidence does not yet support this claim. Recent studies show that lean diets have similar results to low fat diets in reducing body weight. Also, they do not show a considerable improvement in the health risk factors like blood lipids, blood pressure and insulin resistance compared to low-fat diets.

Lean and green diet is a special variant of the low-fat diet, which further makes use of lean proteins instead of fat in promoting weight loss and improving health risk. Lean protein sources include skinless poultry, fish (e.g. cod and haddock), lean cuts of meat, eggs and vegetable proteins such as lentils and beans. This kind of diet improves the metabolism by increasing the metabolic rate that speeds up weight loss. It also reduces the risk of obesity, because following the lean and green diet does not increase body fat as much as low-fat diets.

The emphasis is on consuming a small amount of meat and fish that are eaten twice a day, together with other protein sources such as eggs, lentils and beans. The diet includes vegetables in addition to fruits that are rich in vitamins (e.g. carrots). The green food includes different varieties of beans like green lentils, black-eyed peas and soybeans. Lean and Green diet is one of the healthy diets that should be consumed frequently, because it complements all other healthy diets.

The pros of lean and green diet are that it does not increase the risk of obesity, reduces body weight and improves health. The cons of lean and green diet are that it is not very popular and not many people know about it. On the other hand, lean and green diet is a healthy variant of low-fat diet that is low in fat, high in fiber content and rich in nutrients such as vitamins B6, B12 and C. It should be consumed by everyone who wants to follow a healthy diet plan.

The lean and green diet is probably not for everyone, but it is an excellent way to achieve optimal health. It makes the body function better, repairs tissues and fights cancer. Because it is a low-fat diet, it also decreases the risk of heart disease and stroke by regulating cholesterol levels. The lean and green diet is a good source of fiber that reduces the risk of obesity, diabetes, digestive illnesses like constipation and diarrhea. It is also associated with lowering blood pressure levels. People with some medical conditions such as kidney disorders (or other renal diseases) may consult their doctor before following this diet. The lean and green diet is better for the people who need to lose weight quickly. It is also a good way of reducing overall cardiovascular risk. However, this diet is not appropriate for people with kidney diseases, because it requires more protein than their body can optimally use.

Chapter 1. Appetizer and Snack Recipes

1. Pesto Zucchini Noodles

Difficulty: Average
Preparation Time: 10 minutes
Cooking Time: 30 minutes
Servings: 4
Ingredients:

- 4 zucchinis, spiralized (2 green)
- 1 tbsp avocado oil (1/2 condiment)
- 2 garlic cloves, chopped (1/2 condiment)
- 2/3 cup olive oil (1/2 condiment)
- 1/3 cup parmesan cheese, grated (1/2 healthy fat)
- 2 cups fresh basil (1/4 green)
- 1/3 cup almonds (1/2 healthy fat)
- 1/8 tsp. black pepper (1/8 condiment)
- 3/4 tsp. sea salt (1/8 condiment)

Directions:

1. Add zucchini noodles into a colander and sprinkle with 1/4 teaspoon of salt.
2. Cover and let sit for 30 minutes.
3. Drain zucchini noodles well and pat dry.
4. Preheat the oven to 400°F.
5. Place almonds on a parchment-lined baking sheet and bake for 6-8 minutes.
6. Transfer toasted almonds into the food processor and process until coarse.
7. Add olive oil, cheese, basil, garlic, pepper, and remaining salt in a food processor with almonds and process until pesto texture.
8. Cook avocado oil in a large pan over medium-high heat.
9. Add zucchini noodles and cook for 4-5 minutes.
10. Pour pesto over zucchini noodles, mix well, and cook for 1 minute.
11. Serve immediately with baked salmon.

Nutrition:

- 525 Calories
- 47g Fat
- 17g Protein

2. Herbed Wild Rice

Difficulty: Average
Preparation Time: 10 minutes
Cooking Time: 4 to 6 hours
Servings: 8
Ingredients:

- 3 cups wild rice, rinsed and drained (2 lean)
- 6 cups Roasted Vegetable Broth (2 condiment)
- 1/2 teaspoon salt (1/8 condiment)
- 1/2 tsp. dried thyme leaves (1/8 condiment)
- ½ tsp. dried basil leaves (1/4 green)
- 1 bay leaf (1/4 green)
- 1/3 cup fresh flat-leaf parsley (1/4 green)

Directions:

1. In a 6-quart slow cooker, mix the wild rice, vegetable broth, salt, thyme, basil, and bay leaf.
2. Close and cook over low heat for 4 to 6 hours.
3. You can cook this dish longer until the wild rice pops, taking about 7 to 8 hours.
4. Remove and discard the bay leaf.
5. Stir in the parsley and serve.

Nutrition:

- 258 Calories
- 2g Fat
- 6g Protein

3. Barley Risotto

Difficulty: Easy
Preparation Time: 15 minutes
Cooking Time: 7 to 8 hours
Servings: 8
Ingredients:

- 2 1/4 cups hulled barley, rinsed (2 green)
- 4 garlic cloves, minced (1 condiment)
- 1 (8-ounce) package button mushrooms, chopped (1 healthy fat)
- 6 cups low-sodium vegetable broth (2 condiment)
- ½ tsp. dried marjoram leaves (1/4 green)
- 1/8 tsp. black pepper (1/4 condiment)
- 2/3 cup grated Parmesan cheese (1/2 healthy fat)

Directions:

1. In a 6-quart slow cooker, mix the barley, garlic, mushrooms, broth, marjoram, and pepper.
2. Cover and cook on low for 7 to 8 hours, or until the barley has absorbed most of the liquid and is tender, and the vegetables are tender.
3. Stir in the Parmesan cheese and serve.

Nutrition:

- 288 Calories
- 6g Fat
- 13g Protein

4. Risotto with Green Beans and Sweet Potatoes

Difficulty: Easy
Preparation Time: 20 minutes
Cooking Time: 4 to 5 hours
Servings: 8
Ingredients:

- 1 large sweet potato (1 healthy fat)
- 5 garlic cloves, minced (1 condiment)
- 2 cups short-grain brown rice (2 healthy fat)
- 1 teaspoon dried thyme leaves (1/4 green)
- 7 cups low-sodium vegetable broth (1 condiment)

- 2 cups green beans, cut in half crosswise (1 green)
- 3 tablespoons unsalted butter (1/2 healthy fat)
- 1/2 cup Parmesan cheese (1/2 healthy fat)

Directions:
1. In a 6-quart slow cooker, mix the sweet potato, garlic, rice, thyme, and broth.
2. Cover and cook over low heat for 3 to 4 hours.
3. Mix in the green beans.
4. Cover and cook over low heat for 37 minutes.
5. Stir in the butter and cheese. Cover and cook at low for 20 minutes, then stir and serve.

Nutrition:
- 385 Calories
- 10g Fat
- 10g Protein

5. Maple Lemon Tempeh Cubes

Difficulty: Easy
Preparation Time: 10 minutes
Cooking Time: 30 to 40 minutes
Servings: 4
Ingredients:
- Tempeh; 1 packet (1/2 healthy fat)
- Coconut oil; 2 to 3 teaspoons (1/4 healthy fat)
- Lemon juice; 3 tablespoons (1/4 condiment)
- Maple syrup; 2 teaspoons (1/4 condiment)
- Bragg's Liquid Aminos or low-sodium tamari or (optional); 1 to 2 teaspoons (1/4 condiment)
- Water; 2 teaspoons (1/4 condiment)
- Dried basil; 1/4 teaspoon (1/4 green)
- Powdered garlic; 1/4 teaspoon (1/4 condiment)
- Black pepper (freshly grounded); to taste (1/4 condiment)

Directions:
1. Heat your oven to 400 ° C.
2. Cut your tempeh block into squares in bite form.

3. Cook coconut oil at medium to high heat in a non-stick skillet.
4. When melted and heated, add the tempeh and cook on one side for 2-4 minutes, or until the tempeh turns down into a golden-brown color.
5. Flip the tempeh bits and cook for 2-4 minutes.
6. Mix the lemon juice, tamari, maple syrup, basil, water, garlic, and black pepper while tempeh is browning.
7. Drop the mixture over tempeh, then swirl to cover the tempeh.
8. Sauté for 2-3 minutes, then turn the tempeh and sauté 1-2 minutes more.
9. The tempeh, on both sides, should be soft and orange.

Nutrition:
- 22 Carbohydrates
- 17g Fats
- 21g Protein

6. Quinoa with Vegetables

Difficulty: Average
Preparation Time: 10 minutes
Cooking Time: 5 to 6 hours
Servings: 8
Ingredients:
- 2 cups quinoa, rinsed and drained (1 healthy fat)
- 2 carrots, peeled and sliced (1 green)
- 1 cup sliced cremini mushrooms (1 green)
- 3 garlic cloves, minced (1/4 condiment)
- 4 cups low-sodium vegetable broth (1 condiment)
- 1/2 teaspoon salt (1/4 condiment)
- 1 teaspoon dried marjoram leaves (1/4 green)
- 1/8 tsp. black pepper (1/4 condiment)

Directions:
1. In a 6-quart slow cooker, mix all of the ingredients.
2. Cook over low heat for 5 to 6 hours, covered.
3. Stir the mixture and serve.

Nutrition:

- 204 Calories
- 3g Fat
- 7g Protein

7. Beef with Broccoli or Cauliflower Rice

Difficulty: Average
Preparation Time: 10 minutes
Cooking Time: 30 minutes
Servings: 2
Ingredients:
- 1 lb. raw beef round steak, cut into strips (1 lean)
- 1 Tbsp + 2 tsp. low sodium soy sauce (1/4 condiment)
- 1 Splenda packet (1/4 condiment)
- 1/2 C water (1/4 condiment)
- 1 1/2 C broccoli florets (1 green)
- 1 tsp. sesame or olive oil (1/4 condiment)
- 2 Cups cooked, grated cauliflower or frozen riced cauliflower (1 green)

Directions:
1. Stir steak with soy sauce and let sit for about 15 minutes.
2. Heat oil over medium-high heat and stir-fry beef for 3-5 minutes or until browned.
3. Remove from pan.
4. Place broccoli, Splenda, and water.
5. Cover and cook for 5 minutes or until broccoli starts to turn tender, stirring sometimes.
6. Add beef back in and heat up thoroughly.
7. Serve the dish with cauliflower rice.

Nutrition:
- 16g Fats
- 9g Protein
- 211 Calories

8. Chicken Zucchini Noodles

Difficulty: Easy
Preparation Time: 10 minutes
Cooking Time: 25 minutes
Servings: 2
Ingredients:
- 1 large zucchini, spiralized (1 green)

- 1 chicken breast, skinless & boneless (1 lean)
- 1/2 tbsp jalapeno, minced (1/4 green)
- 2 garlic cloves, minced (1/4 condiment)
- 1/2 tsp. ginger, minced (1/8 condiment)
- 1/2 tbsp fish sauce (1/4 condiment)
- 2 tbsp coconut cream (1/4 healthy fat)
- 1/2 tbsp honey (1/4 condiment)
- 1/2 lime juice (1/8 condiment)
- 1 tbsp peanut butter (1/4 healthy fat)
- 1 carrot, chopped (1/4 green)
- 2 tbsp cashews, chopped (1/2 healthy fat)
- 1/4 cup cilantro (1/4 green)
- 1 tbsp olive oil (1/8 condiment)

Directions:
1. Cook olive oil in a pan over medium-high heat.
2. Season chicken breast with pepper and salt.
3. Once the oil is hot, add chicken breast into the pan and cook for 3-4 minutes per side or until cooked.
4. Remove chicken breast from pan.
5. Shred chicken breast with a fork and set aside.
6. In a small bowl, mix peanut butter, jalapeno, garlic, ginger, fish sauce, coconut cream, honey, and lime juice.
7. Set aside.
8. In a large mixing bowl, combine spiralized zucchini, carrots, cashews, cilantro, and shredded chicken.
9. Pour peanut butter mixture over zucchini noodles and toss to combine.
10. Serve immediately and enjoy.

Nutrition:
- 353 Calories
- 21g Fat
- 25g Protein

9. Spinach and Feta Pasta

Difficulty: Easy
Preparation Time: 15 minutes
Cooking Time: 25 minutes
Servings: 4
Ingredients:
- 8 ounces uncooked penne pasta (1 healthy fat)
- 1-ounce olive oil (1/8 condiment)
- 1 minced garlic clove (1/8 condiment)
- 24 ounces tomatoes, chopped (2 healthy fat)
- 8 ounces fresh mushrooms, sliced (2 healthy fat)
- 16 ounces packed spinach leaves (3 green)
- A pinch of salt and pepper (1/8 condiment)
- 1 pinch red pepper flakes (1/8 condiment)
- 8 ounces crumbled feta cheese (1/2 healthy fat)

Directions:
1. Boil salted water and cook pasta for 5-10 minutes or until the noodles are soft but firm to the taste. Drain the water from the pot.
2. Heat oil in a large frying pan on Medium-High heat. Sauté garlic.
3. Add tomatoes, mushrooms, spinach, salt, pepper, and red flakes in the pan and mix thoroughly, cooking for 2-3 minutes or until mixture is heated through.
4. Reduce heat and add pasta and cheese. Stir thoroughly until heated completely and serve.

Nutrition:
- 17g Protein
- 4.6g Fats
- 233 Calories

10. Shrimp Pesto Pasta

Difficulty: Easy
Preparation Time: 15 minutes
Cooking Time: 20 minutes
Servings: 8
Ingredients:

- 16 ounces linguine pasta (2 healthy fat)
- 4 ounces butter (1/4 healthy fat)
- 16 ounces heavy cream (1/2 healthy fat)
- 1/2 teaspoon black pepper, ground (1/2 condiment)
- 8 ounces Parmesan cheese, grated (1/2 healthy fat)
- 2 1/2 ounces pesto sauce (2 condiment)
- 16 ounces large peeled shrimp, deveined (3 lean)

Directions:
1. Boil salted water and cook noodles for 10 minutes
2. Drain the pool and set it aside.
3. Cook butter in a large frying pan on medium heat. Add cream and pepper, cooking for 8 minutes, and stirring continuously.
4. Add parmesan cheese to the sauce and mix thoroughly. Pour in pesto and cook for 5 minutes or until the mixture reaches the desired thickness.
5. Then, add shrimp and cook for 5 minutes or until shrimp is pink.
6. Arrange shrimp over the linguine noodles and serve.

Nutrition:
- 627 Calories
- 40g Protein
- 30g Fat

11. Slow Cooker Spaghetti

Difficulty: Easy

Preparation Time: 10 minutes
Cooking Time: 20 minutes
Servings: 8
Ingredients:

- 1-ounce olive oil (1/4 condiment)
- 4 ounces Italian sausage (1 lean)
- 16 ounces ground beef (2 lean)
- 1 teaspoon Italian seasoning, dried (1/8 condiment)
- 1/2 teaspoon marjoram, dried (1/8 condiment)
- 1 teaspoon of garlic powder (1/8 condiment)
- 29-ounce canned tomato sauce (1 condiment)
- 6 ounces canned tomato paste (1 condiment)
- 1 4 1/2 ounces canned Italian-style tomatoes, diced (1 healthy fat)
- 1/4 teaspoon thyme leaves, dried (1/4 green)
- 1/4 teaspoon basil, dried (1/4 green)
- 1/2 tsp. oregano (1/8 green)
- 1/3-ounce garlic powder (1/8 condiment)
- 1/2-ounce white sugar (1/4 condiment)

Directions:
1. Preheat oil in a huge frying pan on medium heat. Sautee onions and sausage in the oil until onions are translucent and sausage is browned evenly.
2. Move the sausage into the pot of your slow cooker.
3. Cook marjoram, ground beef, seasoning, and 1 teaspoon of garlic in the same frying pan for 10 minutes or until meat is crumbly and browned evenly.
4. Transfer beef to the slow cooker. Stir in the rest of the ingredients to the mixture in the slow cooker and cook on Low for 8 hours.

Nutrition:
- 343 Calories

- 29g Protein
- 9g Fat

12. Beef Lo Mein

Difficulty: Average
Preparation Time: 15 minutes
Cooking Time: 20 minutes
Servings: 4
Ingredients:

- 8 ounces uncooked spaghetti (2 healthy fat)
- 1 teaspoon sesame oil (1/8 condiment)
- 1/2-ounce peanut oil (1/8 condiment)
- 4 minced cloves garlic (1/8 condiment)
- 1/2-ounce ginger, minced (1/4 condiment)
- 32 ounces mixed vegetables (2 green)
- 16 ounces thinly sliced flank steak (2 lean)
- 1 1/2-ounce soy sauce (1/4 condiment)
- 1-ounce brown sugar (1/4 condiment)
- 1/2-ounce oyster sauce (1/4 condiment)
- 1/2-ounce garlic-flavored chili paste (1/4 condiment)

Directions:
1. Boil salted water and cook spaghetti noodles for 12 minutes
2. Drain the noodles and pour them into a large bowl.
3. Toss the noodles with sesame oil and cover the bowl to keep the noodles warm.
4. Cook peanut oil in a large frying pan on Medium-High heat and cook garlic and ginger in oil for 30 seconds.
5. Add vegetables to the frying pan and cook for 5 minutes, then add beef and cook for another 5 minutes or until heated through.
6. Toss all ingredients together for 3 minutes until hot.

Nutrition:
- 6g Fats
- 7.1g Protein
- 153 Calories

---

13. Chicken Tetrazzini

Difficulty: Difficult
Preparation Time: 10 minutes
Cooking Time: 20 minutes
Servings: 1-2
Ingredients:

- 16 ounces uncooked linguine pasta (2 healthy fat)
- 4 ounces butter (1/2 healthy fat)
- 24 ounces fresh mushrooms, sliced (1 healthy fat)
- 8 ounces green bell pepper, minced (2 green)
- 21 (½ oz) condensed cream of mushroom soup (4 condiment)
- 16 ounces chicken broth (2 condiment)
- 16 ounces Cheddar cheese, shredded (1 healthy fat)
- 4 ounces cooking sherry (1/4 condiment)
- 1 teaspoon Worcestershire sauce (1/8 condiment)
- 1 teaspoon salt (1/8 condiment)
- 1/4 tsp. black pepper (1/8 condiment)
- 32 ounces boneless and skinless cooked chicken breast, chopped (4 lean)
- 8 ounces Parmesan cheese, grated (1 healthy fat)

Directions:
1. Cook pasta in a boiling water with salt for 10 minutes or until noodles are tender but firm to the taste.
2. Preheat oven to 375°F.
3. Cook butter in a big pan on medium heat and cook mushrooms, and pepper in the butter until tender.
4. Add mushroom soup and broth until warmed through. Add the pasta, cheddar cheese, Worcestershire, sherry, salt, pepper, and chicken to the mushroom soup and mix thoroughly.
5. Place the mixture in a huge baking dish and sprinkle Parmesan and paprika over

the top. Bake for 35 minutes.

Nutrition:
- 233 Calories
- 12g Fat
- 33g Protein

14. Mozzarella Chili Casserole

Difficulty: Easy
Preparation Time: 10 minutes
Cooking Time: 20 minutes
Servings: 4
Ingredients:
- 16 ounces extra-lean ground beef (2 lean)
- 28 ounces spaghetti sauce (2 healthy fat)
- 16 ounces rotini pasta (1 healthy fat)
- 16 ounces shredded mozzarella cheese (1 healthy fat)

Directions:
1. Cook pasta in a boiling water for 10 minutes or until the noodles are tender but firm to the taste.
2. Preheat oven to 350 F
3. Spray a casserole dish with cooking spray and set aside.
4. Cook beef in a large frying pan on medium heat until browned evenly and crumbly. Drain excess grease from the pan.
5. Add spaghetti sauce and pasta to the beef in the pan.
6. In the prepared casserole dish, arrange a layer of meat followed by a layer of cheese and repeat until the ingredients are gone.
7. Bake for 25 minutes or until cheese is melted and bubbly.

Nutrition:
- 288 Calories
- 6g Fats
- 15g Protein

15. Shrimp and Tomato Linguini

Difficulty: Average
Preparation Time: 10 minutes
Cooking Time: 20 minutes

Servings: 6
Ingredients:
- 1-ounce extra-virgin olive oil (1/8 condiment)
- 3 minced garlic cloves (1/4 condiment)
- 32 ounces tomatoes, diced (1/2 healthy fat)
- 8 ounces dry white wine (1/4 condiment)
- 1-ounce butter (8 healthy fat)
- Pinch salt and black pepper (1/8 condiment)
- 16 ounces uncooked linguine pasta (2 healthy fat)
- 16 ounces medium shrimp, peeled and deveined (2 lean)
- 1 teaspoon Cajun seasoning (1/8 condiment)
- 1-ounce extra-virgin olive oil (1/8 condiment)

Directions:
1. Cook 1 oz of olive oil in a large stock pot on Medium Heat.
2. Sauté garlic in the oil for 2 minutes, then add tomatoes and wine to the garlic and oil.
3. Cook the mixture for 30 minutes, stirring frequently, then add butter, salt, and pepper.
4. Using a big pot of salted water and cook the linguine for 10-12 minutes or until al dente.
5. Drain water from the pool and set noodles aside.
6. Sprinkle shrimp with seasoning, salt, and pepper and cook in a frying pan with 1 ounce of olive oil on medium heat.
7. Stir for 5 minutes or until pink in the center.
8. Add shrimp to the pasta sauce, then toss with the linguine in a large bowl and serve.

Nutrition:
- 10.7g Fats
- 3.8g Protein
- 204 Calories

16. Quinoa-Kale Egg Casserole

Difficulty: Average
Preparation Time: 20 minutes
Cooking Time: 6 to 8 hours
Servings: 8
Ingredients:
- 1 1/2 cups Roasted Vegetable Broth (2 condiment)
- 11 eggs (2 lean)
- 1 1/2 cups quinoa (1 healthy fat)
- 3 cups chopped kale (1 green)
- 1 leek, chopped (1 green)
- 1 red bell pepper (1 green)
- 3 garlic cloves, minced (1/4 condiment)
- 1 1/2 cups shredded Havarti cheese (1/2 healthy fat)

Directions:
1. Grease a 6-quart slow cooker with vegetable oil and set aside.
2. In a large bowl, mix the milk, vegetable broth, and eggs, and beat well with a wire whisk.
3. Stir in the quinoa, kale, leek, bell pepper, garlic, and cheese. Transfer mixture into the prepared slow cooker.
4. Cover and cook over low heat for 7 hours

Nutrition:
- 483 Calories
- 27g Fat
- 25g Protein

17. Chicken and Pasta Casserole

Difficulty: Average
Preparation Time: 15 minutes
Cooking Time: 20 minutes
Servings: 6
Ingredients:
- 8 ounces dry fusilli pasta (2 healthy fat)
- 1 1/2 ounces olive oil (1/2 condiment)
- 6 chicken tenderloins, cut into bite-sized chunks (3 lean)
- A pinch of salt and pepper (1/8 condiment)

- A bit of garlic powder (1/8 condiment)
- 1/2-ounce basil, dried (1/8 green)
- 1/2-ounce parsley, dried (1/8 green)
- 10 (3/4 oz.) condensed cream chicken soup (3 condiment)
- 10 (3/4 oz.) condensed cream of mushroom soup (3 condiment)
- 16 ounces frozen mixed vegetables (3 green)
- 8 ounces bread crumbs (1/2 healthy fat)
- 1-ounce Parmesan cheese, grated (1/2 healthy fat)
- 1-ounce melted butter (1/2 healthy fat)

Directions:
1. Preheat oven to 400 degrees Fahrenheit.
2. Slightly grease a baking dish with cooking spray.
3. Boil a large pot of the salted water and cook fusilli noodles for 10 minutes or until tender but firm to the bite.
4. Drain water out of the pot.
5. Heat oil in a large frying pan on medium heat. Cook chicken in the oil with salt, pepper, garlic powder, basil, and parsley for 20 minutes or until juices run clear.
6. Stir in pasta, soups, and vegetables. Pour the mixture into the baking dish.
7. Mix bread crumbs, parmesan, and butter in a small bowl and spread over the pasta.
8. Bake for 20 minutes

Nutrition:
- 416 Calories
- 33g Protein
- 18g Fat

18. Egg and Wild Rice Casserole

Difficulty: Average
Preparation Time: 20 minutes
Cooking Time: 5to 7 hours
Servings: 6

Ingredients:
- 3 cups plain cooked wild rice or Herbed Wild Rice (2 healthy fat)
- 2 cups sliced mushrooms (1 healthy fat)
- 1 red bell pepper (1 green)
- 2 garlic cloves, minced (1/4 condiment)
- 11 eggs (3 lean)
- 1 teaspoon dried thyme leaves (1/4 green)
- 1/4 teaspoon salt (1/8 condiment)
- 1 1/2 cups shredded Swiss cheese (1/4 condiment)

Directions:
1. In a 6-quart slow cooker, layer the wild rice, mushrooms, bell pepper, and garlic.
2. In a huge bowl, scourge eggs with thyme and salt. Pour into the slow cooker. Top with the cheese.
3. Cook over low heat for 5 to 7 hours, covered.

Nutrition:
- 360 Calories
- 17g Fat
- 24g Protein

19. Lean and Green Chicken Pesto Pasta

Difficulty: Average
Preparation Time: 5 minutes
Cooking Time: 15 minutes
Servings: 1
Ingredients:
- 3 cups of raw kale leaves (1 green)
- 2 tbsp. of olive oil (1/4 condiment)
- 2 cups of fresh basil (1/4 green)
- 1/4 teaspoon salt (1/8 condiment)
- 3 tbsp. lemon juice (1/8 condiment)
- 3 garlic cloves (1/4 condiment)
- 2 cups of cooked chicken breast (2 lean)
- 1 cup of baby spinach (1 green)

- 6 ounce of uncooked chicken pasta (3 healthy fat)
- 3 ounces of diced fresh mozzarella (1 healthy fat)
- Basil leaves or red pepper flakes to garnish (1/4 green)

Directions:
1. Start by making the pesto, add the kale, lemon juice, basil, garlic cloves, olive oil, and salt to a blender and blend until smooth.
2. Add salt and pepper to taste.
3. Cook the pasta and strain off the water. Reserve 1/4 cup of the liquid.
4. Get a bowl and mix everything, the cooked pasta, pesto, diced chicken, spinach, mozzarella, and the reserved pasta liquid.
5. Sprinkle the mixture with additional chopped basil or red paper flakes (optional).
6. Now your salad is ready. You may serve it warm or chilled. Also, it can be taken as a salad mix-ins or as a side dish. Leftovers should be stored in the refrigerator inside an air-tight container for 3-5 days.

Nutrition:
- 244 Calories
- 20.5g Protein
- 10g Fats

20. Primavera with Smoked Gouda

Difficulty: Average
Preparation Time: 15 minutes
Cooking Time: 30 minutes
Servings: 8
Ingredients:
- 16 ounces whole-wheat penne pasta (2 healthy fat)
- 1-ounce olive oil (1/8 condiment)
- 2 diced zucchinis (1 green)
- 1 diced green bell pepper (1 green)
- 2 diced carrots (1 green)
- 8-ounce sliced mushrooms (1 healthy fat)
- 3 minced cloves garlic (1/2 condiment)

- 14 1/2 ounces canned stewed tomatoes, chopped (2 green)
- 8-ounce chicken broth (2 condiment)
- 1-ounce fresh parsley, chopped (1/4 green)
- 1/2 teaspoon basil, dried (1/4 green)
- 1/2 teaspoon oregano, dried (1/4 green)
- 1/2 tsp. red pepper flakes (1/8 condiment)
- 1-ounce Parmesan cheese, grated (1/4 healthy fat)
- 5 1/2 ounces smoked Gouda, shredded (1 healthy fat)

Directions:
1. Boil water with salt and cook penne for 11 minutes or until al dente.
2. Drain water from the pot and set aside.
3. Cook olive oil in a huge frying pan. Cook onion, zucchini, pepper, carrots, and mushrooms for 5 minutes or until tender.
4. Add garlic to the mixture and cook for 1 more minute or until fragrant.
5. Stir in broth, tomatoes, parsley, oregano, basil, and pepper flakes. Bring to a boil.
6. Set heat to low and then cook for 2 minutes
7. Sprinkle the pasta with parmesan and gouda before serving.

Nutrition:
- 380 Calories
- 11g Fat
- 54g Protein

Chapter 2. Breakfast Recipes

21. Basil Tomato Frittata

Difficulty: Easy
Preparation Time: 10 minutes
Cooking Time: 15 minutes
Servings: 2
Ingredients:

- 5 eggs (3 lean)
- 1 tbsp olive oil (1/4 condiment)
- 7 oz can artichokes (1 green)
- 1 garlic clove, chopped (1/4 condiment)
- 1/2 cup cherry tomatoes (1/2 healthy fat)
- 2 tbsp fresh basil, chopped (1/2 green)
- 1/4 cup feta cheese, crumbled (1/4 healthy fat)
- 1/4 tsp pepper (1/8 condiment)
- 1/4 tsp salt (1/8 condiment)

Directions:

1. Cook oil in a pan over medium heat.
2. Stir in garlic and sauté for 4 minutes.
3. Add artichokes, basil, and tomatoes and cook for 4 minutes.
4. Beat eggs in a bowl and season with pepper and salt.
5. Pour egg mixture into the pan and cook for 5-7 minutes.
6. Serve and enjoy.

Nutrition:

- 325 Calories
- 22g Fat
- 20g Protein

22. Coconut Bread

Difficulty: Average
Preparation Time: 10 minutes
Cooking Time: 35 minutes
Servings: 12
Ingredients:

- 6 eggs (3 lean)
- 1 tbsp baking powder (1/4 condiment)
- 2 tbsp swerve (1/2 condiment)
- 1/2 cup ground flaxseed (1/4 condiment)
- 1/2 cup coconut flour (1/4 condiment)
- 1/2 tsp cinnamon (1/8 condiment)
- 1 tsp xanthan gum (1/8 condiment)
- 1/3 cup unsweetened coconut milk (1/2 healthy fat)
- 1/2 cup olive oil (1/4 condiment)
- 1/2 tsp salt (1/8 condiment)

Directions:

1. Preheat the oven to 375 F.
2. Add eggs, milk, and oil into the stand mixer and blend until combined.
3. Add remaining ingredients and blend until well mixed.
4. Pour batter in a greased loaf pan.
5. Bake in the oven for 40 minutes.
6. Slice and serve.

Nutrition:

- 150 Calories
- 13.7g Fat
- 3.9g Protein

23. Chia Spinach Pancakes

Difficulty: Easy
Preparation Time: 10 minutes
Cooking Time: 5 minutes
Servings: 6
Ingredients:

- 4 eggs (2 lean)
- ½ cup coconut flour (1/4 condiment)
- 1 cup coconut milk (1/2 healthy fat)
- ¼ cup chia seeds (1/4 healthy fat)
- 1 cup spinach, chopped (1 green)
- 1 tsp baking soda (1/4 condiment)
- ½ tsp pepper (1/8 condiment)
- ½ tsp salt (1/8 condiment)

Directions:

1. Whisk eggs in a bowl until frothy.
2. Combine together all dry ingredients and add in the egg mixture and whisk until smooth. Add spinach and stir well.
3. Greased pan with butter and heat over medium heat.
4. Pour 3-4 tablespoons of batter onto the pan and make the pancake.
5. Cook pancake until lightly golden brown from both sides.
6. Serve and enjoy.

Nutrition:

- 111 Calories
- 7.2g Fat
- 6.3g Protein

24. Olive Cheese Omelet

Difficulty: Easy
Preparation Time: 10 minutes
Cooking Time: 5 minutes
Servings: 4
Ingredients:

- 4 large eggs (2 lean)
- 2 oz cheese (1 healthy fat)
- 12 olives, pitted (2 healthy fat)
- 2 tbsp butter (1/2 healthy fat)
- 2 tbsp olive oil (1 condiment)
- 1 tsp herb de Provence (1/4 green)
- 1/2 tsp salt (1/8 condiment)

Directions:

1. Add all ingredients except butter in a bowl, whisk well until frothy.
2. Melt butter in a pan over medium heat.
3. Pour egg mixture onto a hot pan and spread evenly.

4. Cover and cook for 3 minutes.
5. Turn omelet to other side and cook for 2 minutes more.
6. Serve and enjoy.

Nutrition:
- 250 Calories
- 23g Fat
- 10g Protein

25. Feta Kale Frittata

Difficulty: Easy
Preparation Time: 10 minutes
Cooking Time: 2 hour 10 minutes
Servings: 8
Ingredients:
- 8 eggs, beaten (2 lean)
- 4 oz feta cheese, crumbled (1/2 healthy fat)
- 6 oz bell pepper, roasted and diced (1 green)
- 5 oz baby kale (1 green)
- 1/4 cup green onion, sliced (1/4 green)
- 2 tsp olive oil (1/2 condiment)

Directions:
1. Cook olive oil in a pan over medium-high heat.
2. Stir in kale to the pan and sauté for 4-5 minutes or until softened.
3. Spray slow cooker with cooking spray.
4. Add cooked kale into the slow cooker.
5. Add green onion and bell pepper into the slow cooker.
6. Pour beaten eggs into the slow cooker and stir well to combine.
7. Sprinkle crumbled feta cheese.
8. Cook over low heat for 2 hours.
9. Serve and enjoy.

Nutrition:
- 150 Calories
- 9g Fat
- 10g Protein

26. Fresh Berry Muffins

Difficulty: Average
Preparation Time: 11 minutes

Cooking Time: 26 minutes
Servings: 9
Ingredients:
- 2 eggs (1 lean)
- ½ tsp vanilla (1/4 condiment)
- 1/2 cup fresh blueberries (1/2 healthy fat)
- 1 tsp baking powder (1/8 condiment)
- 6 drops stevia (1/4 condiment)
- 1 cup heavy cream (1/2 healthy fat)
- 2 cups almond flour (1/4 condiment)
- 1/4 cup butter, melted (1/2 healthy fat)

Directions:
1. Set the oven to 350 F.
2. Stir in eggs to the mixing bowl and whisk until well mix.
3. Mix in remaining ingredients to the eggs.
4. Fill in the batter into a greased muffin tray and bake in the oven for 25 minutes. Serve.

Nutrition:
- 190 Calories
- 18g Fat
- 5.4g Protein

27. Cheese Zucchini Eggplant

Difficulty: Easy
Preparation Time: 10 minutes
Cooking Time: 2 hours
Servings: 8
Ingredients:
- 1 eggplant, cut in 1-inch cubes (1 green)
- 1 ½ cup spaghetti sauce (1 healthy fat)
- 1 medium zucchini, cut into 1-inch pieces (1 green)
- 1/2 cup parmesan cheese, shredded (1/2 healthy fat)

Directions:
1. Incorporate all ingredients into the crock pot and stir well.
2. Cover and cook on high for 2 hours.
3. Stir well and serve.

Nutrition:

- 47 Calories
- 1.2g Fat
- 2.5g Protein

28. Broccoli Nuggets

Difficulty: Easy
Preparation Time: 10 minutes
Cooking Time: 15 minutes
Servings: 4
Ingredients:
- 2 egg whites (1 lean)
- 2 cups broccoli florets (2 green)
- 1/4 cup almond flour (1/4 condiment)
- 1 cup cheddar cheese, shredded (1/2 condiment)
- 1/8 tsp salt (1/8 condiment)

Directions:
1. Preheat the oven to 350 F.
2. Add broccoli in bowl and mash using a masher.
3. Stir in remaining ingredients to the broccoli.
4. Place 20 scoops onto a baking tray and press lightly down.
5. Bake in preheated oven for 20 minutes.
6. Serve and enjoy.

Nutrition:
- 145 Calories
- 10.4g Fat
- 10.56g Protein

29. Cauliflower Frittata

Difficulty: Easy
Preparation Time: 10 minutes
Cooking Time: 5 minutes
Servings: 1
Ingredients:
- 1 egg (1 lean)
- ¼ cup cauliflower rice (1 green)
- 1 tbsp olive oil (1 condiment)
- 1/4 tsp turmeric (1/8 condiment)
- Pepper (1/8 condiment)
- Salt (1/8 condiment)

Directions:
1. Incorporate all ingredients except oil into the bowl and mix well to combine.

2. Cook oil in a pan over medium heat.
3. Pour the mixture into the hot oil pan and cook for 3-4 minutes or until lightly golden brown.
4. Serve and enjoy.

Nutrition:
- 196 Calories
- 19g Fat
- 7g Protein

30. Coconut Kale Muffins

Difficulty: Average
Preparation Time: 10 minutes
Cooking Time: 30 minutes
Servings: 8
Ingredients:
- 6 eggs (2 lean)
- Half cup coconut milk, unsweetened (1/2 healthy fat)
- 1 cup kale, chopped (1 green)
- ¼ tsp garlic powder (1/8 condiment)
- ¼ tsp paprika (1/8 condiment)
- 1/4 cup green onion, chopped (1/4 green)

Directions:
1. Preheat the oven to 350 F.
2. Add all ingredients into the bowl and whisk well.
3. Pour mixture into the greased muffin tray and bake in the oven for 30 minutes.
4. Serve and enjoy.

Nutrition:
- 92 Calories
- 7g Fat
- 5g Protein

31. Protein Muffins

Difficulty: Average
Preparation Time: 10 minutes
Cooking Time: 15 minutes
Servings: 12
Ingredients:
- 8 eggs (4 lean)
- 2 scoop vanilla protein powder (1 healthy fat)
- 8 oz cream cheese (1 healthy fat)
- 4 tbsp butter, melted (1/2 healthy fat)

Directions:
1. In a large bowl, scourge cream cheese and melted butter.
2. Add eggs and protein powder and whisk until well combined.
3. Pour batter into the greased muffin pan.
4. Bake at 350 F for 25 minutes.
5. Serve and enjoy.

Nutrition:
- 149 Calories
- 12g Fat
- 8g Protein

32. Healthy Waffles

Difficulty: Easy
Preparation Time: 10 minutes
Cooking Time: 10 minutes
Servings: 4
Ingredients:
- 8 drops liquid stevia (1/8 condiment)
- 1/2 tsp baking soda (1/8 condiment)
- 1 tbsp chia seeds (1/4 healthy fat)
- 1/4 cup water (1/8 condiment)
- 2 tbsp sunflower seed butter (1 healthy fat)
- 1 tsp cinnamon (1/8 condiment)
- 1 avocado, peel, pitted and mashed (1 healthy fat)
- 1 tsp vanilla (1/8 condiment)
- 1 tbsp lemon juice (1/8 condiment)
- 3 tbsp coconut flour (1/2 condiment)

Directions:
1. Preheat the waffle iron.
2. In a small bowl, add water and chia seeds and soak for 5 minutes.
3. Mash together sunflower seed butter, lemon juice, vanilla, stevia, chia mixture, and avocado.
4. Mix together cinnamon, baking soda, and coconut flour.

5. Add wet ingredients to the dry ingredients and mix well.
6. Pour waffle mixture into the hot waffle iron and cook on each side for 3-5 minutes.
7. Serve and enjoy.

Nutrition:
- 220 Calories
- 17g Fat
- 5.1g Protein

33. Cheese Almond Pancakes

Difficulty: Easy
Preparation Time: 10 minutes
Cooking Time: 10 minutes
Servings: 4
Ingredients:
- 4 eggs (2 lean)
- 1/4 tsp cinnamon (1/8 condiment)
- 1/2 cup cream cheese (1/4 healthy fat)
- 1/2 cup almond flour (1/4 condiment)
- 1 tbsp butter, melted (1/4 healthy fat)

Directions:
1. Incorporate all ingredients into the blender and blend until combined.
2. Heat up butter in a pan over medium heat.
3. Pour 3 tablespoons of batter per pancake and cook for 2 minutes on each side.
4. Serve and enjoy.

Nutrition:
- 271 Calories
- 25g Fat
- 10.8g Protein

34. Vegetable Quiche

Difficulty: Average
Preparation Time: 10 minutes
Cooking Time: 30 minutes
Servings: 6
Ingredients:

- 8 eggs (3 lean)
- 1 cup Parmesan cheese, grated (1/2 healthy fat)
- 1 cup unsweetened coconut milk (1/2 healthy fat)
- 1 cup tomatoes, chopped (1 green)
- 1 cup zucchini, chopped (1 green)
- 1 tbsp butter (1/2 healthy fat)
- 1/2 tsp pepper (1/8 condiment)
- 1 tsp salt (1/8 condiment)

Directions:

1. Preheat the oven to 400 F.
2. Heat up butter in a pan over medium heat and then add onion and sauté until onion softens.
3. Add tomatoes and zucchini to the pan and sauté for 4 minutes.
4. Beat eggs with cheese, milk, pepper and salt in a bowl.
5. Pour egg mixture over vegetables and bake in the oven for 30 minutes.
6. Slices and serve.

Nutrition:

- 25 Calories
- 16.7g Fat
- 22g Protein

35. Pumpkin Muffins

Difficulty: Average
Preparation Time: 10 minutes
Cooking Time: 25 minutes
Servings: 10
Ingredients:

- 4 eggs (2 lean)
- 1/2 cup pumpkin puree (1/4 healthy fat)
- 1 tsp pumpkin pie spice (1/8 condiment)
- 1/2 cup almond flour (1/4 condiment)
- 1 tbsp baking powder (1/8 condiment)
- 1 tsp vanilla (1/8 condiment)
- 1/3 cup coconut oil, melted (1/2 condiment)
- 2/3 cup swerve (1/2 condiment)
- 1/2 cup coconut flour (1/4 condiment)
- 1/2 tsp sea salt (1/8 condiment)

Directions:

1. Preheat the oven to 350 F.
2. Scourge coconut flour, pumpkin pie spice, baking powder, swerve, almond flour, and sea salt.
3. Stir in eggs, vanilla, coconut oil, and pumpkin puree until well combined.
4. Pour batter into the greased muffin tray and bake in the oven for 25 minutes.
5. Serve and enjoy.

Nutrition:

- 150 Calories
- 13g Fat
- 5g Protein

36. Cheesy Spinach Quiche

Difficulty: Average
Preparation Time: 10 minutes
Cooking Time: 7 Hours
Servings: 6
Ingredients:

- 8 eggs (2 lean)
- 2 cups fresh spinach (2 green)
- 1/2 cup feta cheese (1/2 healthy fat)
- 1/2 cup parmesan cheese, shredded (1/2 healthy fat)
- 1/4 cup cheddar cheese, shredded (1/4 healthy fat)
- 3 garlic cloves, minced (1/4 condiment)
- 2 cups unsweetened almond milk (1 healthy fat)
- 1/4 tsp salt (1/8 condiment)

Directions:

1. In a huge bowl, scourge eggs and almond milk.
2. Add spinach, parmesan cheese, feta cheese, garlic, and salt and stir well to combine.
3. Spray crock pot with cooking spray.
4. Pour egg mixture into the crock pot.
5. Drizzle shredded cheddar cheese over the top of the egg mixture.
6. Cover and cook on low for 7 hours.

Nutrition:

- 365 Calories
- 32.5g Fat
- 16.1g Protein

37. Chicken Chili

Difficulty: Average
Preparation Time: 10 minutes
Cooking Time: 30 minutes
Servings: 1
Ingredients:

- 1 (¼ pound) boneless chicken breast (1 lean)
- 1/4 tablespoon olive oil (1/8 condiment)
- 1/4 cup green spring onion, diced (1/2 green)
- 1/3 cup bell pepper, seeded and chopped (1/2 green)
- ½ cup jalapenos, seeded and diced (1/4 green)
- ½ cloves garlic, minced (1/4 condiment)
- ½ teaspoon salt (1/4 condiment)
- 1/4 teaspoon ground cumin (1/8 condiment)
- 1/4 teaspoon coriander (1/8 condiment)
- 1 cup chicken broth (1 condiment)
- 1/2 cup water (1 condiment)
- ½ (7-oz.) cans green chilies (1/2 green)
- 1 tablespoon thick canned coconut milk, chopped green onions, and coriander for garnish (1 healthy fat)

Directions:

1. Mince the chicken and veggies. Then place a big pot over medium-high heat. Put the peppers, oil, onions, jalapeno, and garlic up.
2. Sauté for 5 minutes, then put the chicken, spices, and salt. Sauté additional 5–8

minutes until chicken is cooked well. Place the green chilies, broth, and coconut milk.

3. Bring to the boil. Cook for 15–20 minutes and shred chicken. Serve topped with green onions and coriander.

Nutrition:

- 226 Calories
- 20g Protein
- 8g Fats

38. Asparagus and Crabmeat Frittata

Difficulty: Easy
Preparation Time: 13 minutes
Cooking Time: 17 minutes
Servings: 1
Ingredients:

- 1½ tablespoon extra-virgin olive oil (1/2 condiment)
- 1-pound asparagus (1 green)
- 1/2 cups liquid egg substitute (1/4 condiment)
- 1/2 teaspoon salt (1/8 condiment)
- 1 ½ teaspoon black pepper (1/8 condiment)
- ¼ cup basil chopped (1/8 green)
- 1/2 teaspoon sweet paprika (1/4 condiment)
- 1/2-pound lump crabmeat (1 lean)
- 1/2 tablespoon finely cut chives (1/2 green)

Directions:

1. Deter the tough ends of the asparagus and cut it into bite-sized pieces.
2. Preheat an oven to 375°F.
3. In a 12-Inch to a 14-inch oven-proof, non-stick skillet, warm the olive oil and sweat the asparagus until tender—season with pepper, paprika, and salt.
4. In a mixing bowl, add the chives, crabmeat, and basil.
5. Pour in the liquid egg substitute and mix until combined.
6. With the cooked asparagus, pour the crab and egg mixture into the skillet and then stir to combine. Bake

over low to medium heat until the eggs start boiling.

7. Place the skillet inside the oven. Then bake for about 15–20 minutes. Wait until the eggs are golden brown. Serve the dish warm.

Nutrition:

- 340 Calories
- 50g Protein
- 10g Fat

39. Mexican Cauliflower Rice

Difficulty: Average
Preparation Time: 10 minutes
Cooking Time: 10 minutes
Servings: 3
Ingredients:

- 1 large cauliflower florets (1 green)
- 2 garlic cloves, minced (1/4 condiment)
- 1 tbsp olive oil (1/4 condiment)
- 1/4 cup vegetable broth (1 condiment)
- 3 tbsp tomato paste (1 condiment)
- 1/2 tsp cumin (1/8 condiment)
- 1 tsp salt (1/8 condiment)

Directions:

1. Stir in cauliflower in a food processor until it looks like rice.
2. Cook oil in a pan over medium heat.
3. Cook onion and garlic for 3 minutes.
4. Add cauliflower rice, cumin, and salt and stir well.
5. Add broth and tomato paste and stir until well combined.
6. Serve and enjoy.

Nutrition

- 90 Calories
- 5g Fat
- 3g Protein

40. Asian Scrambled Egg

Difficulty: Easy
Preparation Time: 10 minutes
Cooking Time: 10 minutes
Servings: 1

Ingredients:

- 1 large egg (1 lean)
- 1/2 teaspoons light soy sauce (1/4 condiment)
- 1/8 teaspoon white pepper (1/8 condiment)
- 1 tablespoon vegetable oil (1/4 condiment)

Directions:

1. Beat the eggs in a bowl.
2. To the beaten egg, add soy sauce, one-teaspoon vegetable oil, and pepper.
3. Preheat a saucepan on high heat.
4. Add two tablespoons of oil to the saucepan.
5. Then add the mixture of the beaten egg.
6. The edges will begin to cook.
7. Lessen the heat to medium and carefully scramble the eggs.
8. Turn off heat and transfer into a bowl.
9. Serve hot and enjoy

Nutrition:

- 200 Calories
- 6.7g Fat
- 6.1g Protein

41. Beef with Broccoli in Rice with Cauliflower

Difficulty: Average
Preparation Time: 5 minutes
Cooking Time: 15 minutes
Servings: 2
Ingredients:

- low sodium soy sauce (1 Tbsp. + 2 tsp) (1 condiment)

- 1 Splenda packet (1/4 condiment)
- 1 tsp sesame or olive oil (1/8 condiment)
- 1 lb. raw beef round steak, cut into strips. (2 lean)
- 1 ½ C broccoli florets (1 lean)
- ½ C water (1 condiment)
- 2 Cups cooked, grated cauliflower (1 lean)

Directions:
1. Combine the steak with soy sauce and let it lie for around 15 minutes.
2. Heat oil over moderate heat and stir the meat for 3-5 minutes or until it is fried.
3. Add Splenda, broccoli, and water. Cook for 5 minutes or until the broccoli begins to soften by stirring.
4. Add meat again and heat well.
5. Serve with cauliflower rice.

Nutrition:
- 4g Fat
- 201 Calories
- 23g Protein

42. Bacon Cheeseburger

Difficulty: Average
Preparation Time: 5 minutes
Cooking Time: 15 minutes
Servings: 4
Ingredients:
- 1 lb. lean ground beef (1 lean)
- 1 clove garlic (1/4 condiment)
- chopped yellow onion (¼ cup)
- 1 Tbsp. yellow mustard (1/4 condiment)
- 3 pieces of turkey bacon, each cut into 8 evenly-sized rectangular pieces (1 lean)
- ½ tsp salt (1/8 condiment)
- 1 Tbsp. Worcestershire sauce (1/2 condiment)
- 4 thin slices cheddar cheese, cut into 6 equal-sized rectangular pieces (1/2 healthy fat)
- 24 dill pickle chips (2 healthy fat)

- lettuce leaves, torn into 24 small square-shaped pieces (2 green)
- 4-6 green leaf (2 green)
- 12 cherry tomatoes (1/2 healthy fat)

Directions:
1. Preheat the broiler to 400°F.
2. Mix the onion, garlic, Worcestershire sauce, salt, and beef in an average-sized dish, and stir well.
3. Form combination into 24 little meatballs. Set meatballs into a foil-lined baking coat and heat for 12-15 minutes. Leave the broiler on.
4. Top all meatballs with a slice of cheese, and then move back to the broiler till cheese melts, around 2 to 3 minutes.
5. Let meatballs to be cold.
6. To assemble tastes: on a toothpick, a slice of bacon, coat a cheese layered meatball, pickle chip, bit of lettuce, pickle chip, and a piece of tomato.

Nutrition:
- 3g Fat
- 234 Calories
- 20g Protein

43. Turkey Caprese Meatloaf Cups

Difficulty: Average
Preparation Time: 20 minutes
Cooking Time: 45 minutes
Servings: 6
Ingredients:
- 2 pounds ground turkey breast (2 lean)
- 1 large egg (1 lean)
- ¼ cup fresh basil leaves, chopped (1/4 green)
- 3 pieces of sun-dried tomatoes (1 green)
- ¼ teaspoon salt and ½ teaspoon pepper, to taste (1/4 condiment)
- 5 ounces low-fat fresh mozzarella, shredded (1 healthy fat)

- ½ teaspoon garlic powder (1/8 condiment)

Directions:
1. Preheat the broiler to 400°F.
2. Whip the egg in a large mixing pan.
3. Add the components and blend everything with your hands until mixed.
4. Spray a 12-cup muffin tin and distribute the turkey mixture among the muffin cups, pressing the mix in. Cook in the preheated oven till the turkey is well-cooked for about 25-30 minutes.
5. Cool the meatloaves fully and store them in a box in the freezer for around five days.

Nutrition:
- 43g Protein
- 181 Calories
- 11g Fat

44. Avocado Chicken Salad

Difficulty: Easy
Preparation Time: 5 minutes
Cooking Time: 10 minutes
Servings: 2
Ingredients:
- ¼ cup fresh cilantro, chopped (1/4 green)
- 10 oz. diced cooked chicken (3 lean)
- 3 oz. chopped avocado (1 healthy fat)
- 1 tbsp. + 1 tsp lime juice (1/4 condiment)
- ½ cup 2% Plain Greek yogurt (1/2 healthy fat)
- ¼ tsp salt (1/8 condiment)
- 12 tsp garlic powder (1/4 condiment)
- Pepper (1/8 tsp) (1/8 condiment)

Directions:
1. Mix all components in an average-sized pan and then Refrigerate until set to serve.
2. Slice the chicken salad in half and take it with your chosen greens.

Nutrition:
- 13g Fat

- 35g Protein
- 265 Calories

45. Zucchini Noodles with Creamy Avocado Pesto

Difficulty: Average
Preparation Time: 10 minutes
Cooking Time: 20 minutes
Servings: 4
Ingredients
- ¼ tsp black pepper (1/8 condiment)
- 6 c of spiralized zucchini (1 green)
- 6 oz. of avocado (1 healthy fat)
- ½ tsp salt (1/8 condiment)
- 1 basil leaves (1/8 green)
- 1/3 oz. pine nuts (1.4 healthy fat)
- 3 garlic cloves (1 condiment)
- 1 Tbsp. olive oil (1/2 condiment)
- Lime juice (2 Tbsp.) (1/2 condiment)

Directions:
1. Spiralize the courgette and placed them down on paper sheets so that the excess liquid is absorbed.
2. In a food processor, put lemon juice, avocados, basil leaves, pine nuts, garlic, sea salt, and pulse until chopped. Then keep olive oil in a quiet stream till creamy and emulsified.
3. Spray olive oil in a skillet over moderate heat and placed zucchini noodles, heating for nearly 2 minutes till tender.
4. Put zucchini noodles in a large pan and stir with avocado pesto. Season with crazed pepper and a little Parmesan and then serve.

Nutrition:
- 30g Protein
- 115 Calories
- 0.2g Fat

46. Crispy Apples

Difficulty: Easy
Preparation Time: 10 minutes
Cooking Time: 10 minutes

Servings: 4
Ingredients:
- 5 apples (2 lean)
- cinnamon powder (2 tbsp.) (1/8 condiment)
- 1 tbsp. maple syrup (1/4 condiment)
- ½ cup water (1/4 condiment)
- ¼ cup brown sugar (1/2 condiment)
- ½ tbsp. nutmeg powder (1/4 condiment)
- ¼ cup flour (1/2 condiment)
- 4 tbsp. butter (1/2 healthy fat)
- ¾ cup oats (1/4 healthy fat)

Directions:
1. Take the apples in a vessel, put in maple syrup, cinnamon, nutmeg, and water.
2. Stir in butter with sugar, salt, flour, and oat and then put a spoonful of the blend over apples, take in the air fryer and heat at 350°F for 10 minutes.
3. Serve while warm.

Nutrition:
- 12.4g Protein
- 5.6g Fat
- 387 Calories

47. Grilled Chicken Power Bowl with Green Goddess Dressing

Difficulty: Difficult
Preparation Time: 5 minutes
Cooking Time: 15 minutes
Servings: 4
Ingredients
- 1 cup shredded red cabbage (1 green)
- 8 cherry tomatoes, halved (2 green)
- 1 ½ skinless, boneless, chicken breasts (1 lean)
- 1 cup rice broccoli (1 green)
- ¼ tsp each salt & pepper (1/8 condiment)
- 1 cup diced zucchini (1 green)
- 1 cup rice or cubed kabocha squash (1 green)

- 1 cup rice yellow summer squash (1 green)
- ¼ cup hemp or pumpkin seeds (1/4 healthy fat)
- 4 radishes, sliced thin (1 green)

Green Goddess Dressing:
- 1 cup fresh basil (1/4 green)
- ¼ tsp each salt & pepper (1/8 condiment)
- low-fat plain Greek yogurt (½ cup) (1/2 healthy fat)
- 4 tbsp. lemon juice (1/4 condiment)
- 1 clove garlic (1/8 condiment)

Directions:
1. Preheat broiler to 350°F.
2. Mix the chicken with pepper and salt.
3. Roast the chicken for 12 minutes until it reaches 165°F temperature. When finished, remove from the broiler and place it aside to rest for around 5 minutes. Slice into bite-sized and keep warm.
4. While the chicken rests, yellow summer squash, zucchini, steam riced kabocha squash, and broccoli in a closed microwave-proof pan for around 5 minutes until soft.
5. Then mix all ingredients into a blender.
6. To serve, put an equivalent quantity of Vegetables Mix into four different bowls. Add an equal number of radishes, cherry tomatoes, and chopped cabbage to several bowls with a quarter of the chicken and a tablespoon of seeds.

Nutrition:
- 43g Protein
- 300 Calories
- 10g Fat

48. Pancakes with Berries

Difficulty: Easy
Preparation Time: 5 minutes
Cooking Time: 20 minutes
Servings: 2
Ingredients
Pancake:

- 50 g spelled flour (1/2 condiment)
- 15 g coconut flour (1/4 condiment)
- 50 g almond flour (1/4 condiment)
- 150 ml of water (1/2 condiment)
- 1 egg (1 lean)

Filling:
- 5 g powdered sugar (1/4 condiment)
- 40 g mixed berries (1 healthy fat)
- 4 tbsp. yogurt (1/3 condiment)
- 10 g chocolate (1/4 healthy fat)

Directions:
1. Put the egg, flour, and also some salt in a mixer jar.
2. Add 150 ml of water and then stir all components.
3. After mixing all ingredients, heat a coated pan.
4. Place it to make the pancake. Once the pancake is firm, turn it over.
5. Take out the pancake, add the second half of the batter to the pan, and repeat.
6. Melt the chocolate over a water bowl.
7. Let the pancakes cool.
8. Whisk the pancakes with the yogurt, then wash the berry and let it drain.
9. Put berries on the yogurt and roll up the pancakes.
10. Sprinkle them with powdered sugar.
11. Decorate the entire thing with the melted chocolate.

Nutrition:
- 9g Fat
- 21g Protein
- 298 Calories

49. Banana Barley Porridge

Difficulty: Easy
Preparation Time: 15 minutes
Cooking Time: 5 minutes
Servings: 2
Ingredients:
- 1/4 cup chopped coconuts (1 lean)
- 1 small sliced and peeled banana (1 lean)
- 1 cup divided unsweetened coconut milk (1/2 healthy fat)
- 3 drops liquid stevia (1/8 condiment)
- 1/2 cup barley (1/4 green)

Directions:
1. In a pan, properly mix barley with half of the stevia and coconut milk.
2. Coat the mixing pan, then refrigerate for around 6 hours.
3. In a vessel, combine the coconut milk with barley mixture.
4. Heat it for nearly 5 minutes. Then cover it with the banana slices and chopped coconuts.
5. Serve.

Nutrition:
- 8.4g Fat
- 159 Calories
- 4.6g Proteins

50. Fried Egg with Bacon

Difficulty: Easy
Preparation Time: 5 minutes
Cooking Time: 10 minutes
Servings: 1
Ingredients
- 30 grams of bacon (1 lean)
- 2 eggs (1 lean)
- salt (1/8 condiment)
- pepper (1/8 condiment)
- olive oil (2 tbsp.) (1/4 condiment)

Directions:
1. Cook oil in the pan and then fry the bacon.
2. Decrease the heat and beat the eggs in the pan.
3. Cook the eggs and season with pepper and salt.
4. At last, serve the fried eggs hot with the bacon.

Nutrition:
- 19g Protein
- 405 Calories
- 38g Fat

51. Amaranth Porridge

Difficulty: Easy
Preparation Time: 5 minutes

Cooking Time: 30 minutes
Servings: 2
Ingredients:
- 1 cup amaranth (1/2 condiment)
- 2 tbsps. coconut oil (1/2 healthy fat)
- 2 cups coconut milk (1/2 healthy fat)
- 1 tbsp. ground cinnamon (1/4 condiment)

Directions:
1. In a pan, add the milk with water, then boil this mixture.
2. You mix in the amaranth and then decrease the heat to medium.
3. Cook on moderate heat and then stew for nearly 30 minutes as you mix it properly.
4. Turn off the temperature.
5. Add in coconut oil and cinnamon and then stir.

Nutrition:
- 35g Fat
- 464 Calories
- 6.7g Protein

52. Alkaline Blueberry Muffins

Difficulty: Average
Preparation Time: 5 minutes
Cooking Time: 20 minutes
Servings: 3
Ingredients:
- 3/4 cup spelt flour (1/2 condiment)
- 1/2 cup blueberries (1 lean)
- grapeseed oil (1/8 condiment)
- 1 cup coconut milk (1 healthy fat)
- 1/3 cup agave (1/4 condiment)

- 3/4 teff flour (1/2 condiment)
- sea salt (1/2 tsp) (1/8 condiment)

Directions:
1. Adjust oven temperature to 365 degrees
2. Grease 6 average size muffin cups with muffin liners.
3. In a dish, mix sea moss, agave, sea salt, coconut milk, and flour gel until they are well blended.
4. You then crimp in blueberries.
5. Coat the muffin vessel lightly with the grapeseed oil.
6. Pour in the muffin batter.
7. Bake around 30 minutes until it changes into brownish and then serve.

Nutrition:
- 5g Fat
- 2g Proteins
- 160 Calories

53. Personal Biscuit Pizza

Difficulty: Easy
Preparation Time: 5 minutes
Cooking Time: 15 minutes
Servings: 1
Ingredients:
- buttermilk cheddar herb biscuit (1 healthy fat)
- 2 tbsp. no-sugar-added tomato sauce (1 condiment)
- 2 tbsp. cold water (1/4 condiment)
- 1 sachet Optavia select (1/2 condiment)
- ¼ cup reduced-fat shredded cheese (1/2 healthy fat)

Directions:
1. Preheat oven temperature to 350°F.
2. Mix water and biscuit, and expanse mixture into a round and small crust shape onto a greased, foil-lined baking coat and bake for 10 minutes
3. Cover with cheese and tomato sauce, and cook around 5 minutes or until cheese is melted.

Nutrition:

- 13g Protein
- 301 Calories
- 8g Fat

54. Cream Cheese Omelet

Difficulty: Easy
Preparation Time: 5 minutes
Cooking Time: 5 minutes
Servings: 4
Ingredients
- 1 tablespoon butter (1/2 healthy fat)
- 2 eggs, beaten (1 lean)
- 2 tablespoons soft cream cheese with chives (1 healthy fat)

Directions:
1. Dissolve the butter in a frypan.
2. Add the cream cheese and eggs; mix and cook until the desired doneness.

Nutrition:
- 15g Protein
- 341 Calories
- 31g Fats

55. Hemp Seed Porridge

Difficulty: Average
Preparation Time: 5 minutes
Cooking Time: 5 minutes
Servings: 6
Ingredients:
- 1 cup coconut milk (1 healthy fat)
- 3 cups cooked hemp seed (1 lean)
- 1 packet Stevia (1/8 condiment)

Directions:
1. In a pan, mix the coconut milk and rice above medium heat for approximately 5 minutes and stir it continuously.
2. Discard the pan from the heater, then mix the Stevia and stir.
3. Serve them in a bowl.

Nutrition:
- 7g Protein
- 1.8g Fat
- 236 Calories

56. Pumpkin Spice Quinoa

Difficulty: Average
Preparation Time: 10 minutes
Cooking Time: 0 minutes
Servings: 2
Ingredients:
- 2 tsps. chia seeds (1 lean)
- 1 cup cooked quinoa (1 healthy fat)
- pumpkin puree (1/4 cup) (1/4 healthy fat)
- 1 large mashed banana (1 lean)
- Pumpkin spice (1 tsp.) (1/4 condiment)
- 1 cup unsweetened coconut milk (1/2 condiment)

Directions:
1. Mix all the components in a container.
2. Seal the top and then shake the container to mix the components well.
3. Refrigerate it overnight.
4. Serve.

Nutrition:
- 11.9g Fat
- 212 Calories
- 7.3g Protein

57. Chicken Lo Mein

Difficulty: Average
Preparation Time: 15 minutes
Cooking Time: 30 minutes
Servings: 4
Ingredients
- 790g boneless, chicken breasts, sliced (2 lean)
- red bell pepper, membranes and seeds removed (1 green)
- ¼ tsp ground black pepper (1/8 condiment)
- oyster sauce (2 tbsp.) (1/4 condiment)
- 1 garlic clove (1/8 condiment)
- 2 tsp peeled and minced fresh ginger-root (1/8 condiment)
- 2 tbsp. soy sauce (1/4 condiment)
- 2 spring onions (1 green)
- 110 g fresh mushrooms, divided (2 healthy fat)

- 2 medium zucchinis (400g), cut, sliced (1 green)
- 2 tbsp. + 2 tsp sesame oil, divided (1 condiment)

Directions:
1. Heat one teaspoon sesame oil above medium-high temperature in a skillet. Place the sliced chicken, season with black pepper, and heat around 165°F until the chicken is done. Dismiss from skillet and placed aside.
2. After the chicken cooks, prepare the sauce by combining the soy sauce, oyster sauce, and sesame oil in a bowl and whisking together, and then set aside.
3. With the same skillet utilize to cook the chicken, heat one teaspoon sesame oil and put the ginger, garlic, and white spring onion pieces; cook for around 1 minute until fragrant. Put the bell peppers and mushrooms and cook for about 3 minutes until just tender. Put zucchini noodles and stir to combine.
4. Put the chicken and mix with sauce; cook until zucchini is tender, and the mixture is cooked for 5 minutes.
5. Decorate with leafy parts of spring onions.

Nutrition:
- 10g Fat
- 9g Protein
- 312 Calories

58. Omelet À La Margherita

Difficulty: Easy
Preparation Time: 10 minutes
Cooking Time: 20 minutes
Servings: 2
Ingredients:
- 3 eggs (1 lean)
- 2 tbsp. heavy cream (1/2 healthy fat)
- 50 g parmesan cheese (1/2 healthy fat)
- pepper (1/8 condiment)
- 1 tbsp. olive oil (1/4 condiment)

- 1 teaspoon oregano (1/8 green)
- salt (1/8 condiment)
- nutmeg (1/8 condiment)

For covering:
- 100 g grated mozzarella (1 healthy fat)
- 3 - 4 stalks of basil (1/4 green)

Directions:
1. Mix the eggs and cream in a medium pan.
2. Add the grated nutmeg, oregano, parmesan, salt, pepper, and stir all the components.
3. Heat the oil in a pan and then add 1/2 of the egg and cream to the pan.
4. Let the omelet set over moderate heat, turn it, and then dismiss it.
5. Repeat with the other 1/2 of the egg batter.
6. Cut the tomatoes into slices and put them on top of the omelets
7. Spread the mozzarella over the tomato slice.
8. Set the omelets on a baking coat.
9. Heat at 180 degrees for 5 to 10 minutes.
10. Garnish with the basil leaves.

Nutrition:
- 402 Calories
- 34g Fat
- 21g Protein

59. Citrus Bacon Thyme Muffins

Difficulty: Average
Preparation Time: 10 minutes
Cooking Time: 20 minutes
Servings: 3
Ingredients
- 4 medium-sized eggs (2 lean)
- 1 cup of bacon bits (1 lean)
- ½ cup of melted ghee (1/2 healthy fat)
- 2 tsp. of lemon thyme (1/8 green)
- ½ tsp. of salt (1/8 condiment)
- 1 tsp. of baking soda (1/8 condiment)

- almond flour (3 cups) (1/4 condiment)

Directions:
1. Preheat oven temperature to 350 F.
2. Add ghee to the mixing pan and melt.
3. Next, add almond flour, eggs, and baking soda.
4. Mix the lemon thyme (if you need flavor, you can use other spices or herbs).
5. Drop salt and mix all ingredients properly.
6. Spray with bacon bits and line the muffin pan with liners.
7. Add the mixture into the pan, filling the pan to about ¾ full.
8. Bake for nearly 20 minutes.
9. Test by entering a toothpick into a muffin, and if it comes out clear, then the muffins are prepared.
10. Serve it quickly and enjoy.

Nutrition:
- 11g Protein
- 300 Calories
- 28g Fat

60. Coconut Chia Pudding with Berries

Difficulty: Easy
Preparation Time: 20 minutes
Cooking Time: 45 minutes
Servings: 2
Ingredient
- 60 g chia seeds (1 healthy fat)
- 1 teaspoon agave syrup (1/2 healthy fat)
- 150 g raspberries and blueberries (1 healthy fat)
- 500 ml coconut milk (1 healthy fat)
- ½ teaspoon ground bourbon vanilla (1/8 condiment)

Directions:
1. Put the agave syrup, vanilla, and chia seeds in a dish. Add the coconut milk into it.
2. Stir thoroughly and soak it for 30 minutes.
3. Meanwhile, rinse the berries and drain them well.

4. Arrange the coconut chia pudding among two glasses.
5. Garnish the berries on the top of the glass.

Nutrition:

- 662 Calories
- 55g Fat
- 8g Protein

Chapter 3. Meat Recipes

61. Balsamic Beef and Mushrooms Mix

Difficulty: Average
Preparation Time: 5 minutes
Cooking Time: 8 hours
Servings: 4
Ingredients

- 2 pounds' beef, cut into strips (1 lean)
- ¼ cup balsamic vinegar (1/4 condiment)
- 2 cups beef stock (1 condiment)
- 1 tablespoon ginger, grated (1/4 condiment)
- Juice of ½ lemon (1/8 condiment)
- 1 cup brown mushrooms, sliced (1 healthy fat)
- Pinch salt and black pepper (1/8 condiment)
- 1 teaspoon ground cinnamon (1/8 condiment)

Directions

1. In your slow cooker, mix all the ingredients, cover and cook on low for 8 hours.
2. Divide everything between plates and serve.

Nutrition

- 446 Calories
- 14g Fat
- 70g Protein

62. Oregano Pork Mix

Difficulty: Easy
Preparation Time: 5 minutes
Cooking Time: 7 hours
Servings: 4
Ingredients

- 2 pounds' pork roast (1 lean)
- 7 ounces' tomato paste (1 condiment)
- 1 yellow onion, chopped (1/2 green)
- 1 cup beef stock (1 condiment)
- 2 tablespoons ground cumin (1/4 condiment)

- 2 tablespoons olive oil (1/4 condiment)
- 2 tablespoons fresh oregano, chopped (1/4 green)
- 1 tablespoon garlic, minced (1/4 condiment)
- ½ cup fresh thyme, chopped (1/4 green)

Direction

1. Heat up a sauté pan with the oil over medium-high heat, add the roast, brown it for 3 minutes on both sides and then transfer to your slow cooker.
2. Add the remaining ingredients, toss a bit, cover and cook on low for 7 hours.
3. Slice the roast, divide it between plates and serve.

Nutrition:

- 301 Calories
- 19g fat
- 13g protein

63. Simple Beef Roast

Difficulty: Easy
Preparation Time: 10 minutes
Cooking Time: 8 hours
Servings: 10
Ingredients

- 5 pounds' beef roast (1 lean)
- 2 tablespoons Italian seasoning (1/4 condiment)
- 1 cup beef stock (1 condiment)
- 1 tablespoon sweet paprika (1/4 condiment)
- 3 tablespoons olive oil (1/4 condiment)

Directions

1. In your slow cooker, mix all the ingredients, cover and cook on low for 8 hours.
2. Carve the roast, divide it between plates and serve.

Nutrition

- 587 Calories
- 24.1g Fat
- 86g Protein

64. Pork and Peppers Chili

Difficulty: Difficult
Preparation Time: 5 minutes
Cooking Time: 8 hours
Servings: 4
Ingredients

- 1 red onion, chopped (1/4 condiment)
- 2 pounds' pork, ground (1 lean)
- 4 garlic cloves, minced (1/4 condiment)
- 2 red bell peppers, chopped (1 green)
- 1 celery stalk, chopped (1 green)
- 25 ounces' fresh tomatoes, peeled, crushed (1 green)
- ¼ cup green chilies, chopped (1/4 green)
- 2 tablespoons fresh oregano, chopped (1/4 green)
- 2 tablespoons chili powder (1/8 condiment)
- Pinch salt and black pepper (1/8 condiment)
- A drizzle of olive oil (1/8 condiment)

Directions

1. Heat up a sauté pan with the oil over medium-high heat and add the onion, garlic and meat. Mix and brown for 5 minutes and then transfer to your slow cooker.
2. Add the rest of the ingredients, toss, cover and cook on low for 8 hours.
3. Divide everything into bowls and serve.

Nutrition

- 448 Calories
- 13g Fat
- 6.3g Protein

Difficulty: Easy
Preparation Time: 10 minutes
Cooking Time: 10 minutes
Servings: 4
Ingredients
- 4 whole wheat tortillas (2 healthy fat)
- 1 cup Mozzarella cheese, shredded (1 healthy fat)
- 1 cup fresh spinach, chopped (1 green)
- 2 tablespoon Greek yogurt (1/2 healthy fat)
- 1 egg, beaten (1/2 healthy fat)
- ¼ cup green olives, sliced (1 green)
- 1 tablespoon olive oil (1/4 condiment)
- 1/3 cup fresh cilantro, chopped (1/4 green)

Directions
1. In the bowl, combine together Mozzarella cheese, spinach, yogurt, egg, olives, and cilantro.
2. Then pour olive oil into the skillet.
3. In the skillet place one tortilla and spread it with Mozzarella mixture.
4. Top it with the second tortilla and spread it with cheese mixture again.
5. Then place the third tortilla and spread it with all remaining cheese mixture.
6. Cover it with the last tortilla and fry it for 5 minutes from each side over the medium heat

Nutrition
- 193 Calories
- 7.7g Fat
- 8.3g Protein

Difficulty: Average
Preparation Time: 10 minutes
Cooking Time: 0 minutes
Servings: 2
Ingredients
- 2 wheat tortillas (1 healthy fat)
- 2 oz. red kidney beans, canned, drained (1/2 healthy fat)
- 2 tablespoons hummus (1/2 healthy fat)
- 2 teaspoons tahini sauce (1/4 condiment)
- 1 cucumber (1 green)
- 2 lettuce leaves (1 green)
- 1 tablespoon lime juice (1/4 condiment)
- 1 teaspoon olive oil (1/8 condiment)
- ½ teaspoon dried oregano (1/4 green)

Directions
1. Mash the red kidney beans until you get a puree.
2. Then spread the wheat tortillas with beans mash from one side.
3. Add hummus and tahini sauce.
4. Cut the cucumber into the wedges and place them over tahini sauce.
5. Then add lettuce leaves.
6. Make the dressing: mix up together olive oil, dried oregano, and lime juice.
7. Drizzle the lettuce leaves with the dressing and wrap the wheat tortillas in the shape of burritos.

Nutrition
- 288 Calories
- 10g Fat
- 12.5g Protein

Difficulty: Easy
Preparation Time: 10 minutes
Cooking Time: 20 minutes
Servings: 4
Ingredients
- 3 sweet potatoes, peeled (1 healthy fat)
- 4 oz. bacon, chopped (1 lean)
- 1 cup chicken stock (1 condiment)
- 1 tablespoon butter (1/4 healthy fat)
- 1 teaspoon salt (1/8 condiment)
- 2 oz. Parmesan, grated (1/2 healthy fat)

Direction
1. Dice sweet potato and put it in the pan.
2. Add chicken stock and close the lid.
3. Boil the vegetables until they are soft.
4. After this, drain the chicken stock.
5. Mash the sweet potato with the help of the potato masher. Add grated cheese and butter.
6. Mix up together salt and chopped bacon. Fry the mixture until it is crunchy (10-15 minutes).
7. Add cooked bacon to the mashed sweet potato and mix up with the help of the spoon.
8. It is recommended to serve the meal warm or hot.

Nutrition
- 304 Calories
- 18g Fat
- 17g Protein

Difficulty: Average
Preparation Time: 10 minutes
Cooking Time: 10 minutes
Servings: 4
Ingredients
- 8 Mozzarella balls, cherry size (2 healthy fat)
- 4 oz. bacon, sliced (1 lean)
- ¼ teaspoon ground black pepper (1/8 condiment)
- ¾ teaspoon dried rosemary (1/4 green)
- 1 teaspoon butter (1/8 healthy fat)

Direction
1. Sprinkle the sliced bacon with ground black pepper and dried rosemary.
2. Wrap every Mozzarella ball in the sliced bacon and secure them with toothpicks.
3. Melt butter.
4. Brush wrapped Mozzarella balls with butter.

5. Line the baking tray with the parchment and arrange Mozzarella balls in it.
6. Bake the meal for 10 minutes at 365F.

Nutrition:
- 323 Calories
- 26.8g Fat
- 20.6g Protein

69. Bulgur Lamb Meatballs

Difficulty: Difficult
Preparation Time: 10 minutes
Cooking Time: 15 minutes
Servings: 6
Ingredients
- 1 and ½ cups Greek yogurt (1 healthy fat)
- ½ teaspoon cumin, ground (1/8 condiment)
- 1 cup cucumber, shredded (1 green)
- ½ teaspoon garlic, minced (1/8 condiment)
- Pinch salt and black pepper (1/8 condiment)
- 1 cup bulgur (1/2 healthy fat)
- 2 cups water (1/8 condiment)
- 1-pound lamb, ground (1 lean)
- ¼ cup parsley, chopped (1/8 green)
- ¼ cup shallots, chopped (1/4 green)
- ½ teaspoon allspice, ground (1/8 condiment)
- ½ teaspoon cinnamon powder (1/8 condiment)
- 1 tablespoon olive oil (1/4 condiment)

Direction
1. Combine the bulgur with the water in a bowl, cover the bowl, leave aside for 10 minutes, drain and transfer to a bowl.
2. Add the meat, the yogurt and the rest of the ingredients except the oil, stir well and shape medium meatballs out of this mix.
3. Preheat oil in a pan at medium-high heat, add the meatballs, cook them for 7 minutes on each side,

arrange them all on a platter and serve as an appetizer.

Nutrition:
- 366 Calories
- 21g Fat
- 19g Protein

70. Hummus with Ground Lamb

Difficulty: Difficult
Preparation Time: 10 minutes
Cooking Time: 15 minutes
Servings: 8
Ingredients
- 10 ounces hummus (1 healthy fat)
- 12 ounces lamb meat, ground (2 lean)
- ½ cup pomegranate seeds (1/2 healthy fat)
- ¼ cup parsley, chopped (1/4 green)
- 1 tablespoon olive oil (1/8 condiment)

Directions
1. Cook oil in a pan over medium-high heat, add the meat, and brown for 15 minutes, stirring often.
2. Spread the hummus on a platter, spread the ground lamb all over, also spread the pomegranate seeds and the parsley and serve with pita chips as a snack.

Nutrition:
- 133 Calories
- 9.7g Fat
- 5g Protein

71. Lamb Stuffed Avocado

Difficulty: Average
Preparation Time: 10 minutes
Cooking Time: 40 minutes
Servings: 4
Ingredients
- 2 avocados (1 healthy fat)
- 1 1/2 cup minced lamb (1 lean)
- 1/2 cup cheddar cheese (1/2 healthy fat)
- 1/2 cup parmesan cheese, grated (1/2 healthy fat)
- 2 tbsp almond, chopped (1/4 healthy fat)

- 1 tbsp coriander, chopped (1/4 green)
- 2 tbsp olive oil (1/8 condiment)
- 1 tomato, chopped (1/4 green)
- 1 jalapeno, chopped (1/4 green)
- Salt and pepper to taste (1/8 condiment)
- 1 tsp. garlic, chopped (1/8 condiment)
- 1-inch ginger, chopped (1/8 condiment)

Direction
1. Cut the avocados in half. Remove the pit and scoop out some flesh to stuff it later.
2. In a skillet, add half of the oil.
3. Toss the ginger, garlic for 1 minute.
4. Add the lamb and toss for 3 minutes.
5. Add the tomato, coriander, parmesan, jalapeno, salt, pepper, and cook for 2 minutes.
6. Take off the heat. Stuff the avocados.
7. Sprinkle the almonds, cheddar cheese, and add olive oil on top.
8. Add to a baking sheet and bake for 30 minutes. Serve.

Nutrition:
- 19.5g Fat
- 16.7g Protein
- 301 Calories

72. Baked Beef Zucchini

Difficulty: Easy
Preparation Time: 10 minutes
Cooking Time: 40 minutes

Servings: 4
Ingredients

- 2 large zucchinis (1 green)
- 1 cup minced beef (1 lean)
- 1 cup mushroom, chopped (1/2 healthy fat)
- 1 tomato, chopped (1/2 green)
- 1/2 cup spinach, chopped (1 green)
- 1 tbsp chives, minced (1/4 green)
- 2 tbsp olive oil (1/8 condiment)
- Salt and pepper to taste (1/8 condiment)
- 1 tbsp almond butter (1/4 healthy fat)
- 1 tsp. garlic powder (1/8 condiment)
- 1 cup cheddar cheese, grated (1/2 healthy fat)
- 1/3 tsp. ginger powder (1/4 condiment)

Direction

1. Preheat the oven to 400 degrees F.
2. Add aluminum foil on a baking sheet.
3. Cut the zucchini in half. Scoop out the seeds and make pockets to stuff them later.
4. In a pan, add the olive oil.
5. Toss the beef until brown.
6. Add the mushroom, tomato, chives, salt, pepper, garlic, ginger, and spinach.
7. Cook for 2 minutes. Take off the heat.
8. Stuff the zucchinis using the mix.
9. Add them onto the baking sheet. Sprinkle the cheese on top.
10. Add the butter on top. Bake for 30 minutes. Serve warm.

Nutrition

- 12.8g Fat
- 7.9g Protein
- 222 Calories

73. Cumin-Lime Steak

Difficulty: Difficult
Preparation Time: 5 minutes
Cooking Time: 30 minutes
Servings: 4
Ingredients

- 20 Once. Steak with lean rib-eye (2 lean)
- 6 Tops of Broccoli (1 green)
- 1/2 cup of beef broth (1 condiment)
- 1/4 tablespoon lime juice (1/4 condiment)
- 1 1/2 spoonful of ground cumin (1/8 condiment)
- 1 1/2 spoonful of ground coriander (1/8 condiment)
- 2 Big, finely chopped cloves of garlic (1/4 condiment)
- 3 Pounds of olive oil (1/8 condiment)

Direction

1. Mix all marinade ingredients (except oil) together in a blender.
2. Add oil to a mixer with the motor working slowly.
3. Refrigerate and cover until ready to use. Pour 1 cup of marinade over steaks in a glass dish, covering with all sides.
4. Cover and leave to cool for 6 hours (or overnight).
5. Grill over medium-sized coals, turning regularly and clean with 1/2 cup marinade left over.
6. Steam broccoli on the side and serve.

Nutrition:

- 0.7g Fats
- 6.1g Protein
- 154 Calories

74. Braised Collard Greens in Peanut Sauce

Difficulty: Average
Preparation Time: 10 minutes
Cooking Time: 60 minutes
Servings: 4
Ingredients

- 2 cups of chicken stock (1 condiment)
- 12 cups of chopped collard greens (2 green)
- 5 tablespoons of powdered peanut butter (1 healthy fat)
- 3 cloves of garlic, crushed (1/4 condiment)
- 1 teaspoon of salt (1/8 condiment)

- 1/2 teaspoon of allspice (1/8 condiment)
- 1/2 teaspoon of black pepper (1/8 condiment)
- 2 teaspoon of lemon juice (1/4 condiment)
- 3/4 teaspoon of hot sauce (1/4 condiment)
- 1 1/2 lb. of pork tenderloin (1 lean)

Directions

1. Get a pot with a tight-fitting lid and combine the collards with the garlic, chicken stock, hot sauce, and half of the pepper and salt.
2. Cook over low heat for 60 minutes.
3. Once the collards are tender, stir lemon juice in the allspice.
4. And powdered peanut butter.
5. Keep warm.
6. Season the pork tenderloin with the remaining pepper and salt, and broil in a toaster oven for 10 minutes when you have an internal temperature of 145F.
7. Make sure to turn the tenderloin every 2 minutes to achieve an even browning all over.
8. After that, you can take away the pork from the oven and allow it to rest for like 5 minutes.
9. Slice the pork as you will like and serve it on top of the braised greens.

Nutrition:

- 320 Calories
- 10g Fat
- 45g Protein

75. High Protein Chipotle Cheddar Quesadilla

Difficulty: Average
Preparation Time: 10 minutes
Cooking Time: 10 minutes
Servings: 4
Ingredients

- Tortillas (4, low carb) (2 healthy fat)
- Cottage cheese (2 cups, low sodium) (1/2 healthy fat)

- Cheddar cheese (2 cups, low fat, shredded) (1/2 healthy fat)
- Bell pepper (1, red, thinly sliced) (1/2 green)
- Portobello mushrooms (1 cup, thinly sliced) (1/2 green)
- Chipotle seasoning (2-3 tbsp) (1/2 condiment)
- Mild salsa (for dipping) (1/4 condiment)

Direction
1. Add the bell pepper (sliced, red), and mushrooms (sliced) into a large grill pan over medium heat.
2. Cook for approximately 10 minutes until soft. Remove then transfer into a bowl (medium). Set aside.
3. Add the chipotle seasoning and cottage cheese in a small bowl. Stir well to incorporate.
4. Place tortillas onto the grill pan and pour vegetable mixture over tortillas.
5. Sprinkle cottage cheese mixture over the top and then top off using the cheddar cheese (shredded).
6. Place an additional tortilla over the top of filling.
7. Cook for roughly 2 minutes and then flip and continue cooking for one more minute.
8. Repeat process with remaining tortillas and filling.
9. Serve immediately with the salsa (mild).

Nutrition:
- 287 Calories
- 32.6g Protein
- 10.6g Fats

76. Zucchini Boats with Beef and Pimiento Rojo

Difficulty: Average
Preparation Time: 10 minutes
Cooking Time: 30 minutes
Servings: 4
Ingredients
- 4 zucchinis (1 green)
- 2 tbsp olive oil (1/4 condiment)

- 1 1/2 lb. ground beef (1 lean)
- 2 tbsp chopped pimiento (1/4 condiment)
- Pinch salt and black pepper (1/8 condiment)
- 1 cup grated yellow cheddar cheese (1/2 healthy fat)

Direction
1. Preheat oven to 350°F.
2. Lay the zucchinis on a flat surface, trim off the ends and cut in half lengthwise. Scoop out the pulp from each half with a spoon to make shells. Chop the pulp.
3. Cook oil in a skillet; add the ground beef, pimiento, zucchini pulp, and season with salt and black pepper.
4. Cook for 6 minutes while stirring to break up lumps until beef is no longer pink. Turn the heat off.
5. Spoon the beef into the boats and sprinkle with cheddar cheese.
6. Situate on a greased baking sheet and cook to melt the cheese for 15 minutes until zucchini boats are tender.
7. Take out, cool for 2 minutes, and serve warm with a mixed green salad.

Nutrition:
- 335 Calories
- 24g Fats
- 18g Protein

77. Tomatillo and Green Chili Pork Stew

Difficulty: Difficult
Preparation Time: 15 minutes
Cooking Time: 45 minutes
Servings: 4
Ingredients
- 2 scallions, chopped (1/4 green)
- 2 cloves of garlic (1/4 condiment)
- 1 lb. tomatillos, trimmed and chopped (1/4 green)
- 8 large romaine or green lettuce leaves, divided (1 green)

- 2 Serrano chilies, seeds, and membranes (1/4 healthy fat)
- 1/2 tsp. of dried Mexican oregano (1/4 green)
- 1 1/2 lb. of boneless pork loin (1 lean)
- 1/4 cup of cilantro, chopped (1/4 green)
- 1/4 tablespoon (each) salt and paper (1/8 condiment)
- 1 jalapeno (1/4 green)
- 1 cup of sliced radishes (1/2 green)
- 4 lime wedges (1/2 condiment)

Direction
1. Combine scallions, garlic, tomatillos, 4 lettuce leaves, Serrano chilies, and oregano in a blender.
2. Then puree until smooth.
3. Put pork and tomatillo mixture in a medium pot. 1-inch of puree should cover the pork; if not, add water until it covers it.
4. Season with pepper & salt and cover it simmers.
5. Simmer over low heat for 22 minutes.
6. Now, finely shred the remaining lettuce leaves.
7. When the stew is done cooking, garnish with cilantro, radishes, finely shredded lettuce, sliced jalapenos, and lime wedges.

Nutrition:
- 370 Calories
- 36g Proteins
- 19g Fat

78. Cheeseburger Pie

Difficulty: Easy
Preparation Time: 20 minutes
Cooking Time: 90 minutes
Servings: 4
Ingredients
- 1 large spaghetti squash (1 green)
- 1 lb. lean ground beef (1 lean)
- 2 eggs (1 lean)
- 1/3 cup low-fat, plain Greek yogurt (1/2 healthy fat)

- 2 Tbsp. Tomato sauce (1/2 condiment)
- 1/2 tsp. Worcestershire sauce (1/2 condiment)
- 2/3 cup reduced-fat cheddar cheese (1 healthy fat)
- 2 oz. dill pickle slices (1/4 green)

Direction

1. Preheat oven to 400°F. Slice spaghetti squash in half lengthwise; dismiss pulp and seeds.
2. Spray insides with cooking spray.
3. Place squash halves cut-side-down onto a foil-lined baking sheet, and bake for 30 minutes.
4. Once cooked, let cool to before scraping squash flesh with a fork to remove spaghetti-like strands; set aside.
5. Push squash strands in the bottom and up sides of the greased pie pan, creating an even layer.
6. Meanwhile, set up pie filling.
7. In a lightly greased, medium-sized skillet, cook beef and onion over medium heat for 8 to 10 minutes, sometimes stirring, until meat is brown. Drain and remove from heat.
8. In a medium-sized bowl, whisk together eggs, tomato paste, Greek yogurt, and Worcestershire sauce. Stir in ground beef mixture.
9. Pour pie filling over squash crust.
10. Sprinkle meat filling with cheese and then top with dill pickle slices.
11. Bake for 40 minutes.

Nutrition:
- 409 Calories
- 24g Fat
- 31g Protein

79. Optavia Pizza Hack

Difficulty: Easy
Preparation Time: 8 minutes
Cooking Time: 17 minutes

Servings: 1
Ingredients

- 1/4 fueling of garlic mashed potato (1 green)
- 1/2 egg whites (1/2 healthy fat)
- 1/4 tablespoon of Baking powder (1/4 condiment)
- 3/4 oz. of reduced-fat shredded mozzarella (1/2 healthy fat)
- 1/8 cup of sliced white mushrooms (1/2 healthy fat)
- 1/16 cup of pizza sauce (1/4 condiment)
- 3/4 oz. of ground beef (1 lean)
- 1/4 sliced black olives (1/4 green)

Directions

1. Start by preheating the oven to 400°
2. Mix your baking powder and garlic potato packet
3. Add egg whites to your mixture and stir well until it blends.
4. Line the baking sheet with parchment paper and pour the mixed batter onto it
5. Situate onto another parchment paper on top of the batter and spread out the batter to a 1/8-inch circle.
6. Then place another baking sheet on top; this way, the matter is between two baking sheets. Place into an oven and bake for about 8 minutes until the pizza crust is golden brown.
7. For the toppings, place your ground beef in a sauté pan and fry till it's brown, and wash your mushrooms very well.
8. After the crust is baked, remove the top layer of parchment paper carefully to prevent the foam from sticking to the pizza crust.
9. Put your toppings on top of the crust and bake for an extra 8 minutes.
10. Once ready, slide the pizza off the parchment paper and into a plate.

Nutrition:
- 478 Calories
- 30g Protein
- 29g Fats

80. Turkey and Tomato Meatloaf Cups

Difficulty: Average
Preparation Time: 10 minutes
Cooking Time: 45 minutes
Servings: 6
Ingredients

- 1 large egg (1 lean)
- 2 pounds ground turkey breast (2 lean)
- 3 pieces of sun-dried tomatoes (1 green)
- 1/4 cup basil leaves (1/4 green)
- 1/2 teaspoon garlic powder (1/2 condiment)
- 5 ounces low-fat fresh mozzarella, shredded (1/2 healthy fat)

Direction

1. Preheat oven to 400°F.
2. Beat the egg in a big mixing bowl.
3. Add the remaining ingredients and mix everything with your hands until evenly combined.
4. Spray a 12-cup muffin tin and divide the turkey mix-among the muffin cups, pressing the mix in.
5. Cook in the preheated oven till the turkey is well, 1/4 teaspoon salt and 1/2 teaspoon pepper, to taste cooked for about 25-30 minutes.
6. Chill the meatloaves entirely and store them in a container in the fridge for up to 5 days.

Nutrition:
- 14g Fats
- 16.9g Protein
- 144 Calories

Chapter 4. Poultry Recipes

81. Beef-Chicken Meatball Casserole

Difficulty: Average
Preparation Time: 14 minutes
Cooking Time: 21 minutes
Servings: 7
Ingredients:

- 1 eggplant (1 green)
- 10 oz. ground chicken (1 lean)
- 8 oz. ground beef (1 lean)
- 1 teaspoon minced garlic (1/4 condiment)
- 1 teaspoon ground white pepper (1/8 condiment)
- 1 tomato (1 green)
- 1 egg (1 healthy fat)
- 1 tablespoon coconut flour (1/4 healthy fat)
- 8 oz. Parmesan, shredded (1/4 healthy fat)
- 2 tablespoon butter (1/4 healthy fat)
- 1/3 cup cream (1/4 healthy fat)

Directions:

1. Combine the ground chicken and ground beef in a large bowl.
2. Add the minced garlic and ground white pepper.
3. In the bowl crack the egg with the ground meat mixture and stir it carefully until well combined.
4. Then add the coconut flour and mix.
5. Make small meatballs from the ground meat.
6. Preheat the air fryer to 360 F.
7. Sprinkle the air fryer basket tray with the butter and pour the cream.
8. Peel the eggplant and chop it.
9. Put the meatballs over the cream and sprinkle them with the chopped eggplant.
10. Slice the tomato and place it over the eggplant.
11. Make a layer of shredded cheese over the sliced tomato.
12. Put the casserole in the air fryer and cook it for 21 minutes.
13. Let the casserole cool to room temperature before serving.

Nutrition:

- 324 Calories
- 16.8g Fat
- 33.9g Protein

82. Lemon Roasted Potatoes

Difficulty: Easy
Preparation Time: 11 minutes
Cooking Time: 60 minutes
Servings: 5
Ingredients:

- 3 cups of chicken broth (1 condiment)
- 1/2 teaspoon of ground black pepper (1/8 condiment)
- 1 teaspoon of oregano (1/8 condiment)
- 2 teaspoons of salt (1/8 condiment)
- 2 lemons, the juice should be extracted (1/8 condiment)
- 1/3 cup of olive oil (1/8 condiment)
- 3 pounds of potatoes, should be peeled and cut into wedges (2 healthy fat)

Directions:

1. Preheat your oven to 400F
2. Get a large bowl and put all the potato wedges. Spray lemon juice and olive oil over the wedges and toss them together to coat. Then season the potatoes with black pepper, oregano, and salt and toss once more to have a coat.
3. Get a 2-inch-deep pan and spread the potatoes wedges inside in one single row.

Next is to pour the chicken broth on top of the potatoes.

4. Roast the potatoes in the already preheated oven until it becomes golden brown and tender in about 1 hour.

Nutrition

- 282.1 Calories
- 4.6g Protein
- 12.2g Fat

83. Italian Chicken Bake

Difficulty: Average
Preparation Time: 15 minutes
Cooking Time: 40 minutes
Servings: 6
Ingredients:

- ¼ cup of parmesan cheese (1/4 healthy fat)
- ½ cup d low fat plain Greek yogurt (1/4 healthy fat)
- 4 tbsps. of cream cheese (1/2 healthy fat)
- 1 cup of low carbohydrate tomato sauce (1/4 condiment)
- ½ tsp. of Italian seasoning (1/4 condiment)
- ½ tsp. of garlic powder (1/4 condiment)
- 10 oz. of shredded chicken (1 lean)

Directions:

1. Preheat your oven to 350F
2. Get a greased glass casserole dish and place the already shredded chicken.
3. Mix all the remaining ingredients except the parmesan cheese
4. Pour the tomato sauce mixture you have over the chicken
5. Then top with parmesan cheese
6. You should bake for 25-30 minutes or until the casseroles begin to bring out bubbles.

Nutrition:

- 411 Calories
- 19g Fat
- 12g Protein

84. Crab Chicken

Difficulty: Difficult
Preparation Time: 9 minutes
Cooking Time: 40 minutes
Servings: 8
Ingredients:

- 1c coarse corn flour (1/4 condiment)
- 1/2 Cup Flour (1/4 condiment)
- 3/4 Cup Baking powder (1/4 condiment)
- 1/4 tablespoon Sare Kosar (1/4 condiment)
- 2 arpagic, finely chopped (1/8 condiment)
- Eat 8 ounces of claw crab meat (2.11 c) (2 lean)
- 4 oz. of Gruyere cheese, chilled (about 1 cup) (1/4 healthy fat)
- 1 c Dough water (1/4 condiment)

Directions:

1. Heat 1 1/2-inch oil in a large Dutch oven over medium heat up to 350 degrees F (deep-fry).
2. Meanwhile, mix the cornmeal, flour, baking powder, cayenne, baking soda, and 3/4 teaspoon salt in a bowl.
3. Add onion and onion and mix to combine. Add the crab meat and cheese and mix with a fork to combine. In the center of a well, add the butter and egg and mix to combine.
4. Spoon soup into the hot oil and be careful not to spill the pan and fry, occasionally turning until browned, 3 to 5 minutes. Transfer to a sheet of paper towel — season with salt, repeat with the remaining dough.

Nutrition:

- 351 Calories
- 4g Fat
- 12g Protein

85. Lean and Green Crunchy Chicken Tacos

Difficulty: Average
Preparation Time: 8 minutes
Cooking Time: 10 minutes
Servings: 4
Ingredients:

- ½ cup low sodium chicken stock (1 condiment)
- 2 chicken breasts, minced (2 lean)
- 1 clove of garlic, minced (1/4 condiment)
- 3 plum tomatoes, chopped (1/2 healthy fat)
- 1 teaspoon cumin powder (1/4 condiment)
- 1 teaspoon cinnamon powder (1/4 condiment)
- 1 teaspoon ground coriander (1/4 condiment)
- ½ red chili, chopped (1/8 condiment)
- 1 tablespoon lime juice (1/4 condiment)
- Meat from 1 ripe avocado (1 healthy fat)
- 1 cucumber (1 green)

Directions:

1. Place a tablespoon of chicken stock in a pan and heat over medium flame. Water sauté the chicken, garlic, and tomatoes for 4 minutes or until the tomatoes have wilted.
2. Season with cumin, cinnamon, and coriander. Reduce the heat to low and cook for another 5 minutes. Set aside and allow to cool.
3. Incorporate onion, chili, lime juice, and mashed avocado. This is the salsa.
4. Scoop the salsa and top on sliced cucumber. Top with cooked chicken.

Nutrition:

- 313 Calories
- 31.8g Protein
- 3.8g Fat

86. Chicken & Turkey Meatloaf

Difficulty: Average
Preparation Time: 9 minutes
Cooking Time: 25 minutes
Servings: 9
Ingredients:

- 3 tablespoon butter (1/2 healthy fat)
- 10 oz. ground turkey (1 lean)
- 7 oz. ground chicken (1 lean)
- 1 teaspoon dried dill (1/8 green)
- ½ teaspoon ground coriander (1/8 condiment)
- 2 tablespoons almond flour (1/4 condiment)
- 1 tablespoon minced garlic (1/8 condiment)
- 3 oz. fresh spinach (1 green)
- 1 teaspoon salt (1/8 condiment)
- 1 egg (1 healthy fat)
- ½ tablespoon paprika (1/4 condiment)
- 1 teaspoon sesame oil (1/8 condiment)

Directions:

1. Put the ground turkey and ground chicken in a large bowl.
2. Sprinkle the meat with dried dill, ground coriander, almond flour, minced garlic, salt, and paprika.
3. Then chop the fresh spinach and add it to the ground poultry mixture.
4. Break the egg into the meat mixture and mix well until you get a smooth texture.
5. Grease the air fryer basket tray with the olive oil.
6. Preheat the air fryer to 350 F.
7. Roll the ground meat mixture gently to make the flat layer.
8. Put the butter in the center of the meat layer.
9. Make the shape of the meatloaf from the ground meat mixture. Use your fingertips for this step.

10. Place the meatloaf in the air fryer basket tray.
11. Cook for 25 minutes.
12. When the meatloaf is cooked, allow it to rest before serving.

Nutrition:
- 142 Calories
- 9.8g Fat
- 13g Protein

87. Lemon Garlic Oregano Chicken with Asparagus

Difficulty: Average
Preparation Time: 8 minutes
Cooking Time: 40 minutes
Servings: 4
Ingredients:
- 1 small lemon, juiced (this should be about 2 tablespoons of lemon juice) (1 condiment)
- 1 ¾ lb. of bone-in, skinless chicken thighs (1 lean)
- 2 tablespoons of fresh oregano, minced (1/4 green)
- 2 cloves of garlic, minced (1/8 condiment)
- 2 lbs. of asparagus, trimmed (1/4 green)
- ¼ teaspoon each or less for black pepper and salt (1/8 condiment)

Directions:
1. Preheat the oven to about 350°F.
2. Put the chicken in a medium-sized bowl. Now, add the garlic, oregano, lemon juice, pepper, and salt and toss together to combine.
3. Roast the chicken in the air fryer oven until it reaches an internal temperature of 165°F in about 40 minutes. Once the chicken thighs have been cooked, remove and keep aside to rest.
4. Now, steam the asparagus on a stovetop or in a microwave to the desired doneness.
5. Serve asparagus with the roasted chicken thighs.

Nutrition:
- 350 Calories

- 10g Fat
- 32g Protein

88. Chicken Coconut Poppers

Difficulty: Difficult
Preparation Time: 14 minutes
Cooking Time: 10 minutes
Servings: 6
Ingredients:
- ½ cup coconut flour (1/4 condiment)
- 1 teaspoon chili flakes (1/4 condiment)
- 1 teaspoon ground black pepper (1/8 condiment)
- 1 teaspoon garlic powder (1/8 condiment)
- 11 oz. chicken breast, boneless, skinless (1 lean)
- 1 tablespoon olive oil (1/8 condiment)

Directions:
1. Cut the chicken breast into sizeable cubes and put them in a large bowl.
2. Sprinkle the chicken cubes with chili flakes, ground black pepper, garlic powder, and stir them well using your hands.
3. After this, sprinkle the chicken cubes with the almond flour.
4. Shake the bowl with the chicken cubes gently to coat the meat.
5. Preheat the air fryer to 365 F.
6. Grease the air fryer basket tray with the olive oil.
7. Place the chicken cubes inside.
8. Cook the chicken poppers for 10 minutes.
9. Turn the chicken poppers over after 5 minutes of cooking.
10. Allow the cooked chicken poppers to cool before serving.

Nutrition:
- 123 Calories
- 4.6g Fat
- 13.2g Protein

89. Lemon Basil Chicken

Difficulty: Easy
Preparation Time: 9 minutes
Cooking Time: 19 minutes
Servings: 5
Ingredients:
- 1 tbsp of extra-virgin olive oil (1/4 condiment)
- 1/2 large finely chopped yellow onion about 1 cup (1 green)
- 4 minced cloves garlic (1/8 condiment)
- 1 1/2 lbs. boneless skinless chicken breasts (1 lean)
- 2 tbsp of low-sodium soy sauce (1/4 condiment)
- 1/4 tsp of ground black pepper (1/8 condiment)
- Loosely packed baby spinach (5 cup) (2 green)
- 1 tbsp of lemon zest (1/8 condiment)
- 2 tablespoons of lemon juice freshly pressed (1/8 condiment)
- 2 cups of fresh basil leaves (1/4 green)
- Kosher salt and pepper (1/8 condiment)
- Prepared brown rice (1 healthy fat)

Directions:
1. Cook olive oil in a big skillet over medium heat. When heated, add the onion and cook for about 4 minutes, stirring frequently, until softened. Connect the garlic and cook for an additional 30 seconds until fragrant.
2. Add the chicken, raise the heat to medium and cook for about 3 minutes, browning on all sides. Stir in the soy sauce and also black pepper. Let cook for about 3 minutes until the chicken is fully cooked through.
3. Stir a few handfuls at a time into the spinach, letting the heat of the pan wilt it as you go. Stir in the lemon zest, basil and lemon juice. Just cook and stir until the basil is wilted, about 1 more minute. As required, taste

and season with additional salt or pepper. Serve warm, as desired, with rice.

Nutrition:
- 318 Calories
- 16g Fats
- 9g Protein

90. Chicken Crust Margherita Pizza

Difficulty: Easy
Preparation Time: 8 minutes
Cooking Time: 30 minutes
Servings: 2
Ingredients:
- ¼ cup of chopped basil (1/4 green)
- 2 plum tomatoes, to be sliced (1/4 green)
- ½ cup of no-sugar-added tomato sauce (like Rao's Homemade) (1/8 condiment)
- ½ tsp. of Italian seasoning (1/8 condiment)
- 2 tbsp. of grated parmesan cheese (1/4 healthy fat)
- 1 egg (1 lean)
- ½ lb. of ground chicken breast (1 lean)

Directions:
1. Preheat oven to 400F.
2. Combine the ground chicken breast, egg, parmesan cheese and Italian seasoning in a medium-sized bowl. Then, form the chicken mixture to a shape similar to a thin and circular crust in a parchment-lined but lightly greased baking sheet. Bake for about 20 minutes when it should have become golden.
3. Top with tomato slices, cheese, and sauce and bake until the cheese becomes melted in about 7-10 minutes.
4. Then top with fresh basil before you serve.

Nutrition:
- 337 Calories
- 21g Fat
- 14g Protein

91. Chicken Stir Fry

Difficulty: Easy
Preparation Time: 20 minutes
Cooking Time: 1 minutes
Servings: 4
Ingredients:
- ½ cup chicken broth, low sodium (1 condiment)
- 12 ounces skinless chicken breasts, cut into strips (2 lean)
- 1 cup red bell pepper, seeded and chopped (1/4 green)
- 8 ounces (1 cup) broccoli, cut into florets (1/2 green)
- 1 teaspoon crushed red pepper (1/4 green)

Directions:
1. Place a small amount of chicken broth in a saucepan. Heat over medium flame and stir in the chicken. Water sauté the chicken for at least 5 minutes while stirring constantly.
2. Place the rest of the ingredients and stir.
3. Cover and cook for another 5 minutes.

Nutrition:
- 137 Calories
- 15g Protein
- 1.2g Fat

92. Greek Island Chicken Shish Kebabs

Difficulty: Easy
Preparation Time: 9 minutes
Cooking Time: 10 minutes
Servings: 6
Ingredients:
- 12 medium of blanks fresh mushroom (1 healthy fat)
- 12 cherry tomatoes (1 green)
- 2 large red or green bell peppers, should be cut into 1-inch pieces (1 green)
- 2 pounds of skinless, boneless chicken breast (2 lean)
- ¼ teaspoon of ground black pepper (1/8 condiment)
- ¼ teaspoon of salt (1/8 condiment)
- ½ teaspoon of dried thyme (1/8 green)
- 1 teaspoon of dried oregano (1/8 green)
- 1 teaspoon of ground cumin (1/8 condiment)
- 2 cloves of garlic, to be minced (1/8 condiment)
- ¼ cup of white vinegar (1/4 condiment)
- ¼ cup of lemon juice (1/4 condiment)
- ¼ cup of olive oil (1/8 condiment)

Directions:
1. Whisk the black pepper, salt, thyme, oregano, cumin, garlic, vinegar, lemon juice, and olive oil together in a large ceramic bowl or glass. Add chicken and toss to get a thorough coat. Get a plastic wrap to cover the bowl and put it in the refrigerator to marinate for at least 2 hours.
2. Put the wooden skewers in water and soak for about 30 minutes before you will use them.
3. Get an outdoor grill, lightly oil the grate, and preheat with medium-high heat.
4. Take the chicken away from the marinade and remove excess liquid from it. Then, pour away the remaining marinade. Next is to thread the marinated chicken with mushrooms, cherry tomatoes, onion, and bell peppers onto the skewers.
5. Then put the skewers on the already preheated grill and cook, turn as frequently as possible until it becomes brown from all of its sides,

wait for about 10 minutes when the chicken should no longer be pink from its center.

Nutrition:
- 289.6 calories
- 33.8g Protein
- 13.1g Fat

93. Chicken Kabobs Mexicana

Difficulty: Average
Preparation Time: 9 minutes
Cooking Time: 10 minutes
Servings: 4
Ingredients:
- 10 cherry tomatoes (1 green)
- 1 red bell pepper, should be cut into 1-inch pieces (1/2 green)
- 1 small zucchini, should be cut into ½ - inch slices (1/2 green)
- 2 breast halves, with the bone and skin removed (2 lean)
- Black pepper and salt to taste (1/8 condiment)
- 1 lime, should be juiced (1/4 condiment)
- 2 tablespoons of chopped fresh cilantro (1/8 green)
- 1 teaspoon of ground cumin (1/8 condiment)
- 2 tablespoons of olive oil (1/8 condiment)

Directions:
1. Get a shallow dish and mix lime juice, chopped cilantro, cumin, and olive oil inside. Then season with pepper and salt. Add chicken and make sure to mix it very well. Cover with a lid for not less than 1 hour.
2. Let your grill preheat over high heat.
3. Thread tomatoes, red bell pepper, onion, zucchini, and chicken onto skewers.
4. Use oil to brush the grill and arrange the skewers on the hot grate. Let it cook for approximately 10 minutes till the chicken is thoroughly cooked. You should turn at

intervals so that all its sides will be well cooked.

Nutrition:
- 165.8 Calories
- 15.2g Protein
- 7.9g Fat

94. Chicken with Veggies and Quinoa

Difficulty: Average
Preparation Time: 11 minutes
Cooking Time: 25 minutes
Servings: 4
Ingredients:
- 1 tablespoon of lime juice (1/4 condiment)
- 8 leaf of fresh basil leaves (1/4 green)
- 4 ounces of crumbled feta cheese (1/2 healthy fat)
- 1 tomato, should be diced (1/2 green)
- 1 zucchini, should be diced (1/2 green)
- 2 tablespoons of extra-virgin olive oil (1/8 condiment)
- 2 breast halves with the bone and skin removed, should be cut into strips (2 lean)
- 2 garlic cloves (1/8 condiment)
- 2 tablespoons of extra-virgin olive oil (1/8 condiment)
- 2 cups of chicken broth (1 condiment)
- 1 cup of rinsed quinoa (1 healthy fat)

Directions:
1. Get a saucepan and add the chicken broth and quinoa and allow to boil, lower the heat to simmer level, and place a lid over the saucepan. Let it simmer until the white line is visible in the grain, the quinoa becomes fluffy, and the broth is absorbed in about 12 minutes.
2. Get a skillet and pour in 2 tablespoons of olive oil, heat it, cook and stir the onion and garlic cloves for 5

minutes. Add the chicken breast strips while stirring and let it cook for about 5 minutes; the chicken should still be a little bit pink at the center from this point. At this point, remove the chicken meat and put it on one side.
3. Pour another 2 tablespoons of olive oil in the skillet and cook and stir the tomato and zucchini till the zucchini become tender in about 5-8 minutes. Put the chicken back inside the skillet and sprinkle with lime juice, basil leaves, and feta cheese. Cook for 10 minutes. Serve with hot quinoa.

Nutrition:
- 445.3 Calories
- 23.3g Protein
- 23.6g Fat

95. Summer Chicken Burgers

Difficulty: Average
Preparation Time: 8 minutes
Cooking Time: 16 minutes
Servings: 7
Ingredients:
- 4 slices of provolone cheese (1/2 healthy fat)
- 4 tablespoons of mayonnaise (1/4 condiment)
- 4 roll (blanks) of hamburger buns (2 healthy fat)
- Pepper and Salt to taste (1/8 condiment)
- 4 breast halves with the bone and skin removed, boneless, skinless chicken breast halves (2 lean)
- 1 large Vidalia onions, to be sliced into rings (1 green)
- 1 tablespoon of butter (1/4 condiment)
- 1 tablespoon of lemon juice (1/4 condiment)
- 1 ripe avocado, should be sliced (1/2 healthy fat)

Directions:
1. Get a small bowl and combine the lemon juice

and sliced avocado. Add water until it covers them up and put them aside. Get an outdoor grill, apply a light oil to grate, and preheat with high heat.

2. Put butter in a large, heavy skillet and place it on medium-high heat. Sauté the onions until they become brown and caramelized, then set aside.

3. Season the chicken with pepper and salt. Situate it on the grill and let it cook until the juices become dry, and it is no longer pink, using about 5 minutes for each side. Situate buns on the grill until they are toast.

4. Next is to spread the buns with mayonnaise to taste, then layer it with avocado, provolone, caramelized onion, and chicken.

Nutrition:
- 587.2 Calories
- 40.6g Protein
- 32.2g Fat

96. Easy Turkey Chili

Difficulty: Easy
Preparation Time: 13 minutes
Cooking Time: 40 minutes
Servings: 5
Ingredients:
- ¼ teaspoon of salt (1/8 condiment)
- ¼ teaspoon of crushed red pepper flakes (1/8 condiment)
- 2 teaspoon of chili powder (1/8 condiment)
- 1 ½ teaspoon of ground cumin (1/8 condiment)
- 1 28 ounces can dice tomatoes (1 green)
- 2 teaspoons of olive oil (1/8 condiment)
- 1 jalapeno pepper, should be diced (1/4 green)
- 1 medium green bell pepper, should be diced (1/4 green)
- 1 medium red bell pepper, should be diced (1/4 green)

- 2 garlic cloves, should be minced (1/4 condiment)
- 1 ½ lb. 99% lean ground turkey (1 lean)

Toppings (Per Serving)
- 3 tablespoon of low-fat shredded cheddar cheese (1/2 healthy fat)
- 2 tablespoons of low-fat plain Greek Yogurt (1/2 healthy fat)
- 1.5 oz. of avocado, diced (1/2 healthy fat)
- 2 tablespoons of chopped scallions (1 green)

Directions:
1. Put a large soup pot on medium-high heat and sauté peppers, garlic, and onions in oil for about 4-5 minutes or till they become tender. Next is to add turkey and cook until it becomes brown with no traces of pink color.

2. Pour in the salt, red pepper flakes, chili powder, cumin, water (optional), and tomatoes and mix very well until they blend. Cover and simmer in low heat for 21 minutes. Serve with the toppings.

Nutrition:
- 360 Calories
- 49g Protein
- 11g Fat

97. Turkey Burger

Difficulty: Average
Preparation Time: 9 minutes
Cooking Time: 10 minutes
Servings: 4
Ingredients:
- 2 tablespoons of chopped fresh cilantro (1/4 green)
- 2 tablespoons of plain yogurt (1/4 healthy fat)
- 1 tablespoon of lemon juice (1/8 condiment)
- 1 ½ teaspoon of garam masala (1/8 condiment)
- 1 ½ teaspoon of salt (1/8 condiment)
- 1 ½ teaspoon of finely grated fresh ginger (1/8 condiment)

- 2 cloves of garlic, should be crushed and minced (1/8 condiment)
- 1 teaspoon of Chile paste (1/8 condiment)
- 1 ½ tablespoon of ground almonds (1/2 healthy fat)
- 1 ½ tablespoon of plain bread crumbs (1/2 healthy fat)
- 1 ½ pound of ground turkey (1 lean)

Directions:
1. Combine cilantro, yogurt, lemon juice, garam masala, salt, ginger, garlic, chili paste, almonds, breadcrumbs, and ground turkey; mix very well with your clean hands or spatula.

2. Use the ground turkey mixture to form a ball shape, divide it into 4 even pieces, and then put in the refrigerator for an hour. Form a patty with each of the pieces using your damp hands.

3. Get your grill preheated with over medium heat and leave the turkey burger patties in the refrigerator until the grill becomes hot. Next is to grill the burgers until you observe that the patties are cooked halfway and turn to the other side; you should grill each of its sides for about 5 minutes. The burger is said to be done when a crack appears on the surface, and its juice starts getting to the top.

Nutrition:
- 301.2 Calories
- 34.4g Protein
- 16.3g Fat

98. Lean and Green Crockpot Chili

Difficulty: Average
Preparation Time: 10 minutes
Cooking Time: 45 minutes
Servings: 8
Ingredients:
- 1-pound boneless skinless chicken breasts, cut into strips (1 lean)

- 2 teaspoons ground cumin (1/8 condiment)
- 1 teaspoon minced garlic (1/4 condiment)
- ½ teaspoon chili powder (1/8 condiment)
- Salt and pepper to taste (1/8 condiment)
- 1 ½ cups water (1/4 condiment)
- 1 can green enchilada sauce (1/8 condiment)
- ½ cup dried beans, soaked overnight (1/4 healthy fat)

Directions:
1. Place all ingredients in a pot.
2. Mix all ingredients until combined.
3. Close the lid and turn on the heat to medium.
4. Bring to a boil and allow to simmer for 45 minutes or until the beans are cooked.
5. Serve with chopped cilantro on top.

Nutrition:
- 84 Calories
- 13.4g Protein
- 1.7g Fat

99. Sheet Pan Chicken Fajita Lettuce Wraps

Difficulty: Average
Preparation Time: 9 minutes
Cooking Time: 45 minutes
Servings: 5
Ingredients:
- ¼ cup of plain non-fat Greek yogurt (1/2 healthy fat)
- 6 leaves from a romaine heart (2 green)
- Juice from half of lime. (1/4 condiment)
- 2 tsp. of fajita seasoning (1/4 condiment)
- 2 tsp. of olive oil (1/4 condiment)
- 2 bell pepper, to be thinly sliced into little strips (1 green)
- 1 lb. of chicken breast, this should also be thinly sliced in strips (1 lean)

Directions:
1. You will need to preheat your oven to 400F
2. Get a large resealable plastic bag and combine all the ingredients except the lettuce. Then mix well to fully coat the vegetables and chicken with seasoning and oil.
3. Get a foil-lined baking sheet and spread the contents of the bag evenly on it. Bake for 25-30 minutes, during which the chicken must have been thoroughly cooked.
4. Serve on the lettuce leaves and top with Greek yogurt if you like.

Nutrition:
- 311 Calories
- 16g Fat
- 9g Protein

100. Ginger Lemon Chicken and Noodles

Difficulty: Average
Preparation Time: 11 minutes
Cooking Time: 15 minutes
Servings: 4
Ingredients:
- Unrefined coconut oil, 4 tsp (1/4 condiment)
- Thai seasoning, 1 tablespoon (or lemongrass, lime, onion, garlic, ginger, red pepper, orange zest, pepper, and salt) (1 condiment)
- Lime juice, 1 tablespoon (1/2 condiment)
- Chicken breasts, skinless, boneless, 1 1/2 lbs. (cut in half if large) (2 lean)

- Zucchini noodles, 4 c prepared (2 healthy fat)

Directions:
1. Add the first three contents of the recipe to a big zipper plastic bag.
2. Shake the plastic bag to combine all the contents to prepare the marinade. Add chicken to the marinade bag, squeeze out the air to seal the bag, and place in the fridge for 4 hours or overnight.
3. Preheat frying pan or a grill pan when ready to cook the chicken. Cook chicken on both sides for 12-15 minutes over medium-high heat; cook both sides of the chicken until it's fully cooked. Check the temperature with a meat thermometer to see if it cooked through.
4. Prepare zucchini noodles While the chicken is cooking.
5. Serve cooked chicken over zoodles, or with any of your favorite side dish.

Nutrition:
- 291 Calories
- 16g Fat
- 11g Protein

101. Chinese Five Spice Chicken

Difficulty: Average
Preparation Time: 20 minutes
Cooking Time: 20 minutes
Servings: 2
Ingredients
- 2 entire chicken breasts bone-in, with skin (2 lean)
- 2 tsp. of five-spice Chinese powder (1/2 condiment)
- 1 tsp. of powdered garlic (1/4 condiment)
- Salt and pepper, for taste (1/8 condiment)
- 1 tbsp. olive oil (1/8 condiment)

Direction
1. Rinse the breasts and pat the chicken dry. Sprinkle with garlic powder, five-spice powder, salt, and

pepper. Cover securely in aluminum foil and cool for at least 2 hours to marinate.
2. Preheat your oven to 175° C (350° F).
3. Remove the wrapping from the chicken breasts and put them in a 9x13 inches baking dish that is lightly greased.
4. Pour olive oil and bake for 45 minutes at 350° F (175° C), or until the juices are cooked through and clear.

Nutrition
- 572 Calories
- 61g Protein
- 33g Fat

102. Feta Chicken with Zucchini

Difficulty: Easy
Preparation Time: 20 minutes
Cooking Time: 20 minutes
Servings: 2
Ingredients
- 2 tbsp. olive oil (1/8 condiment)
- 1 lemon (1/4 condiment)
- 4 boneless, skinless chicken breasts (2 lean)
- One-fourth tsp. kosher salt (1/8 condiment)
- 2 mid-sized zucchinis (1 green)
- One-fourth cup fresh, chopped flat-leaf parsley leaves (1/4 healthy fat)
- 13 tsp. of black pepper (1/8 condiment)
- One-third cup of crumbled Feta (about 2 oz.) (1/2 condiment)

Direction
1. Heat the furnace to 400° F. In a roasting pan, drizzle one-half tablespoon of the oil. In thin stripes, remove the skin from the lemon; set aside. Slice the lemon thinly. In the pan, place half the slices.
2. On top of the lemon slices, place the chicken and season with 1/8 of a teaspoon of salt.

3. Lengthwise, split each zucchini in half, then split each half into one-fourth inch-thick half-moons. Combine the zucchini, parsley, pepper, the remaining oil, slices of lemon, and salt in a bowl; toss.
4. Spread the mixture over the chicken and sprinkle it over the top with the Feta.
5. Roast for 15 to 20 minutes until the chicken is fully cooked. Switch it to a cutting board and cut it into thirds for each piece.
6. Divide the chicken, zucchini mixture, and lemons between individual plates, and sprinkle with the zest.

Nutrition:
- 276 Calories
- 11.6g Protein
- 8.8g Fat

103. Cinnamon Chicken

Difficulty: Average
Preparation Time: 20 minutes
Cooking Time: 20 minutes
Servings: 2
Ingredients
- 4 or 5 (4-6 oz.) boneless chicken breasts without skin (2 lean)
- 2 tbsp. Italian Dressing Low-Calorie (1/4 condiment)
- 1 tsp. of cinnamon (1/4 condiment)
- 1 1/2 tsp. powdered garlic (1/4 condiment)
- 1/4 tsp. salt (optional) (1/8 condiment)
- 1/4 tsp. pepper (1/8 condiment)

Direction
1. Heat the oven to 350 ° C.
2. In a 13x9 baking dish, bring the chicken in. Pour the Italian sauce over it.
3. Blend the remaining ingredients in a small bowl. Sprinkle chicken over it. Bake for 40–45 minutes.

Nutrition:
- 94g Protein
- 26g Fat

- 229 Calories

104. Chicken with Acorn Squash and Tomatoes

Difficulty: Average
Preparation Time: 20 minutes
Cooking Time: 20 minutes
Servings: 2
Ingredients
- 1 small acorn squash (1 green)
- 1 pint of grape tomatoes, halved (1 green)
- 4 garlic cloves, cut (1/4 condiment)
- 3 tbsp. olive oil (1/8 condiment)
- Black pepper and kosher salt (1/8 condiment)
- 4 6-oz boneless, skinless breasts of chicken (2 lean)
- One-half tsp. ground cilantro (1/4 green)
- 2 tbsp. of fresh oregano, chopped (1/4 green)

Direction
1. Heat the furnace to 425° F.
2. Throw in squash, tomatoes, and garlic with 2 tablespoons of oil, one-half teaspoon of salt, and one-fourth teaspoon of pepper on a broad-rimmed baking sheet.
3. Roast the vegetables for 20 to 25 minutes until the squash is tender.
4. Meanwhile, over medium heat, heat the remaining tablespoon of oil in a large skillet.
5. Season the coriander, one-half teaspoon salt, and one-fourth teaspoon pepper with the poultry. Cook, 6 to 7 minutes per hand, until golden brown and cooked through.
6. Serve the squash and tomatoes with the chicken and sprinkle with the oregano.

Nutrition:
- 877 Calories
- 34g Protein
- 39g Fat

105.   Chicken Cordon Blue

Difficulty: Difficult
Preparation Time: 15 minutes
Cooking Time: 20 minutes
Servings: 2
Ingredients

- 2 4-oz boneless chicken breasts, skinless (2 lean)
- 2 large leaves of spinach, washed, stems removed (2 green)
- 2 wedges laughing cow light cheese (1/2 healthy fat)
- 1 oz. of reduced-ham without nitrate sodium (1 lean)
- Paprika to taste (1/8 condiment)
- 1 garlic clove, minced (1/8 condiment)
- 1 tsp. of extra-virgin olive oil (1/8 condiment)
- 1 cup Baby Bella mushrooms, sliced (1/2 green)
- 1/8 tsp. ground black pepper (1/8 condiment)
- 2 tsp. yogurt sauce (1/2 healthy fat)
- 1/2 cup Greek nonfat yogurt (1/2 healthy fat)
- 1 tbsp. Dijon mustard (1/8 condiment)
- 1/2 tsp. buttermilk (1/4 healthy fat)
- 2 tbsp. chives, chopped (1/4 green)

Direction

1. Set up the oven to 400° F.
2. Pound the chicken with a mallet till it is 1/4-inch thick. Take care not to rip a breast apart.
3. On top of each breast lay 1 spinach leaf. Spread a slice of cheese to cover the spinach. Top with 1/2 slice of ham and fold the ham over to match the breast as desired.
4. Roll each breast up gently and protect it with a toothpick. Sprinkle with paprika on the outer side of the breast. Bake for 20 minutes in the oven until the chicken is completely cooked.
5. While the chicken is cooking, sauté the garlic in oil in a non-adhesive skillet over medium-high heat for 1 minute. Add pepper and mushrooms. Stir regularly until soft for 10 minutes. Withdraw from the sun. Cover and set aside.
6. Whisk together the yogurt, mustard, and buttermilk for sauce preparation. Mix the chives in.
7. Divide the mushrooms evenly, about 1/4 cup each, between 2 plates. Then put the chicken on the mushroom bed and drizzle the top with 1/4 cup of yogurt sauce.

Nutrition:

- 180 Calories
- 29g Protein
- 5.35g Fat

106.   Chicken Kampala

Difficulty: Difficult
Preparation Time: 15 minutes
Cooking Time: 1 and 1/2 hours
Servings: 5
Ingredients

- 3 lbs. chicken parts (2 lean)
- 2 tbsp. butter (1 healthy fat)
- 2 tbsp. olive oil (1/4 condiment)
- 2 cloves garlic, minced (1/8 condiment)
- 1 c. canned tomatoes (1/2 condiment)
- 3 oz. tomato paste (1/4 condiment)
- 2 sticks cinnamon (1/8 condiment)
- 1/4 tsp. ground allspice (1/8 condiment)
- 1/4 tsp. sugar (1/8 condiment)
- 1/4 c. red wine (1 healthy fat)

Direction

1. Heat 2 tbsp. butter and 1 tbsp. olive oil in a skillet and stir in chicken. Cook chicken over medium heat for about 15 minutes, stirring often to keep chicken from burning. Once the chicken is browned, remove it from the skillet and add the remaining butter and oil to the pan.
2. Make sure the skillet is still hot before adding the onions and cooking for about 5 minutes over medium heat. Stir in the garlic and tomatoes, cooking for another 5 minutes. Stir in the tomato paste, cinnamon, allspice, sugar, red wine, and chicken, including any juices.
3. Bring to a boil and cover tightly (you can use foil and cover with foil). Reduce heat and simmer, stirring occasionally, for 1 and 1/2 hours.
4. Serve with white rice.

Nutrition:

- 421 Calories
- 56g Protein
- 17g Fat

107.   Garlic and Citrus Turkey with Mixed Greens

Difficulty: Difficult
Preparation Time: 5 minutes
Cooking Time: 15 minutes
Servings: 4
Ingredients

- 4 teaspoons (or oil of your choice and fresh chopped garlic) (1/4 condiment)
- 1 C scallion greens, thinly sliced (1 green)
- 1 3/4 pounds lean ground turkey (1 lean)
- 1 Tablespoon (or lemon, pepper, garlic, onion, parsley, salt & pepper) (1/2 condiment)
- 8 cups mixed green lettuce (2 green)
- 1 lemon cut into wedges for garnish (1/8 condiment)

Direction

1. Heat a large non-stick skillet over medium-high heat with oil and sauté garlic for 1

minute, stirring. Add scallion greens, green onions, ground turkey, and seasonings. Stir and cook for 15 minutes.
2. Split greens between 4 plates and top each plate with 1/4 of the meat mixture.
3. Serve with lemon wedges.
4. Enjoy!

Nutrition:

- 355 Calories
- 38g Protein
- 21g Fat

108. Greek Chicken with Yogurt

Difficulty: Easy
Preparation Time: 10 minutes
Cooking Time: 20 minutes
Servings: 4
Ingredients

- 5 oz. plain Greek yogurt (1/2 healthy fat)
- 2 tbsp mayonnaise (1/4 healthy fat)
- 1/2 cup grated parmesan cheese (1/2 healthy fat)
- 1 tsp garlic powder (1/8 condiment)
- 1/4 tsp salt (1/8 condiment)
- 1/4 tsp black pepper (1/8 condiment)
- 1.5 lb. chicken tenders (whole) or chicken breasts (cut in quarters) (1 lean)
- Parsley (chopped, for garnish) (1/8 green)

Direction

1. Fire up the oven to 480 degrees F.
2. Line a baking sheet with parchment paper. Spray oil on parchment, then place chicken on top (the oil will help prevent the chicken from sticking to the parchment paper).
3. In a small mixing bowl, whisk together the yogurt, mayo, parmesan, garlic powder, salt, and pepper. Toss the chicken tenders or breasts with the yogurt mixture and place them on the baking sheet. Repeat with the remaining chicken and yogurt/spices mixture.
4. Bake for 20 minutes. Garnish with extra parsley and serve immediately with extra Greek yogurt, mayo, and grated parmesan sprinkled on top.

Nutrition:

- 325 Calories
- 42g Protein
- 14g Fat

109. Mexican Chicken in Orange Juice

Difficulty: Average
Preparation Time: 2 hours
Cooking Time: 20 minutes
Servings: 4
Ingredients

- 1 c. fresh orange juice (1/4 condiment)
- 2 Tbsp. fresh lime juice (1/4 condiment)
- 1 dried chipotle chili pepper, stemmed and seeded (1 green)
- 1 c. mild salsa (1/4 condiment)
- 1/4 c. olive oil (1/4 condiment)
- 1 tsp. salt (1/8 condiment)
- 4 boneless, skinless chicken breast halves (2 lean)
- 1 orange, sliced into rings (1 healthy fat)
- 1/4 c. chopped fresh cilantro leaves (1/4 green)

Direction

1. Place all ingredients except chicken and orange slices in a blender. Blend until smooth.
2. Store in refrigerator overnight to allow flavors to blend.
3. Add chicken to orange juice mixture and marinate for 2 hours
4. Prepare grill for medium heat.
5. Remove chicken from marinade; reserve marinade.
6. Place chicken on grill rack coated with nonstick cooking spray and grill for 10 minutes. Turn and cook 10 minutes longer. Situate chicken to cutting board and slice into thin bite-size slices.
7. Pour reserved marinade into a small saucepan. Bring to a boil over high heat. Reduce heat to medium and boil for 5 minutes.
8. Add orange slices to the saucepan and mix well. Heat through.
9. Divide cilantro evenly among 4 dinner plates. Top each of the plates evenly with orange slices and sauced chicken. Garnish with lime slices and serve.

Nutrition:

- 489 Calories
- 55g Protein
- 19g Fat

110. Italian Chicken with White Wine, Peppers, and Anchovy

Difficulty: Average
Preparation Time: 10 minutes
Cooking Time: 25 minutes
Servings: 4
Ingredients
For the Chicken

- 1 tablespoon olive oil (1/8 condiment)
- 4 boneless skinless chicken breasts (2 lean)
- salt and fresh ground pepper to taste (1/8 condiment)
- 1 teaspoon garlic powder (1/8 condiment)
- 1 tablespoon anchovy (1/4 healthy fat)

For the Creamy White Wine Sauce

- 1 tbsp. unsalted butter (1/4 healthy fat)
- 1 big yellow onion diced (1/4 green)
- 3 garlic cloves (1/4 condiment)
- 1 cup dry white wine (1/2 condiment)
- 1 tsp. dried thyme (1/8 green)
- Half cup half and half evaporated milk (1/2 healthy fat)

Direction

1. Heat the olive oil in a heavy large skillet over medium-high heat. Season the chicken with salt, pepper garlic powder and combine it with the anchovy flakes. Add the chicken to the pan and cook until it is golden brown on both sides. Ensure that you are sautéing in the pan, lower the heat to keep it from burning.
2. Whip the wine, thyme, garlic, pepper, and salt in a glass bowl. Add the cream,

mix in the cubes of butter. Keep mixing for a few minutes and then add the peppers. Keep mixing and cook the fusion.

3. Cut the chicken into strips (or very small pieces if desired, the pieces are easier to eat). Combine the chicken with the mixture. Cook the fusion for 10 minutes. Serve with pasta, or on warm pieces of French bread.

Nutrition:
- 742 Calories
- 110g Protein
- 26.8g Fat

111. Tagine of Chicken and Olives

Difficulty: Average
Preparation Time: 3-4 hours
Cooking Time: 45 minutes
Servings: 4
Ingredients
- 5 cloves garlic, finely chopped (1/8 condiment)
- One-fourth teaspoon saffron threads, pulverized (1/4 condiment)
- One-half teaspoon ground ginger (1/8 condiment)
- 1 teaspoon sweet paprika (1/8 condiment)
- One-half teaspoon ground cumin (1/8 condiment)
- One-half teaspoon turmeric (1/8 condiment)
- 1 chicken, slice in 8 to 10 pieces (3 lean)
- 2 tablespoons extra virgin olive oil (1/8 condiment)
- 1 cinnamon stick (1/4 condiment)

- 8 Kalamata olives (1/8 condiment)
- 8 cracked green olives (1/4 green)
- 1 large preserved lemon (1/4 condiment)
- 1 cup chicken stock (1 condiment)
- Juice of 1/2 lemon (1/4 condiment)
- 1 tablespoon chopped flat-leaf parsley (1/4 green)

Direction
1. In a huge plastic food bag, combine the garlic, saffron, ginger, parsley, paprika, cumin, turmeric, salt and pepper. Stir in the chicken and shake the bag to coat the chicken with the spices. Set aside to marinate for 1 hour to 3 hours.
2. Transfer the chicken to a large pot and add the remaining ingredients. If there isn't any liquid in the bag, add enough water to cover the ingredients in the pot. Cover and cook until tender and the liquid are reduced, about 35 to 45 minutes.
3. Serve garnished with lemon juice and parsley.

Nutrition:
- 1090 Calories
- 115g Protein
- 64g Fat

112. Chicken Sancho

Difficulty: Difficult
Preparation Time: 5 minutes
Cooking Time: 1 hour
Servings: 6
Ingredients
- 1 teaspoon olive oil (1/8 condiment)
- 5 scallions, chopped (1 green)
- 1 tomato, chopped (1/2 green)
- 4 cloves garlic, chopped (1/8 condiment)
- 6 skinless chicken thighs on the bone (3 lean)
- 1 cup chopped cilantro (1/8 green)

- 3 medium potatoes (1 healthy fat)
- 3 pieces of yucca (1/4 condiment)
- 1 small green plantain (1/4 green)
- 1 tsp cumin (1/8 condiment)
- 2 chicken bouillon cubes (1/4 condiment)

Direction
1. Heat the oil in a large skillet, brown the chicken, skin side first over medium heat for 2-3 minutes, then take them out.
2. Preheat the oven to 350F.
3. Chop the scallions, tomatoes, and garlic in a food processor
4. Preheat skillet again over medium heat, add the scallion, and garlic, cook for a minute or until the onion is translucent. Add the cilantro and chicken, stir.
5. Prepare the chicken broth by adding the chicken bouillon cubes to a large saucepan and adding 2 cups of water. Boil, decrease the heat and simmer for 6 minutes.
6. Add the potatoes, yucca, and plantain to the skillet, stir. Pour in the chicken broth, cover and cook until the vegetables are tender. Add a pinch or two of salt to taste.
7. Prepare the arroz con coco (rice with coconut milk). Stir 1/2 cup of the coconut milk to rice and cook according to the directions.
8. Into the rice, add the chicken mixture and mix well.
9. Garnish with cilantro

Nutrition:
- 118 Calories
- 34g Protein
- 36g Fat

113. Orange-Five-Spice Roasted Chicken

Difficulty: Average
Preparation Time: 5 minutes
Cooking Time: 1 hour
Servings: 6
Ingredients

- 2 chicken legs (2 lean)
- 1 juice and zest orange (1/4 condiment)
- 1/3 cup soy sauce sub coconut aminos for paleo/whole 30 (1/4 healthy fat)
- ¼ cup apple cider vinegar (1/4 condiment)
- 2 tsp five-spice powder (1/4 condiment)
- 2 tbsp avocado oil or other mild flavored oil (1/4 healthy fat)

Direction

1. Preheat your oven to 425 degrees. Place the Chicken leg(s) into a bowl. Add the rest of your ingredients, toss to combine. If you have a small mixing bowl, place the chicken legs inside of it. This will allow you to toss your other ingredients into the bowl with the legs without making a mess. If you're using a smaller mixing bowl, you may need to set it in a larger bowl so that the chicken leg(s) doesn't tip over when you pour your ingredients into the bowl with the legs.
2. Place in the oven for 30 minutes
3. Remove from the oven and toss the legs again so that they are in a different position in the bowl. Situate the bowl back in the oven for another 30 to 40 minutes.
4. If you want the sauce to thicken even more, place the roasting pan over a medium-high gas flame. Stirring constantly with a rubber spatula. Be careful that the bottom doesn't burn.

Nutrition:

- 179 Calories
- 18g Protein
- 8.36g Fat

114. Citrus Chicken

Difficulty: Average
Preparation Time: 10 minutes
Cooking Time: 3-4 hour
Servings: 3
Ingredients

- 6 bone-in chicken breast halves, skin removed (3 lean)
- 1 tsp. dried oregano (1/8 green)
- 1/2 tsp. seasoned salt (1/8 condiment)
- 1/4 tsp. pepper (1/8 condiment)
- 2 Tbsp olive oil (1/4 condiment)
- 1/4 cup water (1/4 condiment)
- 3 Tbsp lemon juice (1/8 condiment)
- 2 garlic cloves, minced (1/4 condiment)
- 1 teas chicken bouillon granule (1 healthy fat)
- 2 teas minced fresh parsley (1/8 green)

Direction

1. Rinse chicken; pat dry. Place chicken in a 4-qt. slow cooker.
2. Combine the oregano, seasoned salt, pepper, oil, water, lemon juice, garlic, bouillon and parsley; pour over the chicken.
3. Cover and cook over a low heat for 3-4 hours.
4. Serve

Nutrition:

- 379 Calories
- 15.7g Protein
- 8.8g Fat

115. Chunky Chicken Pie

Difficulty: Average
Preparation Time: 10 minutes
Cooking Time: 30 minutes
Servings: 3
Ingredients

- 3 boneless skinless chicken breasts (2 lean)
- 2 tbsp. sunflower oil (1/4 condiment)
- 1 ½ cups milk (1/2 healthy fat)
- 1 cup chicken stock (1 healthy fat)
- 2 tbsp. flour (1/2 condiment)
- 1/3 cup butter (1/2 healthy fat)
- 1 garlic clove, minced (1/2 condiment)
- 1 tbsp. chopped parsley (1/4 green)
- 1 ready to roll short crust pastry, rolled fairly thinly (1 healthy fat)
- beaten egg, to glaze (1/2 healthy fat)

Direction

1. Pound the chicken breasts with a rolling pin until they are about three-eight thick and set aside. In a saucepan, cook the garlic in the oil until pale gold.
2. Precisely Mix the flour and everything, add to the oil and cook 5 minutes over a low heat, stirring at first, until the flour turns clear, and the dish is thick. Add the nutmeg and season with salt, mix well. Take the pan from the heat and let it cool slightly. Add this to the chicken breasts to obtain a heavy pin.
3. Shape into a square by covering them with a piece of wax paper and pounding them with a rolling pin. Spread the chicken mixture evenly over the pastry. Roll the edges of the pastry over the outsides of the chicken mixture to form a rim and bake in a preheated hot oven 220 ° C. until golden brown, about 20 minutes. Serve hot with fresh vegetables.

Nutrition:

- 597 Calories
- 61.4g Protein
- 51g Fat

Difficulty: Difficult
Preparation Time: 10 minutes
Cooking Time: 15 minutes
Servings: 4
Ingredients

- 1 cup chicken breast, cut into bite-sized pieces (1 lean)
- 1 tbsp. cassava flour or all-purpose flour (1/4 condiment)
- 1/3 cup natural taste cooking oil (1/8 condiment)
- 1 tbsp. garlic, crushed and chopped (1/8 condiment)
- 1/2 cup yellow onions, sliced into wedges (1/4 green)
- 1/3 cup dry Thai birds' eye red chilies, deep fried (1/8 green)
- 1/2 cup raw unsalted cashew nuts (1/4 healthy fat)
- 1/3 cup fresh long red chili peppers, thinly julienned (1/4 green)
- 1/3 cup fresh banana chili peppers, cut in thin strips (1/4 green)
- 1/3 cup green onions (spring onions), cut in 2.5 cm pieces (1/4 green)

Seasoning sauce:

- 1 tbsp. light soy sauce (1/4 condiment)
- 1/2 tbsp. dark soy sauce (1/4 condiment)
- 1/2 tbsp. oyster sauce (1/4 condiment)
- 1/4 tsp. ground white pepper (1/4 condiment)
- 3 tbsp. stock or water (1/2 condiment)

Direction

1. In a large bowl, add in chicken. Add in seasonings (1 tbsp. light soy sauce, 1/2 tbsp. dark soy sauce, 1/2 tbsp. oyster sauce, ground white pepper, ground black pepper and a pinch of salt and sugar). Toss to coat evenly. Set aside.

2. In another non-stick pan, heat oil on medium-high heat. Pan-fry the chicken until cooked through, but still tender and juicy. Set aside. Pan-fry garlic, ginger and onions until fragrant and onions are translucent. Do not burn. Set aside.

3. Pour-in the leftover oil. Pan-fry cashew nuts, chilies and chicken. Toss till fragrant. Transfer onto a serving plate and serve hot.

Nutrition:

- 412 Calories
- 15g Protein
- 33g Fat

Difficulty: Difficult
Preparation Time: 5 minutes
Cooking Time: 18 minutes
Servings: 6
Ingredients

- 3 tbsp oil divided (1/4 condiment)
- 1 lb. ground chicken (dark meat) (1 lean)
- 3 tbsp soy sauce divided (1/4 condiment)
- 2 eggs beaten (1 lean)
- 1/2 cup chopped carrot (1/2 green)
- 1/2 cup chopped yellow onion (1/2 green)
- 3 scallions sliced (1 green)
- 2 cloves minced garlic (1 tbsp) (1/2 condiment)
- 3 to 4 cups cauliflower rice (1 healthy fat)
- 1 tbsp sesame oil (1/8 condiment)

Direction

1. In a large pan, sauté garlic, onion, carrots, scallions with 1 tbsp oil. Add the chicken and 1 tbsp soy sauce. Stir and cook for about 4 minutes or until the meat is cooked through.

2. In a small bowl, whip the eggs together with 2 tbsp soy sauce. Stir in the peas. Drop the egg mixture into

the pan with the chicken. Toss in the cashews.

3. Cook and stir until cooked and bubbly. Sprinkle with sesame oil. Serve cauliflower rice on a plate. Top it with chicken, garlic and eggs.

Nutrition:

- 367 Calories
- 19g Protein
- 28g Fat

Difficulty: Average
Preparation Time: 3 hours
Cooking Time: 15 minutes
Servings: 4
Ingredients

- 3 tablespoons fresh lime juice (1/4 condiment)
- 4 teaspoons fish sauce (1/8 condiment)
- 4 teaspoons soy sauce (1/8 condiment)
- 4 teaspoons sugar (1/8 condiment)
- 1 teaspoon grated fresh ginger (1/8 condiment)
- 4 skinless, boneless chicken breasts (2 lean)
- 4 cloves garlic (1 grated, 3 chopped) (1/4 condiment)
- Kosher salt and freshly ground pepper (1/8 condiment)
- 1/4 cup vegetable oil (1/8 condiment)
- 6 ounces dried rice vermicelli (1 healthy fat)
- 1/2-pound snow peas, strings removed (1/2 healthy fat)
- 1 cup fresh cilantro, torn (1/8 green)

Direction

1. Whisk 3 tablespoons of the lime juice, the fish sauce, 3 teaspoons of the soy sauce, 3 teaspoons of the sugar, and the grated ginger in a small bowl. Put the chicken in a Ziplock plastic bag and pour in the marinade. Seal the bag and allow the chicken to marinate for at

least an hour (and up to 3 hours) in the refrigerator.

2. Heat 3 tablespoons of the oil in a large skillet over medium-high heat. Add the chopped garlic and cook, stirring regularly, until golden, about 1 minute. Remove the garlic with a slotted spoon and transfer to a small bowl.
3. Pat the chicken dry with paper towels. Season the chicken with salt and pepper. Add the chicken to the skillet and cook on medium-high heat until almost done, turning it once halfway through cooking, about 5 minutes.
4. Transfer to a plate. Stir in the remaining 1 tablespoon oil to the same skillet. Add the vermicelli and cook, stirring occasionally, until golden brown, about 2 minutes. Add the remaining 2 teaspoons soy sauce and 2 teaspoons sugar and cook, stirring often, until golden brown, about 2 more minutes.
5. Stir in the snow peas and cook, stirring frequently, for 1 minute. Stir in the marinated garlic and season with salt and pepper.
6. Return the chicken to the skillet and cook for 2 minutes, stirring occasionally. Stir in the remaining 1 tablespoon lime juice, then sprinkle with the remaining 1 tablespoon cilantro. Season with salt and pepper. Serve immediately.

Nutrition:
- 604 Calories
- 55g Protein
- 20g Fat

119. Mediterranean Roasted Chicken with Lemon Dill Radishes

Difficulty: Average
Preparation Time: 5 minutes
Cooking Time: 30 minutes

Servings: 4
Ingredients:
- 2 lbs. chicken thighs (Remove skin) (2 lean)
- Pinch Stacey Hawkins Dash of Desperation Seasoning (1/8 condiment)
- 1 Tablespoon garlic (1/4 condiment)
- 1 Tablespoon marjoram (1/4 condiment)
- 1 Tablespoon basil (1/8 green)
- 1 Tablespoon rosemary (1/8 green)

Directions:
1. Preheat the oven to 350 degrees.
2. Put the chicken in a deep baking dish.
3. Chop the vegetables. Then put them with some oil on the baking dish.
4. Pour all the seasoning.
5. Bake for 30 minutes, then put the radishes.
6. The radishes cook with the chicken.
7. Serve at room temperature.

Nutrition:
- 507 Calories
- 37g Protein
- 34g Fat

120. Chicken with Garlic and Spring Onion Cream

Difficulty: Average
Preparation Time: 5 minutes
Cooking Time: 15 minutes
Servings: 4
Ingredients
- 6 medium chicken breasts (3 lean)
- 3 tablespoons butter or 3 tablespoons margarine (2 healthy fat)
- 2 tablespoons all-purpose flour (1/4 condiment)
- One-third cup chopped green onion (1/4 green)
- Three-fourth cup chicken broth (1 healthy fat)
- One-fourth teaspoon salt (1/8 condiment)
- 1 -2 tablespoon Dijon mustard (to taste) (1/8 condiment)
- 1 cup plain yogurt (1/4 healthy fat)

Direction
1. Heat a large skillet, add 1 tablespoon butter. Add chicken breasts to the pan. Cook for 10 minutes on medium heat, until browned on both sides. Remove and set aside on a plate.
2. Flour a chopping board and cut chicken breasts into thin strips when you're free from extra fat.
3. Melt 2 tablespoons butter in the same skillet. Stir in flour and cook for 2 minutes, stirring constantly. Gradually add chicken broth, mustard, salt and pepper. (For a thicker sauce, add 2 tablespoons cornstarch dissolved in 1/2 cup cold water.)
4. Blend in yogurt. Add chicken strips and green onion. Cook until sauce bubbles and thickens, stirring occasionally.
5. Serve with plain white rice or boiled potatoes.

Nutrition:
- 172 Calories
- 13.8g Protein
- 6.34g Fat

Chapter 5. Seafood Recipes

121. Shrimp with Garlic

Difficulty: Easy
Preparation Time: 10 minutes
Cooking Time: 25 minutes
Servings: 2
Ingredients:

- 1 lb. shrimp (1 lean)
- ¼ teaspoon baking soda (1/2 condiment)
- 2 tablespoons oil (1/4 condiment)
- 2 teaspoon minced garlic (1/4 condiment)
- ¼ cup vermouth (1/2 condiment)
- 2 tablespoons unsalted butter (1 healthy fat)
- 1 teaspoon parsley (1/4 green)

Directions:

1. In a bowl toss shrimp with baking soda and salt, let it stand for a couple of minutes
2. In a skillet heat olive oil and add shrimp
3. Add garlic, red pepper flakes and cook for 1-2 minutes
4. Add vermouth and cook for another 4-5 minutes
5. When ready, remove from heat and serve

Nutrition:

- 289 Calories
- 17g Fat
- 7g Protein

122. Crispy Fish

Difficulty: Easy
Preparation Time: 5 minutes
Cooking Time: 15 minutes
Servings: 4

Ingredients:

- Thick fish fillets (1 lean)
- ¼ cup all-purpose flour (1/4 condiment)
- 1 egg (1 lean)
- 1 cup bread crumbs (1/4 condiment)
- 2 tablespoons vegetables (1/2 green)
- Lemon wedge (1/4 condiment)

Directions:

1. In a dish add flour, egg, breadcrumbs in different dishes and set aside
2. Dip each fish fillet into the flour, egg and then bread crumbs bowl
3. Place each fish fillet in a heated skillet and cook for 4-5 minutes per side
4. When ready remove from pan and serve with lemon wedges

Nutrition:

- 189 Calories
- 17g Fat
- 7g Protein

123. Moules Marinieres

Difficulty: Easy
Preparation Time: 10 minutes
Cooking Time: 30 minutes
Servings: 4
Ingredients:

- 2 tablespoons unsalted butter (1/2 healthy fat)
- 1 leek (1/2 green)
- 1 shallot (1/2 green)
- 2 cloves garlic (1/4 condiment)
- 2 bay leaves (1/4 green)
- 1 cup white wine (1/2 condiment)
- 2 lb. mussels (2 lean)
- 2 tablespoons mayonnaise (1/2 healthy fat)
- 1 tablespoon lemon zest (1/4 condiment)
- 2 tablespoons parsley (1/4 green)
- 1 sourdough bread (1 healthy fat)

Directions:

1. In a saucepan melt butter, add leeks, garlic, bay leaves,

shallot and cook until vegetables are soft
2. Bring to a boil, add mussels, and cook for 1-2 minutes
3. Transfer mussels to a bowl and cover
4. Whisk in remaining butter with mayonnaise and return mussels to pot
5. Add lemon juice, parsley lemon zest and stir to combine

Nutrition:

- 321 Calories
- 17g Fat
- 9g Protein

124. Steamed Mussels with Coconut-Curry

Difficulty: Average
Preparation Time: 15 minutes
Cooking Time: 20 minutes
Servings: 4
Ingredients:

- 6 sprigs cilantro (1/4 green)
- 2 cloves garlic (1/4 condiment)
- 2 shallots (1/4 green)
- ¼ teaspoon coriander seeds (1/2 healthy fat)
- ¼ teaspoon red chili flakes (1/4 condiment)
- 1 teaspoon zest (1/4 condiment)
- 1 can coconut milk (1 healthy fat)
- 1 tablespoon vegetable oil (1/4 condiment)
- 1 tablespoon curry paste (1/4 condiment)
- 1 tablespoon brown sugar (1/4 condiment)
- 1 tablespoon fish sauce (1/4 condiment)
- 2 lb. mussels (2 lean)

Directions:

1. In a bowl combine lime zest, cilantro stems, shallot, garlic, coriander seed, chili and salt
2. In a saucepan heat oil add, garlic, shallots, pounded paste and curry paste
3. Cook for 3-4 minutes, add coconut milk, sugar and fish sauce

4. Bring to a simmer and add mussels
5. Stir in lime juice, cilantro leaves and cook for a couple of more minutes
6. When ready, remove from heat and serve

Nutrition:
- 209 Calories
- 7g Fat
- 17g Protein

125. Tuna Noodle Casserole

Difficulty: Average
Preparation Time: 15 minutes
Cooking Time: 20 minutes
Servings: 4
Ingredients:
- 2 oz. egg noodles (1 healthy fat)
- 4 oz. fraiche (2 healthy fat)
- 1 egg (1 lean)
- 1 teaspoon cornstarch (1/8 condiment)
- 1 tablespoon juice from 1 lemon (1/4 condiment)
- 1 can tuna (1 lean)
- ¼ cup parsley (1/4 green)

Directions:
1. Place noodles in a saucepan with water and bring to a boil
2. In a bowl combine egg, crème fraiche and lemon juice, whisk well
3. When noodles are cooked, add crème fraiche mixture to skillet and mix well
4. Add tuna, parsley lemon juice and mix well
5. When ready, remove from heat and serve

Nutrition:
- 214 Calories
- 7g Fat
- 19g Protein

126. Salmon Burgers

Difficulty: Average
Preparation Time: 10 minutes
Cooking Time: 15 minutes
Servings: 4
Ingredients:
- 1 lb. salmon fillets (1 lean)
- ¼ dill fronds (1/4 green)
- 1 tablespoon honey (1/4 condiment)
- 1 tablespoon horseradish (1 green)
- 1 tablespoon mustard (1/4 condiment)
- 1 tablespoon olive oil (1/4 condiment)
- 2 toasted split rolls (1 healthy fat)
- 1 avocado (1 healthy fat)

Directions:
1. Place salmon fillets in a blender and blend until smooth, transfer to a bowl, add dill, honey, horseradish and mix well
2. Add salt and pepper and form 4 patties
3. In a bowl combine mustard, honey, mayonnaise and dill
4. In a skillet heat oil, add salmon patties and cook for 2-3 minutes per side
5. When ready, remove from heat
6. Divided lettuce and onion between the buns
7. Place salmon patty on top and spoon mustard mixture and avocado slices
8. Serve when ready

Nutrition:
- 189 Calories
- 7g Fat
- 12g Protein

127. Seared Scallops

Difficulty: Easy
Preparation Time: 15 minutes
Cooking Time: 20 minutes
Servings: 4
Ingredients:
- 1 lb. sea scallops (1 lean)
- 1 tablespoon canola oil (1 condiment)

Directions:
1. Season scallops and refrigerate for a couple of minutes
2. In a skillet heat oil, add scallops and cook for 1-2 minutes per side
3. When ready, remove from heat and serve

Nutrition:
- 283 Calories
- 8g Fat
- 9g Protein

128. Black Cod

Difficulty: Average
Preparation Time: 15 minutes
Cooking Time: 20 minutes
Servings: 4
Ingredients:
- ¼ cup miso paste (1/4 condiment)
- ¼ cup sake (1/4 condiment)
- 1 tablespoon mirin (1/4 condiment)
- 1 teaspoon soy sauce (1/8 condiment)
- 1 tablespoon olive oil (1/4 condiment)
- 4 black cod filets (2 lean)

Directions:
1. In a bowl combine miso, soy sauce, oil and sake
2. Rub mixture over cod fillets and let it marinade for 20-30 minutes
3. Adjust broiler and broil cod filets for 10-12 minutes
4. When fish is cooked, remove and serve

Nutrition:
- 231 Calories
- 15g Fat
- 8g Protein

129. Miso-Glazed Salmon

Difficulty: Average
Preparation Time: 10 minutes
Cooking Time: 40 minutes
Servings: 4
Ingredients:
- ¼ cup red miso (1/4 healthy fat)
- ¼ cup sake (1/4 condiment)
- 1 tablespoon soy sauce (1/4 condiment)
- 1 tablespoon vegetable oil (1/4 condiment)
- 4 salmon fillets (2 lean)

Directions:
1. In a bowl combine sake, oil, soy sauce and miso
2. Rub mixture over salmon fillets and marinade for 20-30 minutes
3. Preheat a broiler

4. Broil salmon for 5-10 minutes
5. When ready remove and serve

Nutrition:
- 198 Calories
- 10g Fat
- 6g Protein

130. Arugula and Sweet Potato Salad

Difficulty: Easy
Preparation Time: 10 minutes
Cooking Time: 20 minutes
Servings: 4
Ingredients:
- 1 lb. sweet potatoes (1 healthy fat)
- 1 cup walnuts (1/2 healthy fat)
- 1 tablespoon olive oil (1/4 condiment)
- 1 cup water (1/2 condiment)
- 1 tablespoon soy sauce (1/4 condiment)
- 3 cups arugula (2 green)

Directions:
1. Bake potatoes at 400 F until tender, remove and set aside
2. In a bowl drizzle, walnuts with olive oil and microwave for 2-3 minutes or until toasted
3. In a bowl combine all salad ingredients and mix well
4. Pour over soy sauce and serve

Nutrition:
- 189 Calories
- 7g Fat
- 10g Protein

131. Shrimp Curry

Difficulty: Average
Preparation Time: 15 minutes
Cooking Time: 20 minutes
Servings: 4
Ingredients:
- 2 tablespoons peanut oil (1/2 condiment)
- 2 cloves garlic (1/4 condiment)
- 1 teaspoon ginger (1/8 condiment)
- 1 teaspoon cumin (1/8 condiment)
- 1 teaspoon turmeric (1/8 condiment)
- 1 teaspoon paprika (1/8 condiment)
- ¼ red chili powder (1/4 condiment)
- 1 can tomatoes (1/2 condiment)
- 1 can coconut milk (1 healthy fat)
- 1 lb. peeled shrimp (1 lean)
- 1 tablespoon cilantro (1/4 green)

Directions:
1. In a skillet, add ginger, cumin, garlic, chili, paprika and cook on low heat
2. Pour the tomatoes, coconut milk and simmer for 10-12 minutes
3. Stir in shrimp, cilantro, and cook for 2-3 minutes
4. When ready, remove and serve

Nutrition:
- 178 Calories
- 17g Fat
- 9g Protein

132. Salmon Pasta

Difficulty: Easy
Preparation Time: 10 minutes
Cooking Time: 25 minutes
Servings: 2
Ingredients:
- 5 tablespoons butter (1 healthy fat)
- 1 tablespoon all-purpose flour (1/4 condiment)
- 1 teaspoon garlic powder (1/8 condiment)
- 2 cups skim milk (1 healthy fat)
- ¼ cup Romano cheese (1/4 healthy fat)
- ¼ cup canned mushrooms (1/4 healthy fat)
- 8 oz. salmon (4 lean)
- 1 package penne pasta (1 healthy fat)

Directions:
1. Bring a pot with water to a boil
2. Add pasta and cook for 10-12 minutes
3. In a skillet, melt butter, stir in garlic powder, flour, milk and cheese
4. Add mushrooms and cook on low heat for 4-5 minutes
5. Toss in salmon and cook for another 2-3 minutes
6. When ready, serve with cooked pasta

Nutrition:
- 211 Calories
- 18g Fat
- 17g Protein

133. Crab Legs

Difficulty: Average
Preparation Time: 5 minutes
Cooking Time: 20 minutes
Servings: 3
Ingredients:
- 3 lb. crab legs (1 lean)
- ¼ cup salted butter, melted and divided (1/4 healthy fat)
- ½ lemon, juiced (1/2 condiment)
- ¼ tsp. garlic powder (1/8 condiment)

Directions:
1. In a bowl, toss the crab legs and two tablespoons of the melted butter together. Place the crab legs in the basket of the fryer.
2. Cook at 400°F for fifteen minutes, giving the basket a good shake halfway through.
3. Combine the remaining butter with the lemon juice and garlic powder.
4. Crack open the cooked crab legs and remove the meat. Serve with the butter dip on the side and enjoy!

Nutrition:

- 392 Calories
- 10g Fat
- 18g Protein

134. Crusty Pesto Salmon

Difficulty: Easy
Preparation Time: 5 minutes
Cooking Time: 15 minutes
Servings: 2
Ingredients:

- ¼ cup pesto (1/4 condiment)
- 2 x 4-oz. salmon fillets (2 lean)
- 2 tbsp. unsalted butter, melted (1 healthy fat)

Directions:

1. Place the salmon fillets in a round baking dish, roughly six inches in diameter.
2. Brush the fillets with butter, followed by the pesto mixture, ensuring to coat both the top and bottom. Put the baking dish inside the fryer.
3. Cook for twelve minutes at 390°F.
4. The salmon is ready when it flakes easily when prodded with a fork. Serve warm.

Nutrition:

- 290 Calories
- 11g Fat
- 20g Protein

135. Buttery Cod

Difficulty: Easy
Preparation Time: 10 minutes
Cooking Time: 12 minutes
Servings: 2
Ingredients:

- 2 x 4-oz. cod fillets (2 lean)
- 2 tbsp. salted butter, melted (1 healthy fat)
- 1 tsp. Old Bay seasoning (1/8 condiment)
- ½ medium lemon, sliced (1/2 condiment)

Directions:

1. Place the cod fillets in a skillet.
2. Brush with melted butter, season with Old Bay, and top with a few lemon wedges.

3. Wrap the fish in aluminum foil and place it in your deep fryer.
4. Cook for eight minutes at 350 ° F.
5. The cod is done when it is easily peeled. Serve hot

Nutrition:

- 394 Calories
- 5g Fat
- 12g Protein

136. Sesame Tuna Steak

Difficulty: Average
Preparation Time: 5 minutes
Cooking Time: 12 minutes
Servings: 2
Ingredients:

- 1 tbsp. coconut oil, melted (1/4 condiment)
- 2 x 6-oz. tuna steaks (2 lean)
- ½ tsp. garlic powder (1/8 condiment)
- 2 tsp. black sesame seeds (1/4 condiment)
- 2 tsp. white sesame seeds (1/4 condiment)

Directions:

1. Apply the coconut oil to the tuna steaks with a brunch, then season with garlic powder.
2. Combine the black and white sesame seeds. Embed them in the tuna steaks, covering the fish all over. Place the tuna into your air fryer.
3. Cook for eight minutes at 400°F, turning the fish halfway through.
4. The tuna steaks are ready when they have reached a temperature of 145°F. Serve immediately.

Nutrition:

- 160 Calories
- 6g Fat
- 26g Protein

137. Lemon Garlic Shrimp

Difficulty: Easy
Preparation Time: 10 minutes
Cooking Time: 15 minutes
Servings: 2
Ingredients:

- 1 medium lemon (1/4 condiment)
- ½ lb. medium shrimp, shelled and deveined (1 lean)
- ½ tsp. Old Bay seasoning (1/4 condiment)
- 2 tbsp. unsalted butter, melted (1/2 healthy fat)
- ½ tsp. minced garlic (1/8 condiment)

Directions:

1. Grate the rind of the lemon into a bowl. Cut the lemon in half and juice it over the same bowl. Toss in the shrimp, Old Bay, and butter, mixing everything to make sure the shrimp is completely covered.
2. Transfer to a round baking dish roughly six inches wide, then place this dish in your fryer.
3. Cook at 400°F for six minutes. The shrimp is cooked when it turns a bright pink color.
4. Serve hot, drizzling any leftover sauce over the shrimp.

Nutrition:

- 490 Calories
- 9g Fat
- 12g Protein

138. Foil Packet Salmon

Difficulty: Average
Preparation Time: 5 minutes
Cooking Time: 15 minutes
Servings: 2
Ingredients:

- 2 x 4-oz. skinless salmon fillets (2 lean)
- 2 tbsp. unsalted butter, melted (1/2 healthy fat)
- ½ tsp. garlic powder (1/8 condiment)
- 1 medium lemon (1/2 condiment)
- ½ tsp. dried dill (1/4 green)

Directions:

1. Take a sheet of aluminum foil and cut it into two squares measuring roughly 5" x 5". Lay each of the salmon fillets at the center of each piece. Brush both

fillets with a tablespoon of butter and season with a quarter-teaspoon of garlic powder.
2. Halve the lemon and grate the skin of one half over the fish. Cut four half-slices of lemon, using two to top each fillet. Season each fillet with a quarter-teaspoon of dill.
3. Fold the tops and sides of the aluminum foil over the fish to create a kind of packet. Place each one in the fryer.
4. Cook for twelve minutes at 400°F.
5. The salmon is ready when it flakes easily. Serve hot.

Nutrition:
- 240 Calories
- 13g Fat
- 21g Protein

139. Foil Packet Lobster Tail

Difficulty: Difficult
Preparation Time: 5 minutes
Cooking Time: 15 minutes
Servings: 2
Ingredients:
- 2 x 6-oz. lobster tail halves (2 lean)
- 2 tbsp. salted butter, melted (1/2 healthy fat)
- ½ medium lemon, juiced (1/4 condiment)
- ½ tsp. Old Bay seasoning (1/8 condiment)
- 1 tsp. dried parsley (1/8 green)

Directions:
1. Lay each lobster on a sheet of aluminum foil. Pour a light drizzle of melted butter and lemon juice over each one, and season with Old Bay.
2. Fold down the sides and ends of the foil to seal the lobster. Place each one in the fryer.
3. Cook at 375°F for twelve minutes.
4. Just before serving, top the lobster with dried parsley.

Nutrition:

- 510 Calories
- 18g Fat
- 26g Protein

140. Avocado Shrimp

Difficulty: Easy
Preparation Time: 10 minutes
Cooking Time: 20 minutes
Servings: 2
Ingredients:
- 2 lb. shrimp (2 lean)
- 1 tbsp. seasoned salt (1/4 condiment)
- 1 avocado (1 healthy fat)
- ½ cup pecans, chopped (1/2 healthy fat)

Directions:
1. Preheat the fryer at 400°F.
2. Put the chopped onion in the basket of the fryer and spritz with some cooking spray. Leave to cook for five minutes.
3. Add the shrimp and set the timer for a further five minutes. Sprinkle with some seasoned salt, then allow to cook for an additional five minutes.
4. During these last five minutes, halve your avocado and remove the pit. Cube each half, then scoop out the flesh.
5. Take care when removing the shrimp from the fryer. Place it on a dish and top with the avocado and the chopped pecans.

Nutrition:
- 195 Calories
- 14g Fat
- 36g Protein

Chapter 6. Vegetable Recipes

141. Italian Style Genoese Zucchini

Difficulty: Average
Preparation Time: 10 minutes
Cooking Time: 2 minutes
Servings: 4
Ingredients:

- 2 medium zucchinis, spiralized (1 green)
- 2 cups basil leaves (1/2 green)
- Juice from 1 lemon, freshly squeezed (1/4 condiment)
- 3 cloves of garlic, minced (1/4 condiment)
- 1/2 cup cashew nuts, soaked in water overnight then drained (1/2 healthy fat)

Directions:

1. Place zucchini strips on a plate.
2. Place the rest of the ingredients in a food processor and pulse until smooth.
3. Pour sauce over the zucchini and serve.

Nutrition:

- 101 Calories
- 3.1g Protein
- 7.8g Fat

142. Wedding of Broccoli and Tomatoes

Difficulty: Difficult
Preparation Time: 7 minutes
Cooking Time: 2 minutes
Servings: 3
Ingredients:

- 1 head broccoli, cut into florets then blanched (1 green)
- 1/4 cup tomatoes, diced (1/2 green)
- Salt and pepper to taste (1/8 condiment)
- Chopped parsley for garnish (1/8 green)

Directions:

1. Place all ingredients in a bowl.
2. Toss to coat all ingredients.
3. Serve.

Nutrition:

- 52 Calories
- 1.1g Protein
- 0.1g Fat

143. Green Buddha Smile

Difficulty: Average
Preparation Time: 10 minutes
Cooking Time: 10 minutes
Servings: 6
Ingredients:

- 2 pounds boneless and skinless chicken breast (1 lean)
- 2 tablespoons lemon juice, freshly squeezed (1/2 condiment)
- Salt and pepper to taste (1/8 condiment)
- 1-pound Brussels sprouts, trimmed and halved (1 green)
- 3 cloves of garlic, minced (1/8 condiment)
- 3/4 cup plain Greek yogurt (1/2 healthy fat)
- 1 teaspoon stone-ground mustard (/18 condiment)
- 1/4 cup balsamic vinegar (1/4 condiment)
- 2 cups cooked quinoa (1 healthy fat)
- 1 cup chopped red apple, cored, and chopped (1/4 healthy fat)
- 1/4 cup pepitas (1/4 condiment)
- 1 avocado, sliced (1/2 healthy fat)
- 1 1/2 cup arugula (1 green)
- 1 tablespoon fresh basil (1/4 green)

Directions:

1. Place chicken and lemon juice in a bowl. Season with salt and pepper to taste. Allow to marinate in the fridge for at least 30 minutes.
2. Fire up the grill to 375F and cook the chicken for 6 minutes on each side. Add in the Brussels sprouts and cook for 3 minutes on each side. Set the chicken and Brussels sprouts aside.
3. In a bowl, mix together the garlic, yogurt, mustard, and vinegar. Season with salt to taste. Set aside.
4. In a bowl, place the quinoa and top with apple, pepitas, avocado, and arugula. Top with grilled chicken and Brussels sprouts.
5. Drizzle with the sauce and garnish with basil.

Nutrition:

- 411 Calories
- 44g Protein
- 4g Fat

144. Zucchini Fettuccine with Mexican Taco

Difficulty: Easy
Preparation Time: 9 minutes
Cooking Time: 20 minutes
Servings: 6
Ingredients:

- 1 tablespoon olive oil (1/8 condiment)
- 1-pound lean ground turkey (1 lean)
- 1 clove garlic, minced (1/8 condiment)
- 1 tablespoon chili powder (1/8 condiment)
- 1/4 teaspoon garlic powder (1/8 condiment)
- 1/4 teaspoon onion powder (1/8 condiment)
- 1/4 teaspoon dried oregano (1/8 green)
- 1 1/2 teaspoon ground cumin (1/8 condiment)
- 1/4 cup water (1/4 condiment)

- 1/4 cup diced tomatoes (1/4 green)
- 2 large zucchinis, spiralized (1 green)
- 1/2 cup shredded cheddar cheese (1/2 healthy fat)

Directions:
1. Place oil in a pot and heat over medium flame.
2. Sauté the turkey for 2 minutes before adding the garlic and onions. Stir for another minute.
3. Season with chili powder, garlic powder, onion powder, oregano, and ground cumin. Sauté for another minute.
4. before adding the water and tomatoes.
5. Close the lid and allow to simmer for 7 minutes.
6. Add in the zucchini and cheese and allow to cook for 3 more minutes.

Nutrition:
- 145 Calories
- 15g Protein
- 2.1g Fat

145. Green Beans

Difficulty: Easy
Preparation Time: 9 minutes
Cooking Time: 12 minutes
Servings: 4
Ingredients:
- 11 oz. green beans (2 green)
- 1 tablespoon of onion powder (1/4 condiment)
- 1 tablespoon of olive oil (1/4 condiment)
- 1/2 teaspoon of salt (1/4 condiment)
- 1/4 teaspoon of red pepper flakes (1/4 condiment)

Directions:
1. Wash the green beans thoroughly and put them in the bowl.
2. Sprinkle the green beans with lion's powder, salt, chilis, and olive oil.
3. Shake the green bean carefully.
4. Preheat the 400F air refrigerator.

5. Place the green beans in the deep fryer and cook for 8 minutes.
6. Next, shake the green beans and cook them for 4 minutes or more at 400 F.
7. When time remains: shake the green beans.
8. Serve them with joy!

Nutrition:
- 302 Calories
- 7.2g Fat
- 3.2g Protein

146. Cream of Mushrooms Satay

Difficulty: Average
Preparation Time: 9 minutes
Cooking Time: 2 minutes
Servings: 6
Ingredients:
- 7 oz. cremini mushrooms (1 healthy fat)
- 2 tablespoon coconut milk (1/2 healthy fat)
- 1 tablespoon butter (1/4 healthy fat)
- 1 teaspoon chili flakes (1/8 condiment)
- ½ teaspoon balsamic vinegar (1/8 condiment)
- ½ teaspoon curry powder (1/8 condiment)
- ½ teaspoon white pepper (1/8 condiment)

Directions:
1. Wash the mushrooms carefully.
2. Then sprinkle the mushrooms with chili flakes, curry powder, and white pepper.
3. Preheat the air fryer to 400 F.
4. Toss the butter in the air fryer basket and melt it.
5. Put the mushrooms in the air fryer and cook for 2 minutes.
6. Shake the mushrooms well and sprinkle with the coconut milk and balsamic vinegar.
7. Cook the mushrooms for 4 minutes more at 400 F.

8. Then skewer the mushrooms on the wooden sticks and serve.

Nutrition:
- 116 Calories
- 9.5g Fat
- 3g Protein

147. Tortoreto Mushrooms with Cheddar

Difficulty: Difficult
Preparation Time: 10 minutes
Cooking Time: 6 minutes
Servings: 2
Ingredients:
- 2 Portobello mushroom hats (1 healthy fat)
- 2 slices Cheddar cheese (1 healthy fat)
- ¼ cup panko breadcrumbs (1/2 healthy fat)
- ½ teaspoon salt (1/8 condiment)
- ½ teaspoon ground black pepper (1/8 condiment)
- 1 egg (1 lean)
- 1 teaspoon oatmeal (1/4 condiment)
- 2 oz. bacon, chopped cooked (1 lean)

Directions:
1. Crack the egg into the bowl and whisk it.
2. Combine the ground black pepper, oatmeal, salt, and breadcrumbs in a separate bowl.
3. Dip the mushroom hats in the whisked egg.
4. After this, coat the mushroom hats in the breadcrumb mixture.
5. Preheat the air fryer to 400 F.
6. Place the mushrooms in the air fryer basket tray and cook for 3 minutes.
7. After this, put the chopped bacon and sliced cheese over the mushroom hats and cook the meal for 3 minutes.
8. When the meal is cooked – let it chill gently.

Nutrition:
- 376 Calories

- 24g Fat
- 25g Protein

148. Lentil Triumph Hamburger with Carrots

Difficulty: Average
Preparation Time: 10 minutes
Cooking Time: 12 minutes
Servings: 4
Ingredients:
- 6 oz. lentils, cooked (2 green)
- 1 egg (1 lean)
- 2 oz. carrot, grated (1 green)
- 1 teaspoon semolina (1/8 condiment)
- ½ teaspoon salt (1/8 condiment)
- 1 teaspoon turmeric (1/8 condiment)
- 1 tablespoon butter (1/4 healthy fat)

Directions:
1. Crack the egg into the bowl and whisk it.
2. Add the cooked lentils and mash the mixture with the help of the fork.
3. Then sprinkle the mixture with the grated carrot, semolina, salt, and turmeric.
4. Mix it up and make the medium burgers.
5. Put the butter into the lentil burgers. It will make them juicy.
6. Preheat the air fryer to 360 F.
7. Put the lentil burgers in the air fryer and cook for 12 minutes.
8. Flip the burgers into another side after 6 minutes of cooking.
9. Then chill the cooked lentil burgers and serve them.

Nutrition:
- 404 Calories
- 9g Fat
- 25g Protein

149. Stir-Fried Sweet Potatoes with Parmesan

Difficulty: Easy
Preparation Time: 10 minutes
Cooking Time: 35 minutes

Servings: 2
Ingredients:
- 2 sweet potatoes, peeled (1 healthy fat)
- ½ yellow onion, sliced (1/2 green)
- ½ cup cream (1/2 healthy fat)
- ¼ cup spinach (1/4 green)
- 2 oz. Parmesan cheese, shredded (1/2 healthy fat)
- ½ teaspoon salt (1/8 condiment)
- 1 tomato (1 green)
- 1 teaspoon olive oil (1/8 condiment)

Directions:
1. Chop the sweet potatoes.
2. Chop the tomato.
3. Chop the spinach.
4. Spray the air fryer tray with the olive oil.
5. Then place on the layer of the chopped sweet potato.
6. Add the layer of the sliced onion.
7. After this, sprinkle the sliced onion with the chopped spinach and tomatoes.
8. Sprinkle the casserole with salt and shredded cheese.
9. Pour cream.
10. Preheat the air fryer to 390 F.
11. Cover the air fryer tray with the foil.
12. Cook the casserole for 35 minutes.
13. When the casserole is cooked – serve it.

Nutrition
- 93 Calories
- 1.8g Fat
- 2g Protein

150. Rosemary Scent Cauliflower Bundles

Difficulty: Difficult
Preparation Time: 10 minutes
Cooking Time: 30 minutes
Servings: 4
Ingredients:
- 1/3 cup of almond flour (1/2 condiment)
- 4 cups of riced cauliflower (2 green)

- 1/3 cup of reduced-fat, shredded mozzarella or cheddar cheese (1/2 healthy fat)
- 2 eggs (1 lean)
- 2 tablespoons of fresh rosemary, finely chopped (1/4 green)
- ½ teaspoon of salt (1/8 condiment)

Directions:
1. Preheat your oven to 400°F
2. Combine all the listed ingredients in a medium-sized bowl
3. Scoop cauliflower mixture into 12 evenly-sized rolls/biscuits onto a lightly-greased and foil-lined baking sheet.
4. Bake until it turns golden brown, which should be achieved in about 30 minutes.

Nutrition:
- 254 Calories
- 24g Protein
- 8g Fat

151. Cauliflower Sprinkled with Curry

Difficulty: Average
Preparation Time: 10 minutes
Cooking Time: 5 hours
Servings: 4
Ingredients:
- 1 cauliflower head, florets separated (1 green)
- 2 carrots, sliced (1 green)
- ¾ cup coconut milk (1/2 healthy fat)
- 2 garlic cloves, minced (1/4 condiment)
- 2 tablespoons curry powder (1/4 condiment)

- A pinch of salt and black pepper (1/4 condiment)
- 1 tablespoon red pepper flakes (1/8 condiment)
- 1 teaspoon garam masala (1/8 condiment)

Directions:
1. In your slow cooker, mix all the ingredients.
2. Cover, cook on high for 5 hours, divide into bowls and serve.

Nutrition:
- 160 Calories
- 11g Fat
- 3.6g Protein

152. Avocado in Garlic and Paprika Breading

Difficulty: Easy
Preparation Time: 10 minutes
Cooking Time: 10 minutes
Servings: 2
Ingredients:
- 2 avocados cut into wedges 25 mm thick (1 healthy fat)
- 50g Pan crumbs bread (1/4 healthy fat)
- 2g garlic powder (1/8 condiment)
- 2g onion powder (1/8 condiment)
- 1g smoked paprika (1/4 condiment)
- 1g cayenne pepper (1/8 condiment)
- Salt and pepper to taste (1/8 condiment)
- 60g all-purpose flour (1/2 healthy fat)
- 2 eggs, beaten (1 lean)

Directions:
1. Cut the avocados into 25 mm thick pieces.
2. Combine the crumbs, garlic powder, onion powder, smoked paprika, cayenne pepper and salt in a bowl.
3. Separate each wedge of avocado in the flour, then dip the beaten eggs and stir in the breadcrumb mixture.
4. Preheat the air fryer.
5. Place the avocados in the preheated air fryer baskets, spray with oil spray, and cook at 205°C (400°F) for

10 minutes. Turn the fried avocado halfway through cooking and sprinkle with cooking oil.
6. Serve with tomato sauce or ranch sauce.

Nutrition:
- 123 Calories
- 11g Fat
- 4g Protein

153. Tomatoes in The Mushroom

Difficulty: Easy
Preparation Time: 10 minutes
Cooking Time: 50 minutes
Servings: 4
Ingredients:
- 8 large mushrooms (2 healthy fat)
- 250g of minced meat (2 lean)
- 4 cloves of garlic (1/4 condiment)
- Extra virgin olive oil (1/8 condiment)
- Flour, beaten egg and breadcrumbs (1 healthy fat)
- Fried Tomato Sauce (1 condiment)

Directions:
1. Remove the stem from the mushrooms and chop it. Peel the garlic and chop. Put some extra virgin olive oil in a pan and add the garlic and mushroom stems.
2. Sauté and add minced meat. Sauté well until the meat is well cooked and season.
3. Fill the mushrooms with the minced meat.
4. Press well and take the freezer for 30 minutes.
5. Pass the mushrooms with flour, beaten egg and breadcrumbs. Beaten egg and breadcrumbs.
6. Place the mushrooms in the basket of the air fryer.
7. Select 20 minutes, 180°C (350°F).
8. Distribute the mushrooms once cooked in the dishes.
9. Heat the tomato sauce and cover the stuffed mushrooms.

Nutrition:

- 160 Calories
- 11g Fat
- 4g Protein

154. Brown Rice and Baby Spinach

Difficulty: Average
Preparation Time: 10 minutes
Cooking Time: 15 minutes
Servings: 6
Ingredients:
- 2 tablespoons extra-virgin olive oil (1/4 condiment)
- 4 cups fresh baby spinach (2 green)
- 1 garlic clove, minced (1/8 condiment)
- Zest of 1 orange (1/8 condiment)
- Juice of 1 orange (1/8 condiment)
- 1 cup unsalted vegetable broth (1 condiment)
- ½ teaspoon sea salt (1/8 condiment)
- 2 cups cooked brown rice (1 healthy fat)

Directions:
1. In a large skillet over medium-high heat, heat the olive oil until it shimmers.
2. Add the onion and cook for about 5 minutes, stirring occasionally, until soft.
3. Add the spinach and cook for about 2 minutes, stirring occasionally, until it wilts.
4. Add the garlic and cook for 30 seconds, stirring constantly.
5. Stir in the orange zest and juice, broth, sea salt, and pepper. Bring to a simmer.
6. Stir in the rice and cook for about 4 minutes, stirring, until the rice is heated through and the liquid is absorbed.

Nutrition:
- 188 Calories
- 4g Protein
- 6g Fat

155. Delicious Feta with Fresh Spinach

Difficulty: Easy
Preparation Time: 10 minutes
Cooking Time: 0 minutes
Servings: 6
Ingredients:

- 6 cups fresh baby spinach, chopped (3 green)
- ¼ cup scallions, white and green parts, chopped (1 green)
- 1 (16-ounce) package orzo pasta, cooked according to package directions, rinsed, drained, and cooled (1 healthy fat)
- ¾ cup crumbled feta cheese (1/2 healthy fat)
- ¼ cup halved Kalamata olives (1/4 condiment)
- ½ cup red wine vinegar (1/2 condiment)
- ¼ cup extra-virgin olive oil (1/8 condiment)
- 1½ teaspoons freshly squeezed lemon juice (1/8 condiment)
- Sea salt (1/8 condiment)
- Freshly ground black pepper (1/8 condiment)

Directions:

1. In a large bowl, combine the spinach, scallions, and cooled orzo.
2. Sprinkle with the feta and olives.
3. In a small bowl, whisk the vinegar, olive oil, and lemon juice. Season with sea salt and pepper.
4. Add the dressing to the salad and gently toss to combine. Refrigerate until serving.

Nutrition:

- 255 Calories
- 8g Protein
- 8g Fat

156. Celeriac Mix with Cauliflower

Difficulty: Easy
Preparation Time: 10 minutes
Cooking Time: 12 minutes
Servings: 6
Ingredients:

- 1 head cauliflower (1 green)
- 1 small celery root (1 green)
- 1/4 cup butter (1/4 healthy fat)
- 1 tablespoon. chopped rosemary (1/4 green)
- 1 tablespoon. chopped thyme (1/8 green)
- 1 cup cream cheese (1/2 healthy fat)

Directions:

1. Skin the celery root and cut it into small pieces.
2. Cut the cauliflower into similar sized pieces and combine.
3. Toast the herbs in the butter in a large pan until they become fragrant.
4. Add the cauliflower and celery root and stir to combine.
5. Season and cook at medium-high until moisture is released from the vegetables, then cover and cook on low for 10-12 minutes.
6. Once the vegetables are soft, remove them from the heat and place them in the blender.
7. Make it smooth, then put the cream cheese and puree again.
8. Season and serve.

Nutrition:

- 225 Calories
- 20g Fat
- 5g Protein

157. Cheddar Fondue with Tomato Sauce

Difficulty: Average
Preparation Time: 10 minutes
Cooking Time: 30 minutes
Servings: 4
Ingredients:

- 1 garlic clove, halved (1/4 condiment)
- 6 medium tomatoes, seeded and diced (2 green)
- 2/3 cup dry white wine (1 condiment)
- 6 tablespoons. Butter, cubed (2 healthy fat)
- 1-1/2 teaspoons. Dried basil (1/4 green)
- Dash cayenne pepper (1/8 condiment)
- 2 cups shredded cheddar cheese (1/2 healthy fat)
- 1 tablespoon. All-purpose flour (1/4 condiment)
- Cubed French bread and cooked shrimp (1 lean)

Directions:

1. Rub the bottom and sides of a fondue pot with a garlic clove.
2. Set aside and discard the garlic.
3. Combine wine, butter, basil, cayenne and tomatoes in a large saucepan.
4. On a medium-low heat, bring mixture to a simmer, then decrease the heat to low.
5. Mix cheese with flour.
6. Add to tomato mixture gradually while stirring after each addition until cheese is melted.
7. Pour into the Preparation fondue pot and keep warm.
8. Enjoy with shrimp and bread cubes.

Nutrition:

- 118 Calories
- 10g Fat
- 4g Protein

158. Quick Spinach Focaccia

Difficulty: Easy
Preparation Time: 10 minutes
Cooking Time: 25 minutes
Servings: 12
Ingredients:

- 10 eggs (3 lean)
- 2 cups spinach, chopped (1 green)
- 1/4 tsp garlic powder (1/8 condiment)
- 1/4 tsp onion powder (1/8 condiment)
- 1/2 tsp dried basil (1/8 green)
- 1 1/2 cups parmesan cheese, grated (1/2 healthy fat)

Directions:

1. Preheat the oven to 400 F. Grease muffin tin and set aside.
2. In a large bowl, whisk eggs with basil, garlic powder, onion powder, and salt.
3. Add cheese and spinach and stir well.
4. Pour egg mixture into the prepared muffin tin and bake 15 minutes.
5. Serve and enjoy.

Nutrition:
- 110 Calories
- 7g Fat
- 9g Protein

159. Triumph of Cucumbers and Avocados

Difficulty: Easy
Preparation Time: 10 minutes
Cooking Time: 15 minutes
Servings: 4
Ingredients:
- 12 oz cherry tomatoes, cut in half (2 green)
- 5 small cucumbers, chopped (2 green)
- 3 small avocados, chopped (1 healthy fat)
- 1/2 tsp ground black pepper (1/8 condiment)
- 2 tbsp olive oil (1/8 condiment)
- 2 tbsp fresh lemon juice (1/4 condiment)
- 1/4 cup fresh cilantro, chopped (1/8 green)
- 1 tsp sea salt (1/8 condiment)

Directions:
1. Add cherry tomatoes, cucumbers, avocados, and cilantro into the large mixing bowl and mix well.
2. Mix together olive oil, lemon juice, black pepper, and salt and pour over salad.
3. Toss well and serve immediately.

Nutrition:
- 442 Calories
- 37g Fat
- 6.2g Protein

160. Delicious Tomato Broth

Difficulty: Average
Preparation Time: 10 minutes
Cooking Time: 15 minutes
Servings: 2
Ingredients:
- 14 oz can fire-roasted tomatoes (1 green)
- 1/2 tsp dried basil (1/8 green)
- 1/2 cup heavy cream (1/4 healthy fat)
- 1/2 cup parmesan cheese, grated (1/4 healthy fat)
- 1 cup cheddar cheese, grated (1/4 healthy fat)
- 1 1/2 cups vegetable stock (1 condiment)
- 1/4 cup zucchini, grated (1/4 green)
- 1/2 tsp dried oregano (1/8 green)

Directions:
1. Add tomatoes, stock, zucchini, oregano, basil, pepper, and salt into the instant pot and stir well.
2. Seal pot and cook on high pressure for 5 minutes.
3. Release pressure using quick release. Remove lid.
4. Set pot on sauté mode. Add heavy cream, parmesan cheese, and cheddar cheese and stir well and cook until
5. cheese is melted.
6. Serve and enjoy.

Nutrition:
- 460 Calories
- 35g Fat
- 24g Protein

Chapter 7. Soup and Stew Recipes

161. Roasted Tomato Soup

Difficulty: Easy
Preparation Time: 20 minutes
Cooking Time: 50 minutes
Servings: 6
Ingredients:

- 3 pounds of tomatoes in a halved manner (1 green)
- 6 garlic(smashed) (1/2 condiment)
- 4 teaspoon of cooking oil or virgin oil (1/8 condiment)
- Salt to taste (1/8 condiment)
- 1/4 cup of heavy cream(optional) (1/2 healthy fat)
- Sliced fresh basil leaves for garnish (1/8 green)

Directions:

1. Oven medium heat of about 427f, preheat the oven.
2. In your mixing bowl, mix the halved tomatoes, garlic, olive oil, salt and pepper
3. Spread the tomato mixture on the already prepared baking sheet
4. For a process of 20- 28 minutes, roast and stir
5. Then remove it from the oven and the roasted vegetables should now be transferred to a soup pot
6. Stir in the basil leaves
7. Blend in small portions in a blender
8. Serve immediately

Nutrition:

- 5.9g Fat
- 2.3g Protein
- 126 Calories

162. Cheeseburger Soup

Difficulty: Average
Preparation Time: 15 minutes
Cooking Time: 45 minutes
Servings: 4
Ingredients:

- 1 quantity of 14.5 oz. can dice tomato (1 green)

- 1 lb. of 90% lean ground beef (1 lean)
- 3/4 cup of chopped celery (1/2 green)
- 2 teaspoon of Worcestershire sauce (1/8 condiment)
- 3 cups of low sodium chicken broth (1 condiment)
- 1/4 teaspoon of salt (1/8 condiment)
- 1 teaspoon of dried parsley (1/8 green)
- 7 cups of baby spinach (1 green)
- 1/4 teaspoon of ground pepper (1/8 condiment)
- 4 oz. of reduced-fat shredded cheddar cheese (1/2 healthy fat)

Directions:

1. Get a large soup pot and cook the beef until it becomes brown.
2. Add the celery and sauté until it becomes tender.
3. Remove from the heat and drain excess liquid. Stir in the broth, tomatoes, parsley, Worcestershire sauce, pepper, and salt.
4. Cover with the lid and allow it to simmer on low heat for about 20 minutes.
5. Add spinach and leave it to cook until it becomes wilted in about 1-3 minutes.
6. Top each of your servings with 1 ounce of cheese.

Nutrition:

- 400 Calories
- 44g Protein
- 20g Fat

163. Quick Lentil Chili

Difficulty: Easy
Preparation Time: 15 minutes
Cooking Time: 1 hour and 20 minutes
Servings: 10
Ingredients:

- 1 1/2 cups of seeded or diced pepper (1 green)
- 5 cups of vegetable broth (it should have a low sodium content) (1 condiment)
- 1 tablespoon of garlic (1/8 condiment)
- 1/4 teaspoon of freshly ground pepper (1/8 condiment)
- 1 cup of red lentils (1/4 green)
- 3 filled teaspoons of chili powder (1/8 condiment)
- 1 tablespoon of grounded cumin (1/8 condiment)

Directions:

1. Place your pot over medium heat
2. Combine your onions, red peppers, low sodium vegetable broth, garlic, salt and pepper
3. Cook and stir always until the onions are more translucent and all the liquid evaporated. This will take about 10mins.
4. Add the remaining broth, lime juice, chili powder, lentils, cumin and boil.
5. Reduce heat at this point, cover it for about 15minutes to simmer until the lentils are appropriately cooked
6. Drizzle little water if the mixture seems to be thick.
7. The chili will be appropriately done when most of the water is absorbed.
8. Serve and enjoy.

Nutrition:

- 2.3g Protein
- 121 Calories
- 2.9g Fat

164. Lemon-Garlic Chicken

Difficulty: Average
Preparation Time: 5 minutes
Cooking Time: 45 minutes
Servings: 4
Ingredients:

- 1 small lemon, juiced (1/8 condiment)
- 1 3/4 lb. of bone-in, skinless chicken thighs (1 lean)
- 2 tablespoons of fresh oregano, minced (1/8 green)
- 2 cloves of garlic, minced (1/8 condiment)
- 2 lbs. of asparagus, trimmed (1/8 green)
- 1/4 teaspoon each or less for black pepper and salt (1/8 condiment)

Directions:

1. Preheat the oven to about 350F. Put the chicken in a medium-sized bowl.
2. Now, add the garlic, oregano, lemon juice, pepper, and salt and toss together to combine.
3. Roast for 40 minutes.
4. Once the chicken thighs have been cooked, remove and keep aside to rest.
5. Now, steam the asparagus on a stovetop or in a microwave to the desired doneness.
6. Serve asparagus with the roasted chicken thighs.

Nutrition:

- 350 Calories
- 10g Fat
- 32g Protein

165. Creamy Cauliflower Soup

Difficulty: Average
Preparation Time: 15 minutes
Cooking Time: 30 minutes
Servings: 6
Ingredients:

- 5 cups cauliflower rice (1 green)
- 8 oz. cheddar cheese, grated (1 healthy fat)
- 2 cups unsweetened almond milk (1/2 healthy fat)

- 2 cups vegetable stock (1 condiment)
- 2 tbsp water (1/2 condiment)
- 2 garlic cloves, minced (1/4 condiment)
- 1 tbsp olive oil (1/8 condiment)

Directions:

1. Cook olive oil in a large stockpot over medium heat.
2. Add garlic and cook for 1-2 minutes. Add cauliflower rice and water.
3. Cover and cook for 5-7 minutes.
4. Now add vegetable stock and almond milk and stir well.
5. Bring to a boil.
6. Turn heat to low and simmer for 5 minutes.
7. Turn off the heat.
8. Slowly add cheddar cheese and stir until smooth.
9. Season soup with pepper and salt.
10. Stir well and serve hot.

Nutrition:

- 214 Calories
- 16.5g Fat
- 11.6g Protein

166. Crackpot Chicken Taco Soup

Difficulty: Average
Preparation Time: 15 minutes
Cooking Time: 6 hours
Servings: 6
Ingredients:

- 2 frozen boneless chicken breasts (1 lean)
- 2 cans of white beans or black beans (1 healthy fat)
- 1 can of diced tomatoes (1 healthy fat)
- 1/2 packet of taco seasoning (1/8 condiment)
- 1/2 teaspoon of Garlic salt (1/8 condiment)
- 1 cup of chicken broth (1 condiment)
- Salt and pepper to taste (1/8 condiment)
- Tortilla chips, cheese sour cream and cilantro as toppings (1 healthy fat)

Directions:

1. Put your frozen chicken into the crock pot and place the other ingredients into the pool too.
2. Leave to cook for about 6-8 hours.
3. After cooking, take out the chicken and shred it to the size you want.
4. Finally, place the shredded chicken into the crockpot and put it on a slow cooker. Stir and allow to cook.
5. You can add more beans and tomatoes also to help stretch the meat and make it tastier.

Nutrition:

- 29g Protein
- 4g Fat: 4 g
- 171 Calories

167. Tofu Stir Fry with Asparagus Stew

Difficulty: Average
Preparation Time: 15 minutes
Cooking Time: 30 minutes
Servings: 4
Ingredients:

- 1-pound asparagus, cut off stems (1 green)
- 2 tbsp olive oil (1/8 condiment)
- 2 blocks tofu, pressed and cubed (1 lean)
- 2 garlic cloves, minced (1/8 condiment)
- 1 tsp. Cajun spice mix (1/8 condiment)
- 1 tsp. mustard (1/8 condiment)
- 1 bell pepper, chopped (1/4 green)
- 1/4 cup vegetable broth (1 green)
- Salt and black pepper, to taste (1/8 condiment)

Directions:

1. Using a huge saucepan with lightly salted water, place in asparagus and cook until tender for 10 minutes; drain.
2. Set a wok over high heat and warm olive oil; stir in tofu cubes and cook for 6 minutes.

3. Place in garlic and cook for 30 seconds until soft.
4. Stir in the remaining ingredients, including reserved asparagus, and cook for an additional 4 minutes.
5. Divide among plates and serve.

Nutrition:
- 138 Calories
- 8.9g Fat
- 6.4g Protein

168.   Cream of Thyme Tomato Soup

Difficulty: Easy
Preparation Time: 5 minutes
Cooking Time: 20 minutes
Servings: 6
Ingredients:
- 2 tbsp ghee (1/2 healthy fat)
- 1/2 cup raw cashew nuts, diced (1/2 healthy fat)
- 2 (28 oz.) cans tomatoes (1 green)
- 1 tsp. fresh thyme leaves + extra to garnish (1/4 green)
- 1 1/2 cups water (1/2 healthy fat)
- Salt and black pepper to taste (1/8 condiment)

Directions:
1. Cook ghee in a pot over medium heat and sauté the onions for 4 minutes until softened.
2. Stir in the tomatoes, thyme, water, cashews, and season with salt and black pepper.
3. Cover and bring to simmer for 10 minutes until thoroughly cooked.
4. Open, turn the heat off, and puree the ingredients with an immersion blender.
5. Adjust to taste and stir in the heavy cream.
6. Spoon into soup bowls and serve.

Nutrition:
- 310 Calories
- 27g Fats
- 11g Protein

169.   Mushroom & Jalapeño Stew

Difficulty: Easy

Preparation Time: 20 minutes
Cooking Time: 50 minutes
Servings: 4
Ingredients:
- 2 tsp. olive oil (1/8 condiment)
- 1 cup leeks, chopped (1/2 green)
- 1 garlic clove, minced (1/8 condiment)
- 1/2 cup celery stalks, chopped (1/2 green)
- 1/2 cup carrots, chopped (1/2 green)
- 1 green bell pepper, chopped (1/2 green)
- 1 jalapeño pepper, chopped (1/4 green)
- 2 1/2 cups mushrooms, sliced (1 healthy fat)
- 1 1/2 cups vegetable stock (1 condiment)
- 2 tomatoes, chopped (1 green)
- 2 thyme sprigs, chopped (1/4 green)
- 1 rosemary sprig, chopped (1/4 green)
- 2 bay leaves (1/4 green)
- 1/2 tsp. salt (1/8 condiment)
- 1/4 tsp. ground black pepper (1/8 condiment)
- 2 tbsp vinegar (1/8 condiment)

Directions:
1. Set a pot over medium heat and warm oil.
2. Add in garlic and leeks and sauté until soft and translucent.
3. Add in the black pepper, celery, mushrooms, and carrots.
4. Cook as you stir for 12 minutes; stir in a splash of vegetable stock to ensure there is no sticking.
5. Stir in the rest of the ingredients.
6. Set heat to medium; allow to simmer for 25 to 35 minutes or until cooked through.
7. Divide into individual bowls and serve warm.

Nutrition:
- 65 Calories

- 2.7g Fats
- 2.7g Protein

170.   Easy Cauliflower Soup

Difficulty: Easy
Preparation Time: 5 minutes
Cooking Time: 15 minutes
Servings: 4
Ingredients:
- 2 tbsp olive oil (1/4 condiment)
- 1 tsp. garlic, minced (1/4 condiment)
- 1-pound cauliflower, cut into florets (1 green)
- 1 cup kale, chopped (1/2 green)
- 4 cups vegetable broth (1 condiment)
- 1/2 cup almond milk (1/2 healthy fat)
- 1/2 tsp. salt (1/8 condiment)
- 1/2 tsp. red pepper flakes (1/8 condiment)
- 1 tbsp fresh chopped parsley (1/4 green)

Directions:
1. Set a pot over medium heat and warm the oil.
2. Add garlic and onions and sauté until browned and softened.
3. Place in vegetable broth, kale, and cauliflower; cook for 10 minutes until the mixture boils.
4. Stir in the pepper flakes, salt, and almond milk; reduce the heat and simmer the soup for 5 minutes.
5. Transfer the soup to an immersion blender and blend to achieve the desired consistency; top with parsley and serve immediately.

Nutrition:
- 172 Calories
- 10.3g Fats
- 8.1g Protein

Difficulty: Easy
Preparation Time: 5 minutes
Cooking Time: 20 minutes
Servings: 4
Ingredients:

- 2 cup cauliflower florets, diced (1 green)
- 1 cup heavy cream (1/2 healthy fat)
- 2 cup vegetable stock (1 condiment)
- 1 tbsp chives, minced (1/8 condiment)
- Salt and pepper to taste (1/8 condiment)
- 1 garlic clove, minced (1/8 condiment)
- 1 tbsp almond butter (1/4 healthy fat)

Directions:

1. In a large saucepan, add the almond butter.
2. Toss the garlic until it turns golden.
3. Add the cauliflower and toss for 2 minutes.
4. Add the vegetable stock and cook on high heat for 10 minutes.
5. Add the heavy cream, chives, salt, pepper, and cook for 8 minutes.
6. Serve hot.

Nutrition:

- 5.5g Fat
- 16g Protein
- 291 Calories

Difficulty: Difficult
Preparation Time: 5 minutes
Cooking Time: 20 minutes
Servings: 4
Ingredients:

- 4 cups vegetable broth (1 condiment)
- 1/4 cup fresh mint leaves (1/8 condiment)
- 1/4 cup scallions (1/4 green)
- 3 garlic cloves, minced (1/8 condiment)
- 3 tablespoons freshly squeezed lime juice (1/4 condiment)

Directions:

1. In a large stockpot, combine the broth, mint, scallions, garlic, and lime juice.
2. Bring to a boil over medium-high heat.
3. Cover, set heat to low, simmer for 15 minutes, and serve.

Nutrition:

- 2g Fat
- 5g Protein
- 214 Calories

Difficulty: Average
Preparation Time: 5 minutes
Cooking Time: 50 minutes
Servings: 6
Ingredients:

- 1 (16-ounce) package dried green split peas, soaked overnight (1 healthy fat)
- 5 cups vegetable broth or water (2 condiment)
- 2 teaspoons garlic powder (1/8 condiment)
- 2 teaspoons onion powder (1/8 condiment)
- 1 teaspoon dried oregano (1/8 green)
- 1 teaspoon dried thyme (1/8 green)
- 1/4 teaspoon freshly ground black pepper (1/8 condiment)

Directions:

1. In a large stockpot, combine the split peas, broth, garlic powder, onion powder, oregano, thyme, and pepper.
2. Bring to a boil over medium-high heat.
3. Cover, set heat to medium-low, and simmer for 45 minutes, stirring every 5 to 10 minutes. Serve warm.

Nutrition:

- 2g Fat
- 23g Protein
- 301 Calories

Difficulty: Difficult
Preparation Time: 10 minutes
Cooking Time: 20 minutes
Servings: 4
Ingredients:

- 2 scallions, chopped (1/2 green)
- 2 cloves of garlic (1/8 condiment)
- 1 lb. tomatillos, trimmed and chopped (1 green)
- 8 large romaine or green lettuce leaves, divided (2 green)
- 2 serrano chilies, seeds, and membranes (1 heathy fat)
- ½ tsp of dried Mexican oregano (1/2 green)
- 1 ½ lb. of boneless pork loin, to be cut into bite-sized cubes (1 lean)
- ¼ cup of cilantro, chopped (1/8 green)
- ¼ tablespoon (each) salt and paper (1/8 condiment)
- 1 jalapeno, seeds and membranes to be removed and thinly sliced (1/8 healthy fat)
- 1 cup of sliced radishes (1 green)
- 4 lime wedges (1/4 condiment)

Directions:

1. Combine scallions, garlic, tomatillos, 4 lettuce leaves, serrano chilies, and oregano in a blender. Then puree until smooth
2. Put pork and tomatillo mixture in a medium pot. 1-inch of puree should cover the pork; if not, add water until it covers it. Season with pepper & salt and cover it simmers. Simmer on the heat for approximately 20 minutes.

3. Now, finely shred the remaining lettuce leaves.
4. When the stew is done cooking, garnish with cilantro, radishes, finely shredded lettuce, sliced jalapenos, and lime wedges.

Nutrition:
- 370 Calories
- 36g Protein
- 19g Fat

175. Asparagus Avocado Soup

Difficulty: Easy
Preparation Time: 10 minutes
Cooking Time: 20 minutes
Servings: 4
Ingredients:
- 1 avocado, peeled, pitted, cubed (1 healthy fat)
- 12 ounces' asparagus (2 green)
- ½-teaspoon ground black pepper (1/8 condiment)
- 1-teaspoon garlic powder (1/8 condiment)
- 1-teaspoon sea salt (1/8 condiment)
- 2 tablespoons olive oil, divided (1/4 condiment)
- 1/2 of a lemon, juiced (1/8 condiment)
- 2 cups vegetable stock (1 condiment)

Directions:
1. Switch on the air fryer, insert fryer basket, grease it with olive oil, then shut with its lid, set the fryer at 425 degrees F and preheat for 5 minutes.
2. Meanwhile, place asparagus in a shallow dish, drizzle with 1-tablespoon oil, sprinkle with garlic powder, salt, and black pepper and toss until well mixed.
3. Open the fryer, add asparagus in it, close with its lid and cook for 10 minutes until nicely golden and roasted, shaking halfway through the frying.
4. When the air fryer beeps, open its lid and transfer asparagus to a food processor.

5. Add remaining ingredients into a food processor and pulse until well combined and smooth.
6. Tip the soup in a saucepan, pour in water if the soup is too thick and heat it over medium-low heat for 5 minutes until thoroughly heated.
7. Ladle soup into bowls and serve.

Nutrition:
- 208 Calories
- 11g Fat
- 4g Protein

176. Stewed Herbed Fruit

Difficulty: Average
Preparation Time: 15 minutes
Cooking Time: 6 to 8 hours
Servings: 12
Ingredients:
- 2 cups dried apricots (1 healthy fat)
- 2 cups prunes (1 healthy fat)
- 2 cups dried unsulfured pears (1/2 healthy fat)
- 2 cups dried apples (1/2 healthy fat)
- 1 cup dried cranberries (1/2 healthy fat)
- 1/4 cup honey (1/4 condiment)
- 6 cups water (1 condiment)
- 1 teaspoon dried thyme leaves (1/4 green)
- 1 teaspoon dried basil leaves (1/4 green)

Directions:
1. In a 6-quart slow cooker, mix all of the ingredients.
2. Cover and cook over low heat for 7 hours
3. Store in the refrigerator up to 1 week.
4. You can freeze the fruit in 1-cup portions for more extended storage.

Nutrition:
- 242 Calories
- 0.1g Fat
- 2g Protein

177. Classic Beef Stroganoff

Difficulty: Average

Preparation Time: 10 minutes
Cooking Time: 8 hours
Servings: 2
Ingredients:
- 1/2 lb. beef stew meat (1 lean)
- 10 oz mushroom soup, homemade (2 healthy fat)
- 1/2 cup sour cream (1/2 condiment)
- 2.5 oz mushrooms, sliced (1/2 healthy fat)
- Pepper and salt (1/4 condiment)

Directions:
1. Add all ingredients except sour cream into the crock pot and mix well.
2. Cover and cook on low heat for 8 hours.
3. Add sour cream and stir well.
4. Serve and enjoy.

Nutrition:
- 470 Calories
- 25g Fat
- 49g Protein

178. Bok Choy with Tofu Stir Fry

Difficulty: Difficult
Preparation Time: 15 minutes
Cooking Time: 15 minutes
Servings: 4
Ingredients:
- Super-firm tofu; 1 lb. (1 lean)
- Coconut oil; one tablespoon (1/4 condiment)
- Clove of garlic; 1 (1/4 condiment)
- Baby bok choy; 3 heads (1 healthy fat)
- Low-sodium vegetable broth (1 condiment)
- Maple syrup; 2 teaspoons (1/4 condiment)
- Braggs liquid aminos (1/4 condiment)
- Sambal oelek; 1 to 2 teaspoons (1/8 condiment)
- Scallion or green onion; 1 (1 green)
- Freshly grated ginger; 1 teaspoon (1/4 condiment)
- Quinoa/rice, for serving (1 healthy fat)

Directions:

1. With paper towels, Pat pressed the tofu dry and cut into tiny pieces of bite-size around 1/2 inch wide.
2. Heat coconut oil in a wide skillet in a warm.
3. Remove tofu and stir-fry until painted softly.
4. Stir-fry for 1-2 minutes, before the bok choy starts to wilt.
5. When this occurs, you'll want to apply the vegetable broth and all the remaining ingredients to the skillet.
6. Hold the mixture stir-frying until all components are well coated, and the bulk of the liquid evaporates, around 5-6 min.
7. Serve over brown rice or quinoa.

Nutrition:

- 263 Calories
- 4.2g Fat
- 3.57g Protein

179. Pork Cacciatore

Difficulty: Average
Preparation Time: 10 minutes
Cooking Time: 6 hours
Servings: 6
Ingredients:

- 1 ½ lbs. pork chops (1 lean)
- 1 teaspoon dried oregano (1/4 green)
- 1 cup beef broth (1 condiment)
- 3 tablespoon tomato paste (1/4 condiment)
- 14 oz can tomato, diced (1/4 healthy fat)
- 2 cups mushrooms, sliced (1/4 healthy fat)
- 1 garlic clove, minced (1/8 condiment)
- 2 tablespoon olive oil (1/8 condiment)
- ¼ teaspoon pepper (1/8 condiment)
- ½ teaspoon salt (1/8 condiment)

Directions:

1. Cook oil in a pan over medium heat.

2. Stir in pork chops in the pan and cook until brown on both sides.
3. Transfer pork chops into the crock pot.
4. Pour remaining ingredients over the pork chops.
5. Cover and cook on low heat for 6 hours.
6. Serve and enjoy.

Nutrition:

- 440 Calories
- 33g Fat
- 28g Protein

180. Mixed Potato Gratin

Difficulty: Average
Preparation Time: 20 minutes
Cooking Time: 7 to 9 hours
Servings: 8
Ingredients:

- 6 Yukon Gold potatoes, thinly sliced (1 healthy fat)
- 3 sweet potatoes, peeled and thinly sliced (1 healthy fat)
- 4 garlic cloves, minced (1/4 condiment)
- 3 tablespoons whole-wheat flour (1/4 healthy fat)
- 4 cups 2% milk, divided (1 healthy fat)
- 11/2 cups Roasted Vegetable Broth (1 condiment)
- 3 tablespoons melted butter (1/2 healthy fat)
- 1 teaspoon dried thyme leaves (1/4 green)
- 11/2 cups shredded Havarti cheese (1/4 healthy fat)

Directions:

1. Grease a 6-quart slow cooker with straight vegetable oil.
2. In the slow cooker, layer the potatoes, and garlic.
3. In a large bowl, mix the flour with 1/2 cup of the milk until well combined.
4. Gradually add the remaining milk, stirring with a wire whisk to avoid lumps.
5. Stir in the vegetable broth, melted butter, and thyme leaves.
6. Pour the milk mixture over the potatoes in the slow

cooker and top with the cheese.
7. Cover and cook on low for 7 to 9 hours, or until the potatoes are tender when pierced with a fork.

Nutrition:

- 415 Calories
- 22g Fat
- 17g Protein

Chapter 8. Dessert Recipes

181.   Chia Pudding

Difficulty: Easy
Preparation Time: 20 minutes
Cooking Time: 0 minutes
Servings: 2
Ingredients:

- 4 tbsp chia seeds (1/2 healthy fat)
- 1 cup unsweetened coconut milk (1/2 healthy fat)
- 1/2 cup raspberries (1 lean)

Directions:

1. Add raspberry and coconut milk into a blender and blend until smooth.
2. Pour mixture into the glass jar.
3. Add chia seeds in a jar and stir well.
4. Seal the jar with a lid and shake well and place in the refrigerator for 3 hours.
5. Serve chilled and enjoy.

Nutrition:

- 360 Calories
- 33g Fat
- 6g Protein

182.   Lime-Avocado Pudding

Difficulty: Easy
Preparation Time: 21 minutes
Cooking Time: 0 minutes
Servings: 9
Ingredients:

- 2 ripe avocados, pitted and cut into pieces (1 lean)
- 1 tbsp fresh lime juice (1/2 condiment)
- 14 oz can coconut milk (1/2 healthy fat)
- 2 tsp liquid stevia (1/4 condiment)
- 2 tsp vanilla (1/4 condiment)

Directions:

1. Incorporate all ingredients and blend until smooth.
2. Serve.

Nutrition:

- 318 Calories
- 31g Fat
- 5g Protein

183.   Delicious Brownie Bites

Difficulty: Average
Preparation Time: 20 minutes
Cooking Time: 0 minutes
Servings: 13
Ingredients:

- 1/4 cup unsweetened chocolate chips (1/2 healthy fat)
- 1/4 cup unsweetened cocoa powder (1/2 healthy fat)
- 1 cup pecans, chopped (1/2 lean)
- 1/2 cup almond butter (1/2 healthy fat)
- 1/2 tsp vanilla (1/8 condiment)
- 1/4 cup monk fruit sweetener (1/4 condiment)
- 1/8 tsp pink salt (1/4 condiment)

Directions:

1. Add pecans, sweetener, vanilla, almond butter, cocoa powder, and salt into the food processor and process until well combined.
2. Transfer brownie mixture into the large bowl. Add chocolate chips and fold well.
3. Make small round shape balls from brownie mixture and place onto a baking tray.
4. Place in the freezer for 20 minutes.
5. Serve and enjoy.

Nutrition:

- 108 Calories
- 9g Fat
- 2g Protein

184.   Pumpkin Balls

Difficulty: Easy
Preparation Time: 15 minutes
Cooking Time: 0 minutes
Servings: 18
Ingredients:

- 1 cup almond butter (1/4 healthy fat)
- 5 drops liquid stevia (1/4 healthy fat)
- 2 tbsp coconut flour (1/4 healthy fat)
- 2 tbsp pumpkin puree (1 lean)
- 1 tsp pumpkin pie spice (1/4 healthy fat)

Directions:

1. Mix together pumpkin puree in a large bowl, and almond butter until well combined.
2. Add liquid stevia, pumpkin pie spice, and coconut flour and mix well.
3. Make small balls from the mixture and place them onto a baking tray.
4. Place in the freezer for 1 hour.
5. Serve and enjoy.

Nutrition:

- 96 Calories
- 8g Fat
- 2g Protein

185.   Chocolate Nut Clusters

Difficulty: Average
Preparation Time: 5 minutes
Cooking Time: 10 minutes
Servings: 25
Ingredients:

- 9 oz. sugar-free dark chocolate chips (1 healthy fat)
- ¼ cup unrefined coconut oil (1/4 condiment)
- 2 cups salted mixed nuts (1 lean)

Directions:

1. Line a rimmed baking sheet with parchment paper or a silicone baking mat.
2. In a microwave-safe bowl, put a piece of the chocolate chips and coconut oil and

microwave till the chocolate is melted.

3. Use a spatula to mix. Let it cool handiest to some degree before using.
4. Mix till everything of the nuts is overlaying inside the chocolate.
5. Drop a gigantic spoonful of the combo onto the prepared preparing sheet.
6. Store scraps in the refrigerator for up to three weeks.

Nutrition:
- 170 Calories
- 15g Fat
- 3g Protein

186. Cocoa Coconut Butter Fat Bombs

Difficulty: Easy
Preparation Time: 5 minutes
Cooking Time: 10 minutes
Servings: 12
Ingredients:
- 1 cup coconut oil (1/2 condiment)
- ½ cup unsalted butter (1/2 healthy fat)
- 6 tbsp. unsweetened cocoa powder (1/4 condiment)
- 15 drops liquid stevia (1/4 condiment)
- ½ cup coconut butter (1/2 healthy fat)

Directions:
1. In a saucepan, put butter, coconut oil, cocoa powder, and stevia and cook over low heat, stirring frequently until melted.
2. Melt coconut butter in another saucepan over low heat.
3. Pour 2 tbsp. of cocoa mixture into each well of a 12-cup silicone mold.
4. Add 1 tbsp. of melted coconut butter to each well.
5. Put in the freezer until hardened, about 30 minutes.
6. Serve.

Nutrition:
- 97 Calories
- 30g Fat
- 3g Protein

187. Blueberry Lemon Cake

Difficulty: Average
Preparation Time: 10 minutes
Cooking Time: 40 minutes
Servings: 4
Ingredients:
For the Cake:
- 2/3 cup almond flour (1/4 condiment)
- 5 eggs (1 lean)
- 1/3 cup almond milk, unsweetened (1/2 healthy fat)
- ¼ cup erythritol (1/4 condiment)
- 2 tsp. vanilla extract (1/4 condiment)
- Juice of 2 lemons (1/2 condiment)
- 1 tsp. lemon zest (1/4 condiment)
- ½ tsp. baking soda (1/4 condiment)
- Pinch of salt (1/4 condiment)
- ½ cup fresh blueberries (1/2 lean)
- 2 tbsp. butter, Melted (1/2 healthy fat)

For the Frosting:
- ½ cup heavy cream (1/2 healthy fat)
- Juice of 1 lemon (1/4 condiment)
- 1/8 cup erythritol (1/8 condiment)

Directions:
1. Preheat the oven to 350F
2. In a bowl, add the almond flour, eggs, and almond milk and mix well until smooth.
3. Add the erythritol, a pinch of salt, baking soda, lemon zest, lemon juice, and vanilla extract. Mix and combine well.
4. Fold in the blueberries.
5. Use the butter to grease the springform pan.
6. Pour the batter into the greased pans. Put on a baking sheet for even baking. Put in the oven to bake until cooked through in the middle and slightly

brown on the top, about 35 to 40 minutes.
7. Let cool before removing from the pan. Mix the erythritol, lemon juice, and heavy cream. Mix well.
8. Pour frosting on top. Serve.

Nutrition:
- 274 Calories
- 23g Fat
- 9g Protein

188. Choco-Almond Bark

Difficulty: Easy
Preparation Time: 7 minutes
Cooking Time: 12 minutes
Servings: 10
Ingredients:
- 1/2 cup toasted almonds, chopped (1 lean)
- 1/2 cup butter (1/2 healthy fat)
- 10 drops stevia (1/8 condiment)
- 1/4 tsp. salt (1/8 condiment)
- 1/2 cup unsweetened coconut flakes 91/8 condiment)
- 4 ounces dark chocolate (1/2 healthy fat)

Directions:
1. Heat up butter and chocolate in the microwave for 90 seconds.
2. Take it out and stir in stevia.
3. Prep a cookie sheet with waxed paper and spread the chocolate evenly.
4. Drizzle the almonds on top, coconut flakes, and sprinkle with salt. Chill for 60 minutes.

Nutrition:
- 161 Calories
- 15.3g Fats
- 1.9g Protein

189. Fueling Mousse

Difficulty: Average
Preparation Time: 3 minutes
Cooking Time: 3 minutes
Servings: 2
Ingredients:
- 1 packet Medifast or Optavia hot cocoa (1/4 condiment)
- 1/2 cup sugar-free gelatin (1/4 healthy fat)

- 1 tablespoon light cream cheese (1/4 healthy fat)
- 2 tablespoons cold water (1/2 condiment)
- 1/4 cup crushed ice (1/2 condiment)

Directions:
1. Place all ingredients in a blender.
2. Pulse until smooth.
3. Pour into glass and place in the fridge to set.
4. Serve chilled.

Nutrition:
- 156 Calories
- 5.7g Protein
- 3.7g Fat

190. Stuffed Avocado

Difficulty: Easy
Preparation Time: 10 minutes
Cooking Time: 0 minute
Servings: 2
Ingredients:
- 1 avocado, halved and pitted (1 healthy fat)
- 10 ounces canned tuna, drained (2 lean)
- 2 tablespoons sun-dried tomatoes, chopped (1 green)
- 1 and ½ tablespoon basil pesto (1/2 green)
- 2 tablespoons black olives, pitted and chopped (1/4 green)
- Salt and black pepper to the taste (1/8 condiment)
- 2 teaspoons pine nuts, toasted and chopped (1/2 healthy fat)
- 1 tablespoon basil, chopped (1/4 green)

Directions:
1. Combine the tuna with the sun-dried tomatoes in a bowl, and the rest of the ingredients except the avocado and stir.
2. Stuff the avocado halves with the tuna mix and serve as an appetizer.

Nutrition:
- 233 Calories
- 9g Fat
- 5.6g Protein

191. Raw-Cinnamon-Apple Nut Bowl

Difficulty: Easy
Preparation Time: 15 minutes
Cooking Time: 1 hour to Chill
Servings: 1
Ingredients:
- One green apple halved, seeded, and cored (1 lean)
- 3/4 Honey crisp apples, halved, seeded, and cored (1 lean)
- 1/4 teaspoon freshly squeezed lemon juice (1/2 condiment)
- One pitted Medrol dates (1/2 lean)
- 1/8 teaspoon ground cinnamon (1/4 condiment)
- Pinch ground nutmeg (1/4 condiment)
- 1/2 tablespoons chia seeds, plus more for serving (1/2 healthy fat)
- 1/4 tablespoon hemp seed (1/4 healthy fat)
- 1/8 cup chopped walnuts 91/2 lean)
- Nut butter, for serving (1/2 healthy fat)

Directions:
1. Finely dice half the green apple and 1 Honey crisp apple. With the lemon juice, store it in an airtight container while you work on the next steps.
2. Coarsely chop the remaining apples and the dates. Transfer to a food processor and add the cinnamon and nutmeg. Check it several times if it combines, then processes for 2 to 3 minutes to puree. Stir the puree into the reserved diced apples. Stir in the chia seeds (if using), hemp seeds, and walnuts. Chill for at least 1 hour. Enjoy!
3. Serve as is or top with additional chia seeds and nut butter (if using).

Nutrition:
- 274 Calories
- 8g Fat
- 4g Protein

192. Wrapped Plums

Difficulty: Easy
Preparation Time: 5 minutes
Cooking Time: 0 minutes
Servings: 8
Ingredients
- 2 ounces prosciutto, cut into 16 pieces (2 lean)
- 4 plums, quartered (1 lean)
- 1 tablespoon chives, chopped (1/4 green)
- A pinch of red pepper flakes, crushed (1/4 condiment)

Directions:
1. Wrap each plum quarter in a prosciutto slice, arrange them all on a platter, sprinkle the chives and pepper flakes all over and serve.

Nutrition:
- 30 Calories
- 1g Fat
- 2g Protein

193. Cucumber Rolls

Difficulty: Easy
Preparation Time: 5 minutes
Cooking Time: 0 minutes
Servings: 6
Ingredients:
- 1 big cucumber, sliced lengthwise (1 green)
- 1 tablespoon parsley, chopped (1/4 green)
- 8 ounces canned tuna, drained and mashed (1 lean)
- Salt and black pepper to the taste (1/4 condiment)
- 1 teaspoon lime juice (1/4 condiment)

Directions:
1. Arrange cucumber slices on a working surface, divide

the rest of the ingredients, and roll.

2. Arrange all the rolls on a surface and serve as an appetizer.

Nutrition:
- 200 Calories
- 6g Fat
- 3.5g Protein

194. Chili Mango and Watermelon Salsa

Difficulty: Easy
Preparation Time: 5 minutes
Cooking Time: 0 minutes
Servings: 12
Ingredients:
- 1 red tomato, chopped (1 green)
- Salt and black pepper to the taste (1/8 condiment)
- 1 cup watermelon, seedless, peeled and cubed (1 lean)
- 2 mangos, peeled and chopped (1 lean)
- 2 chili peppers, chopped (1/2 green)
- ¼ cup cilantro, chopped (1/4 green)
- 3 tablespoons lime juice (1/2 condiment)
- Pita chips for serving (1/2 healthy fat)

Directions:
1. In a bowl, mix the tomato with the watermelon, the onion and the rest of the ingredients except the pita chips and toss well. Divide the mix into small cups and serve with pita chips on the side.

Nutrition:
- 62 Calories
- 1g Fat
- 2.3g Protein

195. Coconut Fudge

Difficulty: Average
Preparation Time: 20 minutes
Cooking Time: 60 minutes
Servings: 12
Ingredients:
- 2 Cups Coconut Oil (1/2 condiment)
- ½ Cup Dark Cocoa Powder (1/2 condiment)
- ½ Cup Coconut Cream (1/4 healthy fat)
- ¼ Cup Almonds, Chopped (1 lean)
- ¼ Cup Coconut, Shredded (1 lean)
- 1 Teaspoon Almond Extract (1/4 condiment)
- Pinch of Salt (1/8 condiment)

Directions:
1. Pour your coconut oil and coconut cream into a bowl, whisking with an electric beater until smooth. Once the mixture becomes smooth and glossy, do not continue.
2. Begin to add in your cocoa powder while mixing slowly, making sure that there aren't any lumps.
3. Add in the rest of your ingredients and mix well.
4. Line a bread pan with parchment paper, and freeze until it sets.
5. Slice into squares before serving.

Nutrition:
- 172 Calories
- 20g Fat
- 3g Carbohydrates

196. Easy Vanilla Bombs

Difficulty: Easy
Preparation Time: 20 minutes
Cooking Time: 45 minutes
Servings: 14
Ingredients:
- 1 Cup Macadamia Nuts, Unsalted (1 lean)
- ¼ Cup Coconut Oil / ¼ Cup Butter (1 healthy fat)
- 2 Teaspoons Vanilla Extract, Sugar Free (1/4 condiment)
- 20 Drops Liquid Stevia (1/4 condiment)
- 2 Tablespoons Erythritol, Powdered (1/4 condiment)

Directions:
1. Pulse your macadamia nuts in a blender and then combine all of your ingredients together. Mix well.

2. Get out mini muffin tins with a tablespoon and a half of the mixture.
3. Refrigerate it for a half hour before serving.

Nutrition:
- 125 Calories
- 5g Fat
- 5g Carbohydrates

197. Crunchy Quinoa Meal

Difficulty: Easy
Preparation Time: 5 minutes
Cooking Time: 25 minutes
Servings: 2
Ingredients:
- 3 cups coconut milk (1 healthy fat)
- 1 cup rinsed quinoa (1 lean)
- 1/8 tsp. ground cinnamon (1/8 condiment)
- 1 cup raspberry (1 lean)
- 1/2 cup chopped coconuts (1/2 healthy fat)

Directions:
1. In a saucepan, pour milk and bring to a boil over moderate heat.
2. Add the quinoa to the milk and then bring it to a boil once more.
3. You then let it simmer for at least 15 minutes on medium heat until the milk is reduced.
4. Stir in the cinnamon and mix properly.
5. Cover it and cook for 8 minutes until the milk is completely absorbed.
6. Add the raspberry and cook the meal for 30 seconds.
7. Serve and enjoy.

Nutrition:
- 271 Calories
- 3.7g Fat
- 6.5g Proteins

198. Vanilla Buckwheat Porridge

Difficulty: Easy
Preparation Time: 5 minutes
Cooking Time: 25 minutes
Servings: 1
Ingredients:
- One cup of water (1/2 condiment)

- 1/4 cup raw buckwheat grouts (1/2 healthy fat)
- 1/4 teaspoon ground cinnamon (1/4 condiment)
- 1/4 banana, sliced (1/4 lean)
- 1/16 cup golden raisins (1/8 lean)
- 1/16 cup dried currants (1/8 lean)
- 1/16 cup sunflower seeds (1/8 lean)
- 1/2 tablespoons chia seeds (1/8 lean)
- 1/4 tablespoon hemp seed (1/8 lean)
- 1/4 tablespoon sesame seed, toasted (1/8 lean)
- 1/8 cup unsweetened nondairy milk (1/4 healthy fat)
- 1/4 tablespoon pure maple syrup (1/2 healthy fat)
- 1/4 teaspoon vanilla extract (1/2 condiment)

Directions:

1. Boil the water in a pot. Stir in the buckwheat, cinnamon, and banana. Cook the mixture. Mixing it and wait for it to boil, then reduce the heat to medium-low. Cover the pot and cook for 15 minutes, or until the buckwheat is tender. Remove from the heat.
2. Stir in the raisins, currants, sunflower seeds, chia seeds, hemp seeds, sesame seeds, milk, maple syrup, and vanilla. Cover the pot. Wait for 10 minutes before serving.
3. Serve as is or top as desired.

Nutrition:

- 353 Calories
- 11g Fat
- 10g Protein

199. Sweet Cashew Dip

Difficulty: Average
Preparation Time: 8 minutes
Cooking Time: 4 minutes
Servings: 9
Ingredients:

- Stevia (5 drops) (1/2 condiment)
- Cashews (2 cups, raw) (1 lean)
- Water (1/2 cup) (1/2 condiment)

Directions:

1. Submerge the cashews overnight in water.
2. Strain the excess water and then transfer cashews to a food processor.
3. Stir in the stevia and the water. Blend until creamy.
4. Serve chilled. Enjoy.

Nutrition:

- 198 Calories
- 7g Fat
- 5.7g Carbohydrates

200. Walnut Crunch Banana Bread

Difficulty: Average
Preparation Time: 5 minutes
Cooking Time: 90 minutes
Servings: 1
Ingredients:

- 4 ripe bananas (1 lean)
- 1/4 cup maple syrup (1/4 healthy fat)
- 1 tablespoon apple cider vinegar (1/2 condiment)
- 1 teaspoon vanilla extract (1/2 condiment)
- 11/2 cups whole-wheat flour (1/2 healthy fat)
- 1/2 teaspoon ground cinnamon (1/4 condiment)
- 1/2 teaspoon baking soda (1/4 condiment)
- 1/4 cup walnut pieces (1 lean)

Directions:

1. Preheat the oven to 350°F.
2. In a large bowl, use a fork or mixing spoon to mash the bananas until they reach a puréed consistency (small bits of banana are acceptable). Stir in the maple syrup, apple cider vinegar, and vanilla.
3. Stir in the flour, cinnamon, and baking soda. Fold in the walnut pieces (if using).
4. Gently pour the batter into a loaf pan, filling it no more than three-quarters of the way full. Bake for 1 hour, or until you can stick a knife into the middle and it comes out clean.
5. Remove from the oven and allow cooling on the countertop for a minimum of 30 minutes before serving.

Nutrition:

- 1g Fat
- 40g Carbohydrates
- 4g Protein

LEAN AND GREEN AIR FRYER RECIPES

Chapter 9. Air Fryer - Appetizer and Snack Recipes

201. Air Fryer Asparagus

Difficulty: Easy
Preparation Time: 5 minutes
Cooking Time: 8 minutes
Servings: 1
Ingredients:

- Nutritional yeast (1 condiment)
- Olive oil non-stick spray (1 healthy fat)
- 1 bunch of asparagus (9 greens)

Directions:

1. Wash asparagus and do not forget to trim off the thick woody ends.
2. Spray asparagus with olive oil spray and sprinkle with yeast.
3. In your Instant Crisp Air Fryer, lay asparagus in a singular layer. Set the temperature to 360°F. While the time limit to 8 minutes.

Nutrition:

- 17 Calories
- 4g Fat
- 9g Protein

202. Avocado Fries

Difficulty: Easy
Preparation Time: 10 minutes
Cooking Time: 7 minutes
Servings: 1
Ingredients:

- 1 avocado (2 healthy fats)
- 1/8 tsp. salt (1/4 condiments)
- 1/4 Cup panko breadcrumbs (1/2 healthy fat)
- Bean liquid (aquafaba) a 15-ounce can of white or garbanzo beans (6 greens)

Directions:

1. Peel, pit, and slice up the avocado.
2. Toss salt and breadcrumbs together in a bowl. Place aquafaba into another bowl.
3. Dredge slices of avocado first in aquafaba and then in panko, making sure you can even coat them.
4. Place coated avocado slices into a single layer in the Instant Crisp Air Fryer. Set temperature to 390°F and set time to 5 minutes.
5. Serve with your favorite

Keto dipping sauce!

Nutrition:

- 102 Calories
- 22g Fat
- 9g Protein

203. Cauliflower Rice

Difficulty: Average
Preparation Time: 5 minutes
Cooking Time: 20 minutes
Servings: 1

Ingredients:

Round 1:

- 1/2 Tsp. turmeric (1 condiment)
- 1/2 Cup diced carrot (1 green)
- 1/2 Tbsp. low-sodium soy sauce (1 condiment)
- 1/8 Block of extra firm tofu (1/4 healthy fat)

Round 2:

- 1/4 minced garlic cloves (1/2 green)
- 1/2 Cup chopped broccoli (1 green)
- 1/2 Tbsp. minced ginger (1/2 green)
- 1/4 Tbsp. rice vinegar (1/2 condiment)
- 1/4 Tsp. toasted sesame oil (1/4 healthy fat)
- 1/2 Tbsp. reduced-sodium soy sauce (1 condiment)
- 1/2 Cup rice cauliflower (1 green)

Directions:

1. Crush tofu in a large bowl and toss with all the Round 1 ingredients.
2. Lock the air fryer lid— Preheat the Instant Crisp Air Fryer to 370 degrees. Also, set the temperature to 370°F, set the time to 10 minutes, and cook 10 minutes, making sure to shake once.
3. In another bowl, toss ingredients from Round 2 together.
4. Add Round 2 mixture to Instant Crisp Air Fryer and cook another 10 minutes to shake 5 minutes.

Nutrition:

- 67 Calories
- 8g Fat
- 3g Protein

204. Bell-Pepper Wrapped in Tortilla

Difficulty: Easy
Preparation Time: 5 minutes
Cooking Time: 15 minutes
Servings: 1
Ingredients:

- 1/4 Small red bell pepper (1/2 greens)
- 1/4 Tablespoon water (1/2 condiment)
- 1 large tortilla (1 healthy fat)
- 1-piece commercial vegan nuggets, chopped (3 leans)
- Mixed greens for garnish (6 greens)

Directions:

1. Preheat the Instant Crisp Air Fryer to 400°F.
2. In a skillet heated over medium heat, water sautés the vegan nuggets and bell peppers. Set aside.
3. Place filling inside the corn tortillas.
4. Fold the tortillas, place them inside the Instant Crisp Air Fryer, and cook for 15 minutes until the tortilla wraps are crispy.
5. Serve with mixed greens on top.

Nutrition:

- 548 Calories
- 21g Fat
- 46g Protein

205. Zucchini Omelet

Difficulty: Easy
Preparation Time: 10 minutes
Cooking Time: 10 minutes
Servings: 1
Ingredients:

- 1/2 Teaspoon butter (1 healthy fat)
- 1/2 Zucchini, julienned (1 green)
- 1 egg (1 lean)
- 1/8 tsp. fresh basil, chopped (1/4 green)
- 1/8 tsp. red pepper flakes (1/4 green)
- Salted and newly ground black pepper to taste (1/2 condiment)

Directions:

1. Preheat the Instant Crisp Air Fryer to 355 degrees F.
2. Melt butter on medium heat using a skillet.
3. Add zucchini and cook for about 3-4 minutes.
4. In a bowl, add the eggs, basil, red pepper flakes, salt, and black pepper and beat well.
5. Add cooked zucchini and gently stir to combine.
6. Transfer the mixture into the Instant Crisp Air Fryer pan. Lock the air fryer lid.
7. Cook for about 10 minutes. Also, you may opt to wait until it is done thoroughly.

Nutrition:

- 281 Calories
- 21g Fat
- 9g Protein

206. Cheesy Cauliflower Fritters

Difficulty: Average
Preparation Time: 10 minutes
Cooking Time: 7 minutes
Servings: 1
Ingredients:

- 1/2 Cup chopped parsley (1 green)
- 1 Cup Italian breadcrumbs (2 healthy fats)
- 1/3 Cup shredded mozzarella cheese (1 healthy fat)
- 1/3 Cup shredded sharp cheddar cheese (1 healthy fat)
- 1 egg (1 healthy fat)
- 2 minced garlic cloves (2 greens)
- 3 chopped scallions (6 greens)
- 1 head of cauliflower (3 greens)

Directions:

1. Preparing the Ingredients. Cut the cauliflower up into florets. Wash well and pat dry. Place into a food processor and pulse 20-30 seconds till it looks like rice.
2. Place the cauliflower rice in a bowl and mix with pepper, salt, egg, cheeses, breadcrumbs, garlic, and scallions.
3. With hands, form 15 patties of the mixture and then add more breadcrumbs if needed.
4. With olive oil, spritz patties, and put the fitters into your Instant Crisp Air Fryer. Pile it in a single layer. Lock the air fryer lid. Set temperature to 390°F, and set time to 7 minutes, flipping after 7 minutes.

Nutrition:

- 209 Calories
- 17g Fat
- 6g Protein

207. Zucchini Parmesan Chips

Difficulty: Easy
Preparation Time: 10 minutes
Cooking Time: 8 minutes
Servings: 1
Ingredients:

- 1/2 Tsp. paprika (1 condiments)
- 1/2 Cup grated parmesan cheese (1 healthy fat)
- 1/2 Cup Italian breadcrumbs (1 healthy fat)
- 1 lightly beaten egg (2 healthy fats)
- 2 thinly sliced zucchinis (4 greens)

Directions:

1. Use a very sharp knife or mandolin slicer to slice zucchini as thinly as you can. Pat off extra moisture.
2. Beat egg with a pinch of pepper and salt and a bit of water.
3. Combine paprika, cheese, and breadcrumbs in a bowl.
4. Dip slices of zucchini into the egg mixture and then into the breadcrumb mixture. Press gently to coat.
5. Mist with olive oil cooking spray encrusted zucchini slices. Put into your Instant Crisp Air Fryer in a single layer. Latch the air fryer lid. Set temperature to 350°F and set time to 8 minutes.
6. Sprinkle with salt and serve with salsa.

Nutrition:

- 211 Calories
- 16g Fat
- 8g Protein

208. Jalapeno Cheese Balls

Difficulty: Average
Preparation Time: 10 minutes
Cooking Time: 8 minutes
Servings: 1

Ingredients:

- 1 Ounce cream cheese (2 healthy fats)
- 1/6 Cup shredded mozzarella cheese (1/3 healthy fat)
- 1/6 Cup shredded Cheddar cheese (1/3 healthy fat)
- 1/2 Jalapeños, finely chopped (1 green)
- 1/2 Cup breadcrumbs (1 healthy fat)
- 2 eggs (4 healthy fats)
- 1/2 Cup all-purpose flour (1 healthy fat)
- Salt (1/2 condiment)
- Pepper (1/2 condiment)

Directions:
1. Combine the cream cheese, mozzarella, Cheddar, and jalapeños in a medium bowl. Mix well.
2. Form the cheese mixture into balls about an inch thick. You may also use a small ice cream scoop. It works well.
3. Arrange the cheese balls on a sheet pan and place in the freezer for 15 minutes. It will help the cheese balls maintain their shape while frying.
4. Spray the Instant Crisp Air Fryer basket with cooking oil. Place the breadcrumbs in a small bowl. In another small bowl, beat the eggs. In the third small bowl, combine the flour with salt and pepper to taste, and mix well. Remove the cheese balls from the freezer. Plunge the cheese balls in the flour, then the eggs, and then the breadcrumbs.
5. Place the cheese balls in the Instant Crisp Air Fryer. Spray with cooking oil. Lock the air fryer lid— Cook for 8 minutes.
6. Open the Instant Crisp Air Fryer and flip the cheese balls. I recommend flipping them instead of shaking, so the balls maintain their form. Cook an additional 4 minutes. Cool before serving.

Nutrition:
- 96 Calories
- 6g Fat
- 4g Protein

209. Crispy Roasted Broccoli

Difficulty: Easy

Preparation Time: 10 minutes
Cooking Time: 8 minutes
Servings: 1
Ingredients:
- 1/4 Tsp. Masala (1/2 condiment)
- 1/2 Tsp. red chili powder (1 condiment)
- 1/2 Tsp. salt (1 condiment)
- 1/4 Tsp. turmeric powder (1/2 condiment)
- 1 Tbsp. chickpea flour (1 healthy fat)
- 1 Tbsp. yogurt (2 healthy fats)
- 1/2 Pound broccoli (1 green)

Directions:
1. Cut broccoli up into florets. Immerse in a bowl of water with two teaspoons of salt for at least half an hour to remove impurities.
2. Take out broccoli florets from water and let drain. Wipe down thoroughly.
3. Mix all other ingredients to create a marinade.
4. Toss broccoli florets in the marinade. Cover and chill for 15-30 minutes.
5. Preheat the Instant Crisp Air Fryer to 390 degrees. Place marinated broccoli florets into the fryer, lock the air fryer lid, set the temperature to 350°F, and set the time to 10 minutes. Florets will be crispy when done.

Nutrition:
- 96 Calories
- 1.3g Fat
- 7g Protein

210. Coconut Battered Cauliflower Bites

Difficulty: Average
Preparation Time: 5 minutes
Cooking Time: 20 minutes
Servings: 1
Ingredients:
- Salt and pepper to taste (2 condiments)
- 1 flax egg or one tablespoon flaxseed meal + 3 tablespoon water (1 healthy fat)
- 1 small cauliflower, cut into florets (2 greens)
- 1 teaspoon mixed spice (1 condiment)
- 1/2 teaspoon mustard powder (1 condiment)
- 2 tablespoons maple syrup (2 healthy fats)
- 1 clove of garlic, minced (1 green)
- 2 tablespoons soy sauce (2 condiments)
- 1/3 Cup oats flour (1/2 healthy fat)
- 1/3 Cup plain flour (1/2 healthy fat)
- 1/3 Cup desiccated coconut (1/2 lean)

Directions:
1. In a mixing bowl, mix oats, flour, and desiccated coconut. Season with salt and pepper to taste. Set aside.

2. In another bowl, place the flax egg and add a pinch of salt to taste. Set aside.
3. Season the cauliflower with mixed spice and mustard powder.
4. Dredge the florets in the flax egg first, then in the flour mixture.
5. Place inside the Instant Crisp Air Fryer, lock the air fryer lid and cook at 400°F or 15 minutes.
6. Meanwhile, place the maple syrup, garlic, and soy sauce in a saucepan and heat over medium flame. Wait for it to boil and adjust the heat to low until the sauce thickens.
7. After 15 minutes, take out the Instant Crisp Air Fryer's florets and place them in the saucepan.
8. Toss to coat the florets and place inside the Instant Crisp Air Fryer and cook for another 5 minutes.

Nutrition:
- 154 Calories
- 2.3g Fat
- 4.6g Protein
-

211.   Crispy Jalapeno Coins

Difficulty: Easy
Preparation Time: 10 minutes
Cooking Time: 5 minutes
Servings: 1
Ingredients:
- 1 egg (1 healthy fat)
- 2-3 Tbsp. coconut flour (1 healthy fat)
- 1 sliced and seeded jalapeno (2 greens)
- Pinch of garlic powder (1 condiment)
- Bit of Cajun seasoning (optional)
- Pinch of pepper and salt (1 condiment)

Directions:
1. Preparing the Ingredients. Ensure your Instant Crisp Air Fryer is preheated to 400 degrees.
2. Mix all dry ingredients.
3. Pat jalapeno slices dry. Dip coins into the egg wash and

then into the dry mixture. Toss to coat thoroughly.
4. Add coated jalapeno slices to Instant Crisp Air Fryer in a singular layer. Spray with olive oil.
5. Lock the air fryer lid. Set temperature to 350°F and set time to 5 minutes. Cook just till crispy.

Nutrition:
- 128 Calories
- 8g Fat
- 7g Protein

212.   Buffalo Cauliflower

Difficulty: Difficult
Preparation Time: 5 minutes
Cooking Time: 15 minutes
Servings: 1
Ingredients:
   Cauliflower:
- 1 Cup panko breadcrumbs (1 healthy fat)
- 1 Tsp. salt (1 condiment)
- 2 Cups cauliflower florets (2 greens)
   Buffalo Coating:
- 1/4 Cup Vegan Buffalo sauce (1/2 condiment)
- 1/4 Cup melted vegan butter (1/2 healthy fat)

Directions:
1. Melt butter in microwave and whisk in buffalo sauce.
2. Dip each cauliflower floret into the buffalo mixture, ensuring it gets coated well. Holdover a bowl till the floret is done dripping.
3. Mix breadcrumbs with salt.
4. Dredge dipped florets into breadcrumbs and place them into Instant Crisp Air Fryer. Lock the air fryer lid. Set temperature to 350°F and set time to 15 minutes. When slightly browned, they are ready to eat!
5. Serve with your favorite Keto dipping sauce!

Nutrition:
- 194 Calories
- 17g Fat
- 10g Protein

213.   Slow Cooker Savory Butternut Squash Oatmeal

Difficulty: Difficult
Preparation Time: 15 minutes
Cooking Time: 6 to 8 hours
Servings: 1
Ingredients:
- 1/4 Cup steel-cut oats (1/2 healthy fat)
- 1/2 Cups cubed (1/2-inch pieces) peeled butternut squash (1 green)
- 3/4 Cups of water (1 healthy fat)
- 1/16 Cup unsweetened nondairy milk (1/8 healthy fat)
- 1/4 Tablespoon chia seed (1/2 healthy fat)
- 1/2 Teaspoons yellow (mellow) miso paste (1 condiment)
- 3/4 Teaspoons ground ginger (1 condiment)
- 1/4 Tablespoon sesame seed, toasted (1/2 healthy fat)
- 1/4 Tablespoon chopped scallion, green parts only (1 green)
- Shredded carrot, for serving (optional) (1 green)

Directions:
1. In a slow cooker, combine the oats, butternut squash, and water.
2. Cover the slow cooker and cook on low for 6 to 8 hours, or until the squash is fork-tender. Using a potato masher or heavy spoon, roughly mash the cooked butternut squash. Stir to combine with the oats.
3. Whisk together the milk, chia seeds, miso paste, and ginger to combine in a large bowl. Stir the mixture into the oats.
4. Top your oatmeal bowl with sesame seeds and scallion for more plant-based fiber, top with shredded carrot (if using).

Nutrition:
- 230 Calories
- 5g Fat

- 7g Protein

214. Carrot Cake Oatmeal

Difficulty: Easy
Preparation Time: 10 minutes
Cooking Time: 15 minutes
Servings: 1
Ingredients:

- 1/8 Cup pecans (1/4 healthy fat)
- 1/2 Cup finely shredded carrot (1 green)
- 1/4 Cup old-fashioned oats (1/2 healthy fat)
- 5/8 Cups unsweetened nondairy milk (1/4 healthy fat)
- 1/2 Tablespoon pure maple syrup (1 healthy fat)
- 1/2 Teaspoon ground cinnamon (1 condiment)
- 1/2 Teaspoon ground ginger (1 condiment)
- 1/8 Teaspoon ground nutmeg (1/4 condiment)
- 1 tablespoon chia seed (1 healthy fat)

Directions:

1. Over medium-high heat in a skillet, toast the pecans for 3 to 4 minutes, often stirring, until browned and fragrant (watch closely, as they can burn quickly). Pour the pecans onto a cutting board and coarsely chop them. Set aside.
2. Using an 8-quart pot at medium-high heat, combine the carrot, oats, milk, maple syrup, cinnamon, ginger, and nutmeg. When it is already boiling, reduce the heat to medium-low. Cook, uncovered, for 10 minutes, stirring occasionally.
3. Stir in the chopped pecans and chia seeds. Serve immediately.

Nutrition:

- 307 Calories
- 17g Fat
- 7g Protein

215. Spiced Sorghum and Berries

Difficulty: Easy
Preparation Time: 5 minutes
Cooking Time: 1 hour
Servings: 1
Ingredients:

- 1/4 Cup whole-grain sorghum (1/2 healthy fat)
- ¼ tsp. ground cinnamon (1/2 condiment)
- 1/4 Teaspoon Chinese five-spice powder (1/2 condiment)
- 3/4 Cups water (1 condiment)
- 1/4 Cup nondairy milk, unsweetened (1/2 healthy fat)
- 1/4 Teaspoon vanilla extract (1/2 healthy fat)
- 1/2 Tablespoons pure maple syrup (1 healthy fat)
- 1/2 Tablespoon chia seed (1 healthy fat)
- 1/8 Cup sliced almonds (1/4 lean)
- 1/2 Cups fresh raspberries, divided (1 lean)

Directions:

1. Using a large pot over medium-high heat, stir together the sorghum, cinnamon, five-spice powder, and water. Wait for the water to a boil, cover the bank, and reduce the heat to medium-low. Cook for 1 hour, or until the sorghum is soft and chewy. If the sorghum grains are still hard, add another water cup and cook for 15 minutes more.
2. Using a glass measuring cup, whisk together the milk, vanilla, and maple syrup to blend. Add the mixture to the sorghum and the chia seeds, almonds, and 1 cup of raspberries. Gently stir to combine.
3. When serving, top with the remaining 1 cup of fresh raspberries.

Nutrition:

- 289 Calories
- 8g Fat
- 9g Protein

216. Spiced Pumpkin Muffins

Difficulty: Average
Preparation Time: 15 minutes
Cooking Time: 20 minutes
Servings: 1
Ingredients:

- 1/6 Tablespoons ground flaxseed (1/4 healthy fat)
- 1/24 Cup of water (1/4 condiment)
- 1/8 Cups whole wheat flour (1/4 healthy fat)
- 1/6 Teaspoons baking powder (1/3 healthy fat)
- 5/6 Teaspoons ground cinnamon (1/4 condiment)
- 1/12 Teaspoon baking soda (1/8 condiment)
- 1/12 Teaspoon ground ginger (1/8 condiment)
- 1/16 Teaspoon ground nutmeg (1/8 condiment)
- 1/32 Teaspoon ground cloves (1/8 condiment)
- 1/6 Cup pumpkin puree (1/3 healthy fat)
- 1/12 Cup pure maple syrup (1/8 healthy fat)
- 1/24 Cup unsweetened applesauce (1/8 healthy fat)
- 1/24 Cup unsweetened nondairy milk (1/8 healthy fat)
- 1/2 Teaspoons vanilla extract (1 healthy fat)

Directions:

1. Preheat the oven to 350°F. Line a 12-cup metal muffin pan with parchment paper liners or use a silicone muffin pan.
2. First, mix the flaxseed and water in a large bowl and then keep it aside.
3. In a medium bowl, stir together the flour, baking powder, cinnamon, baking soda, ginger, nutmeg, and cloves.
4. In a medium bowl, stir up the maple syrup, pumpkin puree, applesauce, milk, and vanilla. Using a spatula, mix the wet ingredients with the dry ones.
5. Fold the soaked flaxseed into the batter until evenly combined, but do not overmix the batter, or your muffins will become dense.

Ladle the batter with a ½ cup per muffin into your prepared muffin pan.

6. Bake for 18 to 20 minutes. Remove the muffins from the pan.
7. Transfer to a wire rack for cooling.
8. Store in an air-tight container at room temperature.

Nutrition:
- 115 Calories
- 1g Fat
- 3g Protein

217. Plant-Powered Pancakes

Difficulty: Easy
Preparation Time: 5 minutes
Cooking Time: 15 minutes
Servings: 8
Ingredients:
- 1 Cup whole-wheat flour (1 healthy fat)
- 1 Teaspoon baking powder (1/2 healthy fat)
- 1/2 Teaspoon ground cinnamon (1/2 condiment)
- 1 Cup plant-based milk (1 healthy fat)
- 1/2 Cup unsweetened applesauce (1 healthy fat)
- 1/4 Cup maple syrup (1/2 healthy fat)
- 1 Teaspoon vanilla extract (1 healthy fat)

Directions:
1. In a large bowl, combine the flour, baking powder, and cinnamon.
2. Stir in the milk, applesauce, maple syrup, and vanilla until no dry flour is left, and the batter is smooth.
3. Preheat a huge, non-stick skillet over medium heat. For each pancake, pour 1/4 cup of batter onto the hot skillet. Once bubbles form over the top of the pancake and the sides begin to brown, flip and cook for 1 to 2 minutes more.
4. Repeat until all of the batters are used and serve.

Nutrition:
- 2g Fat
- 5g Protein
- 591Calories

218. Sweet Cashew Cheese Spread

Difficulty: Easy
Preparation Time: 5 minutes
Cooking Time: 5 minutes
Servings: 10
Ingredients:
- Stevia (5 drops) (1/2 condiment)
- Cashews (2 cups, raw) (3 healthy fats)
- Water (1/2 cup) (1 condiment)

Directions:
1. Soak the cashews overnight in water.
2. Next, drain the excess water, then transfer cashews to a food processor.
3. Add in the stevia and the water.
4. Process until smooth.
5. Serve chilled. Enjoy.

Nutrition:
- 7g Fat
- 5.7g Protein
- 322 Calories

219. Mini Zucchini Bites

Difficulty: Average
Preparation Time: 10 minutes
Cooking Time: 10 minutes
Servings: 6
Ingredients:
- 1 Zucchini, cut into thick circles (2 greens)
- 3 Cherry tomatoes, halved (6 greens)
- 1/2 Cup parmesan cheese, grated (1 healthy fat)
- Salt and pepper to taste (1 condiment)
- 1 Tsp. chives, chopped (1 green)

Directions:
1. Preheat the oven to 390 degrees F.
2. Add wax paper on a baking sheet.
3. Arrange the zucchini pieces.
4. Add the cherry halves to each zucchini slice.
5. Add parmesan cheese, chives, and sprinkle with salt and pepper.
6. Bake for 10 minutes. Serve.

Nutrition:
- 1g Fat
- 7.3g Protein
- 361 Calories

220. Crispy Cauliflowers

Difficulty: Easy
Preparation Time: 10 minutes
Cooking Time: 10 minutes
Servings: 4
Ingredients:
- 2 Cup cauliflower florets, diced (6 greens)
- 1/2 Cup almond flour (1 healthy fat)
- 1/2 Cup coconut flour (1 healthy fat)
- Salt and pepper to taste (1/2 condiment)
- 1 Tsp. mixed herbs (1 green)
- 1 Tsp. chives, chopped (1 green)
- 1 Egg (1 lean)
- 1 Tsp. cumin (1 condiment)
- 1/2 Tsp. garlic powder (1 condiment)
- 1 Cup water (1 condiment)
- Oil for frying (1 condiment)

Directions:
1. Combine the egg, salt, garlic, water, cumin, chives, mixed herbs, pepper, and flour in a mixing bowl.
2. Stir in the cauliflower to the mixture and then fry them in oil until they become golden in color.
3. Serve.

Nutrition:
- 3.3g Protein
- 10.4g Fat
- 259 Calories

Chapter 10. Air Fryer - Breakfast Recipes

221. Air Fried Cauliflower Ranch Chips

Difficulty: Easy
Preparation Time: 5 minutes
Cooking Time: 12 minutes
Servings: 2
Ingredients:

- Raw cauliflower, grated - ½ cup (1/4 green)
- Parsley - ¼ tsp (1/8 green)
- Basil - ¼ tsp (1/8 green)
- Dill - ¼ tsp (1/8 green)
- Chives - ¼ tsp (1/8 green)
- Garlic powder - ¼ tsp (1/8 condiment)
- Onion powder - ¼ tsp (1/8 condiment)
- Pepper, ground - ¼ tsp (1/8 condiment)
- Parmesan cheese - ¼ cup (1/8 healthy fat)
- Cooking spray – as required (1/2 healthy fat)

Directions:

1. Preheat the air fryer to 230°C.
2. Using a medium bowl, mix all the ingredients.
3. Line the air fryer baking tray with parchment paper.
4. Scoop 1 tbsp mixture and place it on the parchment paper without overlapping one another.
5. Bake for 12 minutes by flipping side halfway through.
6. Serve hot.

Nutrition:

- 65 Calories
- 3.6g Fat
- 4g Protein

222. Shrimp Stuffed in Eggplant with Cauliflower Rice

Difficulty: Average
Preparation Time: 10 minutes
Cooking Time: 33 minutes
Servings: 2
Ingredients:

- Eggplant, large – 1 (2 greens)
- Salt, divided - ¼ tsp. (1/4 condiment)
- Shrimp, peeled & deveined - ½ lb. (2 leans)
- Black pepper, ground - ¼ tsp (1/4 condiment)
- Cauliflower, riced – 1 cup (1 green)
- Scallion, without the head, finely chopped – 1 (1 green)
- Greek yogurt, plain, low fat - ¼ cup (1/2 lean)
- Parmesan cheese, shredded - ¼ cup (1/2 healthy fat)

Directions:

1. Wash eggplant and cut into 4 rounds.
2. Remove the flesh and make it into a cup shape.
3. Chop the flesh and keep it ready to use.
4. Rub inside with half portion of the salt.
5. Put in the air fryer grill tray and bake for 18 minutes at 230°C.
6. After baking, keep it aside.
7. Now season the shrimp with pepper and the remaining salt.
8. Place it in the air fryer grill tray and spray some cooking oil.
9. Broil it for 5 minutes by flipping sides halfway through the cooking, until it turns to pink.
10. After that, remove and keep it aside.
11. In the air fry tray, put the chopped eggplant flesh, cauliflower rice, scallions, and air fry or 3-4 minutes until they become tender.
12. Transfer the air fried veggies into a bowl and add the fried shrimps into it.
13. Add yogurt and combine to mix.
14. Now scoop the mix into the eggplant cup.
15. Top it with grated parmesan cheese.
16. Put it in the air fryer baking grill and bake for 15 minutes at 230°C.
17. Serve hot.

Nutrition:

- 269 Calories
- 5.9g Fat
- 33g Protein

223. Air Fried Chicken and Cauliflower Rice

Difficulty: Average
Preparation Time: 10 minutes
Cooking Time: 45 minutes
Servings: 2

Ingredients:

- Chicken breast, chopped – 9 oz (3 leans)
- Cauliflower, grated, cooked - 2½ cup (3 greens)
- Tomatoes, diced - ½ cup (1/2 green)
- Salsa - ¼ cup (1/4 condiment)
- Pepper - ¼ tsp (1/4 condiment)
- Salt - ¼ tsp (1/4 condiment)
- Garlic powder - ¼ tsp (1/4 condiment)
- Parmesan cheese, low fat, shredded – 1 cup (1/2 healthy fat)
- Taco seasoning, low sodium - ½ tsp (1/4 condiment)

- Olive oil – 1 tsp (1/2 healthy fat)

Directions:
1. Wash chicken and drain it thoroughly.
2. Rub taco seasoning with olive oil on the chicken breast.
3. Marinate it for 4 hours.
4. Set the air fryer temperature to 180°C.
5. After that, place it in the air fryer grill and broil for 20 minutes by flipping side halfway through.
6. Once the cooking is over, remove and keep it aside.
7. In an air fryer bowl, mix the grated cauliflower, salsa, pepper, salt, garlic powder, and tomatoes.
8. Transfer the broiled chicken on to it.
9. Layer grated cheese on top of it.
10. Bake at 180°C for 25 minutes, until the cheese starts to melt.
11. Serve hot.

Nutrition:
- 504 Calories
- 29g Fat
- 44g Protein

224. Sweet Potato Pecan Muffins

Difficulty: Average
Preparation Time: 10 minutes
Cooking Time: 20 minutes
Servings: 2
Ingredients:
- Optavia Select Honey Sweet Potatoes – 2 sachets (1/2 condiment)
- Optavia Essential Spiced Gingerbread – 2 sachets (1/2 condiment)
- Water – 1 cup (1/2 condiment)
- Liquid egg substitute – 6 tbsp (3 healthy fat)
- Cashew milk, unsweetened - ¼ cup (1/2 healthy fat)
- Pumpkin pie spice - ½ tsp (1/4 condiment)

- Vanilla extract - ½ tsp (1/4 condiment)
- Baking powder - ½ tsp (1/4 condiment)
- Pecans, chopped - 1½ oz (2 healthy fats)

Directions:
1. Preheat the air fryer to 180°C.
2. Do the directions on the packet to make the Honey Sweet Potatoes.
3. Allow it to cool for some time.
4. Mix the prepared honey sweet potatoes and all the other ingredients, except the pecans.
5. Lightly spray the muffin pan and transfer the mix to the slots evenly.
6. Top it with chopped pecans.
7. Situate it in the air fryer tray and bake for 20 minutes.
8. Serve hot.

Nutrition:
- 383 Calories
- 21g Fat
- 15g Protein

225. Breakfast Scones with Blueberry Almond

Difficulty: Difficult
Preparation Time: 10 minutes
Cooking Time: 20 minutes
Servings: 2
Ingredients:
- Optavia Blueberry Almond Hot Cereal – 2 sachets (1/2 healthy fat)
- Flaxseed ground - ¼ cup (1/4 condiment)
- Sugar substitute, zero-calorie – 1 pkt (1/4 condiment)
- Baking powder - ½ tsp (1/4 condiment)
- Solid butter, unsalted, cut into ½" thickness – 1 tbsp. (1/2 healthy fat)
- Liquid egg white - 1½ tbsp (1 healthy fat)
- Greek yogurt, plain, low fat - 1½ tbsp (1 lean)
- Cinnamon ground – 1/8 tsp (1/4 condiment)

Directions:

1. Combine Blueberry Almond Hot Cereal, baking powder, and sugar substitute in a food processor.
2. Put butter cubes and blitz to form a rough, coarse meal. Let there be rice-sized butter pieces to get the scone structure.
3. Now add Greek yogurt, egg white, almond extract, cashew milk, and process until it turns to a dough form.
4. Line a baking paper in the air fryer baking tray.
5. Make 4 flat circles of dough and place them on the baking paper.
6. Drizzle some cinnamon powder on top.
7. Bake it at 205°C for 20 minutes, until it turns to a golden brown.
8. Allow it to cool and cut into half to make 8 wedges.
9. Serve and enjoy.

Nutrition:
- 277 Calories
- 13.6g Fat
- 7g Protein

226. Cheesy Broccoli Bites

Difficulty: Average
Preparation Time: 5 minutes
Cooking Time: 40 minutes
Servings: 2

Ingredients:
- Frozen broccoli – 3 cups (2 greens)
- Scallions, thinly sliced - ¼ cup (1/2 green)
- Eggs – 2 (1 healthy fat)
- Cottage cheese – 1 cup (1/2 healthy fat)
- Mozzarella cheese, grated - ¾ cup (1/2 healthy fat)
- Parmesan cheese, shredded - ¼ cup (1/4 healthy fat)
- Olive oil – 1 tsp (1/2 condiment)
- Garlic powder - ½ tsp (1/2 condiment)
- Salt – 1/8 tsp (1/4 condiment)

- Water – 2 cups (1 healthy fat)

Directions:
1. Preheat the air fryer to 190°C.
2. Place the broccoli in an air fryer, save bowl, and pour water.
3. Air fryer it for 10 minutes until the broccoli becomes tender.
4. Drain the water and transfer the broccoli into the blender.
5. Blitz it until it chopped well.
6. Now add cottage cheese, scallions, parmesan, mozzarella, eggs, olive oil, salt, and garlic into the blender.
7. Pulse it until it gets mixed well.
8. Transfer it to 12 muffin tins evenly after greasing them.
9. Place it in the air fryer and bake for 30 minutes until the filling becomes firm and its top turns to a golden brown.
10. After baking, remove them from the air fryer.
11. Allow it to settle down the heat and serve.

Nutrition:
- 366 Calories
- 15.1g Fat
- 41g Protein

227. Brine & Spinach Egg Muffins Air Fried

Difficulty: Difficult
Preparation Time: 10 minutes
Cooking Time: 25 minutes
Servings: 2
Ingredients:
For Egg Muffin
- Eggs – 4 (2 healthy fat)
- Liquid egg whites – 1 cup (1/2 healthy fat)
- Greek yogurt, plain, low fat - ¼ cup (1/2 healthy fat)
- Salt - ¼ tsp (1/4 condiment)

For Brie, Spinach & Mushroom Mix
- Brie – 1 oz (1/2 green)
- Spinach, frozen, coarsely chopped – 5 oz (2 greens)

- Mushrooms, chopped – 1 cup. (1/2 green)

Directions:
1. Thaw the frozen spinach for 10 minutes.
2. Wash all the vegetables separately and pat dry.
3. Preheat the air fryer to 190°C.
4. In a large bowl, combine Greek yogurt, egg whites, eggs, cheese, and salt.
5. Add all the vegetables in the bowl mix and combine well.
6. Take 12 muffin tins and lightly spray with cooking oil.
7. Transfer the mixture evenly into the muffin tins.
8. Place them in the air fryer and bake for 25 minutes until the center portion becomes hard.
9. Do a toothpick test by inserting it in the center and check if it comes out clean.
10. Take it out from the air fryer and allow it to settle down the heat before serving.
11. Enjoy your muffin.

Nutrition:
- 278 Calories
- 13.1g Fat
- 33g Protein

228. Mini Pepper Nachos

Difficulty: Average
Preparation Time: 10 minutes
Cooking Time: 13 minutes
Servings: 2
Ingredients:
- Jalapeno pepper, diced - ¼ cup (1/2 green)
- Bell pepper, halved, cored – 12 nos. (2 greens)
- Chicken breast, canned in low sodium water – 6 oz (3 lean)
- Avocado, mashed – 3 oz (2 healthy fats)
- Greek yogurt, plain, low fat - ¼ cup (1/2 healthy fat)
- Cheddar cheese, low fat, divided – 1 cup (1/2 healthy fat)
- Chili powder - ½ tsp (1/2 condiment)

- Scallions, chopped - ¼ cup. (1/2 green)

Directions:
1. Drain the chicken thoroughly.
2. Put the diced jalapeno pepper in the air fryer tray and spray some cooking spray oil.
3. Air fry it at 200°C for 2-3 minutes until they become tender.
4. Transfer them to a large bowl, add chicken, yogurt, avocado, half portion of cheese, jalapeno, chili powder, and combine to mix.
5. In the air fryer tray, arrange the bell pepper and fill the chicken mixture.
6. Top them with the remaining cheese.
7. Bake it for 10 minutes until the cheese starts to melt.
8. Serve with garnished scallion.

Nutrition
- 457 Calories
- 18.5g Fat
- 40g Protein

229. Cheddar Herb Pizza Bites

Difficulty: Average
Preparation Time: 5 minutes
Cooking Time: 10 minutes
Servings: 2
Ingredients:
- Optavia Buttermilk Cheddar Herb Biscuit – 2 sachets (1 condiment)
- Almond milk, unsweetened - ½ cup (1/2 healthy fat)
- Olive oil – 1 tsp (1/2 condiment)
- Basil leaves, julienned - ½ cup (1/2 green)
- Mozzarella stick, cut into 6 small pieces – 2 oz. (1 healthy fat)
- Tomatoes, sliced – 1 medium (1 green)
- Balsamic vinegar – 1 tbsp (1/2 condiment)

Directions:
1. Preheat the air fryer to 230°C.

2. Combine the Buttermilk Cheddar Herb Biscuit, olive oil, and almond milk in a large bowl until they become a smooth paste.
3. Take 6 muffin tin and spray lightly with cooking oil.
4. Distribute the mixture evenly into the muffin tin.
5. Place the muffin tin on the air fryer grill tray, topped with mozzarella and sliced tomato.
6. Sprinkle basil on top and bake for 10 minutes, until the biscuit mixture becomes brown and cheese starts to bubble.
7. Drop balsamic vinegar on top before serving.

Nutrition:
- 203 Calories
- 7g Fat
- 13g Protein

230. Cauliflower & Tomato Egg Muffins Air Fried

Difficulty: Difficult
Preparation Time: 10 minutes
Cooking Time: 25 minutes
Servings: 2
Ingredients:
For Egg Muffin
- Eggs – 4 (2 healthy fats)
- Liquid egg whites – 1 cup (1/2 healthy fat)
- Greek yogurt, plain, low fat - ¼ cup (1/4 healthy fat)
- Salt - ¼ tsp (1/4 condiment)

For Cauliflower, Mozzarella & Tomato Mix
- Cauliflower rice, frozen – 6 oz (3 greens)
- Mozzarella cheese, low fat – 1 oz (1/2 healthy fat)
- Cherry tomatoes – 1 cup (1 green)
- Water – 2 cups (1 condiment)

Directions:
1. Thaw the frozen cauliflower rice for 10 minutes.
2. Preheat the air fryer to 190°C.
3. Cook the cauliflower rice in the air fryer by adding 2

cups of water for 10 minutes.
4. Drain the water using a sieve and keep aside ready.
5. In a large bowl, combine Greek yogurt, egg whites, eggs, cheese, and salt.
6. Add all the vegetables to the bowl mix to combine well.
7. Take 12 muffin tins and lightly spray with cooking oil.
8. Transfer the mixture evenly into the muffin tins.
9. Place them in the air fryer and bake for 25 minutes until the center portion becomes hard.
10. Do a toothpick test by inserting it in the center and check if it comes out clean.
11. Pull it out and allow it to settle down the heat before serving.
12. Enjoy your muffin.

Nutrition:
- 286 Calories
- 9.9g Fat
- 33g Protein

231. Pumpkin Chocolate Cheesecake

Difficulty: Difficult
Preparation Time: 10 minutes
Cooking Time: 40 minutes
Servings: 2
Ingredients:
- Optavia Essential Decadent Double Chocolate Brownie – 4 sachets (2 healthy fat)
- Butter, unsalted, melted – 1 tbsp (1/2 healthy fat)
- Coldwater – 4 tbsp (1 condiment)
- Greek yogurt, plain, low fat – 2 cups (1/2 healthy fat)
- Cream cheese, light, softened – 5 tbsp (2 healthy fat)
- Pumpkin puree – 6 tbsp (3 lean)
- Egg – 2 (1 healthy fat)
- Stevia – 4 packets (1/4 condiment)
- Vanilla extract – 1 tsp (1/2 condiment)

- Pumpkin pie spice – 1 tsp (1/2 condiment)
- Salt – 1/8 tsp (1/4 condiment)

Directions:
1. Mix the Decadent Double Chocolate Brownie, water, and butter in a medium bowl thoroughly.
2. Preheat the air fryer to 175°C.
3. Grease 4 air fry oven-safe springform pan and evenly place the chocolate brownie mixture.
4. Push the mixture firmly to the bottom of the pan to form a thin crust.
5. Bake it for 15 minutes.
6. Now combine the rest of the ingredients in a medium-size bowl until they become a smooth paste.
7. Transfer it evenly to the springform pans.
8. Reduce the baking temperature to 150°C and bake it for 30-35 minutes until the center becomes firm and the edges start to brown.
9. Pull it from the air fryer and allow them to settle down the temperature.
10. Serve fresh.

Nutrition:
- 518 Calories
- 28g Fat
- 29g Protein

232. Cloud Garlic Bread Breakfast

Difficulty: Difficult
Preparation Time: 10 minutes
Cooking Time: 30 minutes
Servings: 2
Ingredients:
- Eggs, medium (separate yellow and white) – 2 (1 healthy fat)
- Cream cheese, low fat - 1½ tbsp (1 healthy fat)
- Sweetener, no-calorie - ½ pkt (1/2 condiment)
- Tartar cream - ¼ tsp (1/4 condiment)

For Garlic Bread

- Butter, unsalted, melted – 1tsp (1/2 healthy fat)
- Garlic powder – 1/8 tsp (1/4 condiment)
- Italian seasoning - ¼ tsp (1/4 condiment)
- Salt – 1/8 tsp (1/4 condiment)

Directions:
1. Combine thoroughly cream cheese, egg yolks, the sweetener in a medium bowl.
2. Beat egg whites in a large bowl along with tartar cream until the whites become stiff peaks.
3. Now carefully fold the yellow yolk mixture into the egg whites without breaking the whites.
4. Line a parchment paper in the air fryer baking tray and place 4 scoops of the mixture without overlapping one another.
5. Set the temperature to 150°C and bake for 20 minutes.
6. Take out the bread, and brush butter on top and sprinkle the seasoning, garlic powder, and salt.
7. Place it again into the air fryer and bake for further 10 minutes until the top becomes golden brown.
8. After baking, allow it to settle down the heat before serving.

Nutrition:
- 115 Calories
- 8.8g Fat
- 6g Protein

233. Portabella Mushrooms Stuffed with Cheese

Difficulty: Difficult
Preparation Time: 15 minutes
Cooking Time: 17 minutes
Servings: 2

Ingredients:
- Portabella mushroom caps, large – 4 (2 leans)

- Soy sauce – 1 tbsp (1/2 condiment)
- Lemon juice – 1 tbsp (1/2 condiment)
- Olive oil, divided – 1 tsp (1/4 condiment)
- Mozzarella cheese, low fat, grated – 2 cups (1 healthy fat)
- Tomato, fresh, diced - ½ cup (1/2 green)
- Clove Garlic, finely grated – 1 clove (1/4 green)
- Cilantro, fresh, chopped – 1 tbsp (1/4 green)

Directions:
1. Make bowls by scooping the flesh from the interior of the mushroom caps.
2. Set the air fryer temperature to 200°C and preheat.
3. Mix the soy sauce, lemon juice, and half a portion of olive oil in a small bowl.
4. Marinate the mixture on the mushroom cap both inside and outside.
5. Line foil coated baking paper in the air fryer tray.
6. Place the marinated mushroom cap in the tray and bake for 10 minutes until they become tender.
7. Now combine tomatoes, mozzarella, garlic, remaining olive oil, and Italian seasoning in a medium bowl.
8. Fill the mushroom caps with the mixture evenly.
9. Bake it in the air fryer for 7 minutes, until the cheese starts to melt.
10. Sprinkle cilantro on top and serve.

Nutrition:
- 250 Calories
- 4.4g Fat
- 40g Protein

234. Air Fryer Mint Cookies

Difficulty: Average
Preparation Time: 5 minutes
Cooking Time: 15 minutes
Servings: 2
Ingredients:

- Optavia Essentials Decadent Double Chocolate Brownie – 2 sachets (1 condiment)
- Optavia Essential Chocolate Mint Cookie Bars (2 healthy fats)
- Almond milk, unsweetened – 2 tbsp (1 healthy fat)
- Egg white – 2 (1/2 healthy fat)

Directions:
1. Preheat the air fryer to 180°C.
2. In a mixer blender, crush the chocolate mint bars.
3. Combine chocolate brownie, crushed chocolate mint bars, almond milk, and egg whites in a large bowl.
4. Evenly transfer the mix to 8 cookies ramekins.
5. Place it in the air fryer grill tray and bake for 15 minutes until the top becomes firm.
6. Allow it to settle down the heat and serve.

Nutrition:
- 187 Calories
- 4.1g Fat
- 5g Protein

235. Red Pepper & Kale Egg Muffins Air Fried

Difficulty: Average
Preparation Time: 10 minutes
Cooking Time: 25 minutes
Servings: 2
Ingredients:
For Egg Muffin

- Eggs – 4 (1 healthy fat)
- Liquid egg whites – 1 cup (1/2 healthy fat)
- Greek yogurt, plain, low fat - ¼ cup (1/4 healthy fat)
- Salt - ¼ tsp (1/4 condiment)

For Red Bell Pepper, Goat Cheese & Kale Mix

- Red bell pepper, cored and chopped – 6 oz. (3 greens)
- Kale, frozen, chopped – 5 oz (2 greens)
- Goat cheese – 1 oz (1/2 healthy fat)

Directions:

1. Thaw the frozen cauliflower rice for 10 minutes.
2. Preheat the air fryer to 190°C.
3. In a large bowl, combine Greek yogurt, egg whites, eggs, cheese, and salt.
4. Add all the vegetables to the bowl mix to combine well.
5. Take 12 muffin tins and lightly spray with cooking oil.
6. Transfer the mixture evenly into the muffin tins.
7. Place them in the air fryer and bake for 25 minutes until the center portion becomes hard.
8. Do a toothpick test by inserting it in the center and check if it comes out clean.
9. Take it out from the air fryer and allow it to settle down the heat before serving.
10. Enjoy your muffin.

Nutrition:
- 323 Calories
- 15.4g Fat
- 34g Protein

236. Asparagus Risotto with Chicken

Difficulty: Difficult
Preparation Time: 20 minutes
Cooking Time: 38 minutes
Servings: 2
Ingredients:
- Chicken breast – 1 lb. (2 lean)
- Pepper ground - ½ tsp (1/4 condiment)
- Salt - ¼ tsp (1/4 condiment)
- Butter, melted – 1 tbsp (1/2 healthy fat)
- Cauliflower, finely grated - ¾ lb. (1 green)
- Asparagus, finely chopped - ¼ lb. (1/2 green)
- Chicken stock - ¼ cup (1/2 condiment)
- Nutritional yeast flakes – 2 tbsp (1 condiment)

Directions:
1. Soak the chicken in running water and pat dry.
2. Preheat the air fryer to 180°C.

3. Season the chicken with pepper and salt.
4. Place it in an air fryer safe casserole and pour melted butter over it.
5. Air fry it for 30 minutes until the internal temperature of the meat reaches 70°C.
6. Pull it out from the air fryer and let it cool.
7. Now place the asparagus and cauliflower rice in the air fryer tray.
8. Pour the chicken stock over it and air fry for 8 minutes until the veggies become tender.
9. After cooking, remove the risotto and mix the yeast.
10. Cut the chicken and serve along with the risotto.

Nutrition:
- 382 Calories
- 8.6g Fat
- 60g Protein

237. Lemon Garlic Oregano Boneless Chicken

Difficulty: Average
Preparation Time: 5 minutes
Cooking Time: 44 minutes
Servings: 2
Ingredients:
- Chicken breast boneless, skinless - ½ lb. (1 lean)
- Lemon juice – 1 tbsp (1/2 condiment)
- Clove Garlic, minced – 1 (1/2 condiment)
- Oregano fresh, minced – 1 tbsp (1/2 green)
- Black pepper, ground - ¼ tsp (1/4 condiment)
- Salt - ¼ tsp (1/4 condiment)
- Asparagus ends trimmed – 1 lb. (2 greens)
- Water – 1 cup (1/2 condiment)

Directions:
1. Soak, wash, and pat dry chicken.
2. Situate the chicken in a big bowl and marinate with pepper, lemon juice, salt, garlic, and oregano.

3. Place the marinated chicken in the air fry grill tray.
4. Broil at 175°C for 40 minutes until the meat's internal temperature reaches 70°C.
5. After broiling, remove it from the air fryer and set it aside.
6. Now place the asparagus in the air fry ray and pour 1 cup water.
7. Air fry at 175°C for 4 minutes until the asparagus becomes tender.
8. Remove it from the air fryer and drain the water.
9. Slice the chicken and serve along with asparagus.

Nutrition:
- 258 Calories
- 11g Fat
- 29g Protein

238. Cloud Focaccia Bread Breakfast

Difficulty: Difficult
Preparation Time: 10 minutes
Cooking Time: 30 minutes
Servings: 2
Ingredients:
- Eggs, medium (separate yellow and white) – 2 (1 healthy fat)
- Cream cheese, low fat - 1½ tbsp (1 healthy fat)
- Sweetener, no-calorie - ½ pkt (1/2 condiment)
- Tartar cream - ¼ tsp (1/4 condiment)

For Focaccia Bread
- Olive oil – ½ tsp
- Rosemary - ½ tsp (1/2 green)
- Salt – 1/8 tsp (1/4 condiment)

Directions:
1. Combine thoroughly cream cheese, egg yolks, the sweetener in a medium bowl.
2. Beat egg whites in a large bowl along with tartar cream until the whites become stiff peaks.
3. Now carefully fold the yellow yolk mixture into the

egg whites without breaking the whites.

4. Line a parchment paper in the air fryer baking tray and place 4 scoops of the mixture without overlapping one another.

5. Set the temperature to 150°C and bake for 20 minutes.

6. Take out the bread, and brush olive oil on top and sprinkle Rosemary and salt.

7. Place it again into the air fryer and bake for further 10 minutes until the top becomes golden brown.

8. After baking, allow it to settle down the heat before serving.

Nutrition:
- 90 Calories
- 6.5g Fat
- 6g Protein

239. Brownie Pies in Peanut Butter

Difficulty: Average
Preparation Time: 10 minutes
Cooking Time: 20 minutes
Servings: 2
Ingredients:
- Optavia Decadent Double Chocolate Brownie – 2 pkt (1 condiment)
- Baking powder - ¼ tsp (1/4 condiment)
- Liquid egg substitute – 3 tbsp (1 healthy fat)
- Vanilla almond milk, unsweetened, divided – 6 tbsp (2 healthy fats)
- Vegetable oil – 1 tsp (1/4 condiment)
- Peanut butter, powdered - ¼ cup (1/2 healthy fat)

Directions:
1. Preheat the air fryer to 180°C.
2. Mix the Decadent Double Chocolate Brownie mixture, egg substitute, baking powder, oil, half of the milk in a large bowl until it becomes a smooth paste.
3. Take 4 muffin tin and spray cooking oil.

4. Evenly fill ¾ portion of the muffin tin and bake in the air fryer for 20 minutes.

5. When the center becomes firm, insert a toothpick and check whether it comes out clean so that you can confirm the doneness of the muffin.

6. Remove it from the air fryer and allow them to cool down.

7. Now mix the remaining milk and powdered peanut butter in a medium bowl.

8. Slice the muffin horizontally and spread the peanut butter paste onto one half.

9. Situate the other half on top and serve.

Nutrition:
- 281 Calories
- 9.8g Fat
- 7g Protein

240. Chicken Continental Salad

Difficulty: Easy
Preparation Time: 15 minutes
Cooking Time: 40 minutes
Servings: 2
Ingredients:
Salad making:
- Eggplant, chopped - ½ cup. (1/2 green)
- Zucchini, chopped - ½ cup. (1/2 green)
- Cherry tomatoes halved - ½ cup. (1/2 green)
- Romaine lettuce – 3 cups (2 greens)
- Parmesan cheese, shredded - ¼ cup (1/4 healthy fat)
- Chicken breast - ¾ lb. (1 lean)
- Salt - ¼ tsp (1/4 condiment)
- Pepper ground - ¼ tsp (1/4 condiment)

Dressing:
- Fresh lemon juice - ½ tsp (1/2 condiment)
- Dijon mustard - ¼ tsp (1/4 condiment)
- Worcestershire sauce - ½ tsp (1/4 condiment)
- Clove garlic – 1 (1/4 condiment)
- Salt - ½ tsp (1/4 condiment)
- Pepper ground - ¼ tsp (1/4 condiment)
- Parmesan cheese, shredded – 1 tbsp (1/2 healthy fat)
- Mayonnaise, light – 1 tbsp (1/2 healthy fat)
- Olive oil, extra virgin - 1½ tsp (1 condiment)

Directions:
- Preheat the air fryer to 200°C.
- Clean, wash, and drain the chicken breast.
- Rub salt, pepper on the chicken breast, and keep aside for 15 minutes for marinating.
- Line a baking paper in the air fryer tray and spray some cooking on to it.
- Place zucchini and eggplant on the baking paper.
- Start baking by shaking intermittently for 20 minutes until they become tender.
- For preparing the dressing, combine all the ingredients in the dressing section in a medium bowl.
- Put the tomatoes, lettuce, air fried veggies in the dressing mixture, and toss well.
- Place the marinated chicken on the air fryer grill tray and broil for 20 minutes until the inside meat temperature reaches 75°C.
- After cooking, remove it and allow it to cool down.
- Slice the chicken and serve along with the dressing.

Nutrition:
- 370 Calories
- 14.3g Fat
- 45g Protein

Chapter 11. Air Fryer - Meat Recipes

241. Low Carb Pork Dumplings with Dipping Sauce

Difficulty: Difficult
Preparation Time: 30 minutes
Cooking Time: 20 minutes
Servings: 6
Ingredients

- 18 dumpling wrappers (1 healthy fat)
- One teaspoon olive oil (1/4 condiment)
- Bok choy: 4 cups(chopped) (2 leans)
- Rice vinegar: 2 tablespoons (1/2 condiment)
- Diced ginger: 1 tablespoon (1/4 condiment)
- Crushed red pepper: 1/4 teaspoon (1/2 green)
- Diced garlic: 1 tablespoon (1/2 condiment)
- Lean ground pork: 1/2 cup (2 leans)
- Lite soy sauce: 2 teaspoons (1/2 condiment)
- Honey: 1/2 tsp. (1/4 healthy fat)
- Toasted sesame oil: 1 teaspoon (1/4 condiment)
- Finely chopped scallions (1 green)

Directions

1. In a large skillet, heat the olive oil, add the bok choy, cook for 6 minutes and add the garlic, ginger and cook for one minute. Transfer this mixture to a paper towel and pat dry any excess oil

2. In a bowl, add the mixture of bok choy, chopped chili and lean ground pork and mix well.
3. Place gnocchi wrap on a plate and add a spoon to fill half of the wrapper. With water, seal the edges and fold them.
4. Spray air fryer basket with air, add dumplings into air fryer basket, and cook at 375 F for 12 minutes or until golden brown.
5. Meanwhile, to make the sauce, combine the sesame oil, rice vinegar, shallot, soy sauce and honey in a mixing bowl.
6. Serve the gnocchi with the sauce.

Nutrition:

- 140 Calories
- 5g Fat
- 12g Protein

242. Gluten-Free Air Fryer Chicken Fried Brown Rice

Difficulty: Average
Preparation Time: 10 minutes
Cooking Time: 20 minutes
Servings: 2
Ingredients

- Chicken Breast: 1 Cup (1 lean)
- White Onion: 1/4 cup chopped (1/2 green)
- Celery: 1/4 Cup chopped (1/2 green)
- Cooked brown rice: 4 Cups (2 healthy fat)
- Carrots: 1/4 cup chopped (1/2 green)

Directions

1. Place the foil on the air fryer basket, make sure to leave room for airflow, roll up on the sides
2. Spray the film with olive oil. Mix all the ingredients.
3. On top of the foil, add all the ingredients to the air fryer basket.
4. Give a splash of olive oil in the mixture.

5. Cook for five minutes at 390 ° F.
6. Open the air fryer and give the mixture a spin
7. cook for another five minutes at 390 ° F.
8. Remove from air fryer and serve hot.

Nutrition

- 350 Calories
- 6g Fat
- 22g Protein

243. Air Fryer Cheesy Pork Chops

Difficulty: Average
Preparation Time: 5 minutes
Cooking Time: 8 minutes
Servings: 2
Ingredients

- 4 lean pork chops (2 leans)
- Salt: half tsp. (1/4 condiment)
- Garlic powder: ½ tsp. (1/4 condiment)
- Shredded cheese: 4 tbsp. (1 healthy fat)
- Chopped cilantro (1 green)

Direction

1. Let the air fryer preheat to 350 degrees.
2. With garlic, coriander and salt, rub the pork chops. Put the air fryer on. Let it cook for four minutes. Turn them over and then cook for extra two minutes.
3. Drizzle the cheese on top and cook for another two minutes or until the cheese has melted.
4. Serve with salad.

Nutrition

- 467 Calories
- 61g Protein
- 22g Fat

244. Air Fryer Pork Chop & Broccoli

Difficulty: Average
Preparation Time: 20 minutes
Cooking Time: 20 minutes
Servings: 2
Ingredients

- Broccoli florets: 2 cups (1 green)
- Bone-in pork chop: 2 pieces (1 lean)
- Paprika: 1/2 tsp. (1/4 condiment)
- Avocado oil: 2 tbsp. (1 healthy fat)
- Garlic powder: 1/2 tsp. (1/4 condiment)
- Onion powder: 1/2 tsp. (1/4 condiment)
- Two cloves of crushed garlic (1/4 condiment)
- Salt: 1 teaspoon divided (1/4 condiment)

Direction

1. Let the air fryer preheat to 350 degrees. Spray the basket with cooking oil
2. Add a spoon. Oil, onion powder, half a teaspoon. of salt, garlic powder and paprika in a bowl mix well, rub this spice mixture on the sides of the pork chop
3. Add the pork chops to the fryer basket and cook for five minutes
4. Meanwhile, add a teaspoon. oil, garlic, half a teaspoon of salt and broccoli in a bowl and coat them well
5. Turn the pork chop and add the broccoli, let it cook for another five minutes.
6. Remove from air fryer and serve.

Nutrition

- 483 Calories
- 20g Fat
- 23g Protein

245. Mustard Glazed Air Fryer Pork Tenderloin

Difficulty: Average
Preparation Time: 10 minutes
Cooking Time: 18 minutes
Servings: 4
Ingredients

- Yellow mustard: 1/4 cup (1/2 green)
- One pork tenderloin (1 lean)
- Salt: 1/4 tsp (1/4 condiment)
- Honey: 3 Tbsp. (1/2 healthy fat)
- black pepper: 1/8 tsp (1/4 condiment)
- Minced garlic: 1 Tbsp. (1/4 condiment)
- Dried rosemary: 1 tsp (1/4 green)
- Italian seasoning: 1 tsp (1/8 condiment)

Direction

1. Using a knife, cut the top of the pork tenderloin. Add the garlic (minced) into the cuts. Then sprinkle with kosher salt and pepper.
2. In a bowl, add the honey, mustard, rosemary, and Italian seasoning mixture until well blended. Rub this mustard mix all over the pork.
3. Leave to marinate in the refrigerator for at least two hours.
4. Place the pork tenderloin in the basket of the air fryer. Cook for 18-20 minutes at 400 F. With an instant read thermometer, verify that the internal temperature of the pig should be 145 F.
5. Remove from air fryer and serve with a side of salad.

Nutrition

- 390 Calories
- 59g Protein
- 11g Fat

246. Air Fryer Pork Taquitos

Difficulty: Average
Preparation Time: 10 minutes
Cooking Time: 20 minutes
Servings: 10
Ingredients

- Pork tenderloin: 3 cups, cooked & shredded (2 leans)
- Shredded mozzarella: 2 and 1/2 cups, fat-free (1 healthy fat)
- 10 small tortillas (1 healthy fat)
- Salsa for dipping (1 condiment)
- 1 juice of a lime (1/4 condiment)

Direction

1. Allow the air fryer to preheat to 380 F.
2. Add the lime juice to the pork and mix well
3. With a damp towel over the tortilla, microwave for ten seconds to soften it
4. Add the pork filling and cheese on top, in a tortilla, roll the tortilla tightly.
5. Situate the tortillas on a greased baking sheet
6. Sprinkle oil on the tortillas. Bake for 7-10 minutes or until the tortillas are golden, turn them halfway.
7. Serve with salad.

Nutrition

- 253 Calories
- 18g Fat
- 20g Protein

247. Pork Rind Nachos

Difficulty: Average
Preparation Time: 5 minutes
Cooking Time: 5 minutes
Servings: 2
Ingredients

- 2 tbsp. of pork rinds (1 lean)
- 1/4 cup shredded cooked chicken (1/2 lean)
- 1/2 cup shredded Monterey jack cheese (1/4 healthy fat)
- 1/4 cup sliced pickled jalapeños (1/4 green)
- 1/4 cup guacamole (1/4 healthy fat)
- 1/4 cup full-fat sour cream (1/4 healthy fat)

Direction

1. Place the pork rinds in a 6-inch round pan. Fill with grilled chicken and Monterey jack cheese. Place the pan in the basket with the air fryer.
2. Set the temperature to 370 ° F and set the timer for 5 minutes or until the cheese has melted.
3. Eat immediately with jalapeños, guacamole, and sour cream.

Nutrition

- 295 calories

- 30g protein
- 27g fat

248. Air Fried Jamaican Jerk Pork

Difficulty: Difficult
Preparation Time: 10 minutes
Cooking Time: 20 minutes
Servings: 4
Ingredients

- Pork, cut into three-inch pieces (1 lean)
- Jerk paste: ¼ cup (1/4 condiment)

Direction

1. Rub the jerk dough on all the pork pieces.
2. Chill to marinate for 4 hours in the refrigerator.
3. Allow the air fryer to preheat to 390 F. Spray with olive oil
4. Before placing it in the air fryer, allow the meat to rest for 20 minutes at room temperature.
5. Cook for 20 minutes at 390 ° F in the air fryer, turn halfway.
6. Remove from air fryer and let sit for ten minutes before slicing.
7. Serve with microgreens.

Nutrition

- 234 Calories
- 31g Protein
- 9g Fat

249. Air Fryer Whole Wheat Crusted Pork Chops

Difficulty: Average
Preparation Time: 10 minutes
Cooking Time: 12 minutes
Servings: 4
Ingredients

- Whole-wheat breadcrumbs: 1 cup (1/2 healthy fat)
- Salt: ¼ teaspoon (1/4 condiment)
- Pork chops: 2-4 pieces (center cut and boneless) (2 leans)
- Chili powder: half teaspoon (1/4 condiment)
- Parmesan cheese: 1 tablespoon (1/4 healthy fat)
- Paprika: 1½ teaspoons (1/2 condiment)

- One egg beaten (1 healthy fat)
- Onion powder: half teaspoon (1/4 condiment)
- Granulated garlic: half teaspoon (1/4 condiment)

Direction

1. Allow the air fryer to preheat to 400 F.
2. rub kosher salt on each side of the pork chops, let it rest
3. Add the beaten egg to a large bowl
4. Add the parmesan, breadcrumbs, garlic, pepper, paprika, chili powder and onion powder to a bowl and mix well
5. Dip the pork chop in the egg and then in the breadcrumbs
6. Put it in the air fryer and spray it with oil.
7. Leave to cook for 12 minutes at 400 F. Turn it upside down halfway through cooking. Cook for another six minutes.
8. Serve with salad.

Nutrition

- 425 calories
- 20g fat
- 31g protein

250. Air Fried Philly Cheesesteak Taquitos

Difficulty: Average
Preparation Time: 20 minutes
Cooking Time: 6-8 hours
Servings: 6
Ingredients

- Dry Italian dressing mix: one package (1 condiment)
- Super Soft Corn Tortillas: one pack (1 healthy fat)
- Green peppers: two pieces, chopped (1/2 green)
- 12 cups of lean beef steak strips (3 leans)
- Beef stock: 2 cups (1 condiment)
- Lettuce shredded, one cup (1/2 green)
- Provolone cheese: ten slices (1 healthy fat)

Direction

1. In a slow cooker, add onion, beef, broth, pepper and seasonings.

2. Cover then cook at low heat for 6 or 8 hours.
3. Heat the tortillas for two minutes in the microwave.
4. Allow the air fryer to preheat to 350F.
5. Remove the cheesesteak from the slow cooker, add 2-3 tablespoons of steak to the tortilla.
6. Add some cheese, roll the tortilla well, and place in a deep fryer basket.
7. Make all the tortillas you want.
8. Lightly brush with olive oil
9. Cook for 6-8 minutes.
10. Flip the tortillas over and brush more oil as needed.
11. Serve with chopped lettuce and enjoy

Nutrition

- 220 calories
- 21g protein
- 16g fat

251. Beef Lunch Meatballs

Difficulty: Easy
Preparation Time: 10 minutes
Cooking Time: 15 minutes
Servings: 4
Ingredients:

- ½ pound beef, ground (1/2 lean)
- ½ pound Italian sausage, chopped (1/2 lean)
- ½ tsp. garlic powder (1/4 condiment)
- ½ tsp. onion powder (1/4 condiment)
- Salt and black pepper to the taste (1/4 condiment)
- ½ cup cheddar cheese, grated (1/2 healthy fat)
- Mashed potatoes for serving (1/2 healthy fat)

Directions:

1. In a bowl, mix the beef with the sausage, garlic powder, onion powder, salt, pepper and cheese, mix well and form 16 meatballs with this mixture.
2. Situate the meatballs in your air fryer and cook them at 370 ° F for 15 minutes.

3. Serve the meatballs with some mashed potatoes on the side.

Nutrition:
- 132 Calories
- 6.7g Fat
- 5.5g Protein

252. Roasted Garlic Bacon and Potatoes

Difficulty: Easy
Preparation Time: 5 minutes
Cooking Time: 25 minutes
Servings: 4
Ingredients:
- 4 medium-sized potatoes (1 healthy fat)
- 4 strips of streaky bacon (1 lean)
- 2 sprigs of rosemary (1 green)
- 6 cloves of garlic, smashed, unpeeled (1/2 condiment)
- 3 tsp of vegetable oil (1/2 condiment)

Directions:
1. Preheat Air fryer to 390°F.
2. Put the smashed garlic, bacon, potatoes, rosemary, and then the oil in a bowl. Stir thoroughly.
3. Place into air fryer basket and roast until golden for about 25 minutes.

Nutrition:
- 114 Calories
- 8.1g Fat
- 6.2g Protein

253. Chinese Pancetta Lunch Mix

Difficulty: Average
Preparation Time: 10 minutes
Cooking Time: 12 minutes
Servings: 4
Ingredients:
- 2 eggs (1 healthy fat)
- 2 pounds Pancetta, cut into medium cubes (1 lean)
- 1 cup cornstarch (1/2 condiment)
- 1 tsp. sesame oil (1/2 condiment)
- Salt and black pepper to the taste (1/2 condiment)
- A pinch of Chinese five-spice (1/2 condiment)
- 3 tbsp. canola oil (1/2 healthy fat)
- Sweet ketchup for serving (1/2 condiment)

Directions:
1. In a bowl, mix five spices with salt, pepper, and cornstarch and mix.
2. Scourge eggs with the sesame oil and beat well.
3. Dip the bacon cubes into the cornstarch mixture, then dip the eggs and place them in the air fryer you greased with canola oil.
4. Bake at 340 ° F for 12 minutes, shaking the fryer once.
5. Serve the bacon for lunch with the sweet ketchup on the side.

Nutrition:
- 125 Calories
- 7.9g Fat
- 8.3g Protein

254. Teriyaki Glazed Halibut Steak

Difficulty: Average
Preparation Time: 30 minutes
Cooking Time: 10-15 minutes
Servings: 3
Ingredients
- 1-pound halibut steak (1 lean)

For the Marinade:
- 3 oz. soy sauce, low sodium (1/4 condiment)
- ½ cup mirin (1/4 condiment)
- 2 tbsp. lime juice (1/8 condiment)
- ¼ cup sugar (1/8 condiment)
- ¼ cup orange juice (1/8 condiment)
- ¼ tsp. ginger ground (1/8 condiment)
- ¼ tsp. crushed red pepper flakes (1/8 condiment)
- 1 each garlic clove (smashed) (1/8 condiment)

Direction
1. Place all ingredients for the teriyaki glaze/marinade in a saucepan. Bring to a boil and reduce by half, then allow to cool.
2. When it cools, pour half of the icing/marinade into a zip-up bag along with the halibut, then refrigerate for 30 minutes.
3. Preheat Air fryer to 390 ° F. Place marinated halibut in the Air fryer and cook 10-12 minutes. Rub some of the remaining glaze on the halibut steak.
4. Spread on white rice with basil/mint chutney.

Nutrition
- 116 Calories
- 7g Fat
- 7.2g Protein

255. Pancetta Chops with Pineapple-Jalapeno Salsa

Difficulty: Average
Preparation Time: 20 minutes
Cooking Time: 20 minutes
Servings: 3
Ingredients
- 3 pieces of Pancetta Chops (roughly 10 ounces each) (1 lean)
- 2 tablespoons parsley (1/2 green)
- 1 tablespoon of ground Coriander (1/4 condiment)
- ¾ cup of olive oil (1/4 condiment)
- 1 tablespoon of finely chopped rosemary (1/4 green)
- 4 ounces of tomatoes, diced (1/4 green)
- 2 cloves of garlic, chopped (1/4 condiment)
- 4 ounces of pineapple, diced (1/2 healthy fat)
- 8 Jalapenos (1/2 green)
- 3 tsps. of Dijon Mustard (1/4 condiment)
- 1½ tsp. of sugar (1/8 condiment)

- 4 ounces of lemon juice (1/8 condiment)
- 3 tbsp. of finely chopped Cilantro (1/2 green)
- 2½ tsp. of salt (1/8 condiment)

Direction

1. Place the rosemary, sugar, mustard, coriander, ¼ cup of olive oil, 1 tablespoon of coriander, 1 ½ teaspoons of salt and 1 tablespoon of parsley in a mixing bowl and mix thoroughly. Add the bacon cutlets and mix.
2. Fill in marinade into a resealable plastic bag and refrigerate for about 3 hours.
3. Heat your deep fryer to 390 ° F.
4. Place the jalapenos in a bowl and season with 1 tsp. of oil to cover them evenly. Transfer the jalapenos to the air fryer and cook for about 7 minutes. Remove from the deep fryer and set aside to cool.
5. Once cooled, peel, remove the seeds and chop the jalapenos into small pieces and transfer them to a bowl. Add the pineapple, tomatoes, garlic and lemon juice, the rest of the oil, parsley, coriander and salt. Stir and set the sauce aside.
6. Remove the bacon chops from the refrigerator and allow to rest for 30 minutes at room temperature before cooking.
7. Place the ribs in the air fryer and roast at 390 ° F for about 12 minutes. The bacon cutlets are well cooked when the internal temperature is 140 ° F.

Nutrition
- 104 Calories
- 8.7g Fat
- 6.7g Protein

256. Peppery Roasted Potatoes with Smoked Bacon

Difficulty: Average
Preparation Time: 15 minutes
Cooking Time: 11 minutes
Servings: 2
Ingredients
- 5 small rashers smoked bacon (1 lean)
- 1/3 tsp. garlic powder (1/4 condiment)
- 1 tsp. sea salt (1/4 condiment)
- 2 tsp. paprika (1/4 condiment)
- 1/3 tsp. ground black pepper (1/4 condiment)
- 1 bell pepper (1/2 green)
- 1 tsp. mustard (1/4 condiment)
- 2 habanero peppers, halved (1/2 green)

Direction
1. Simply toss all the ingredients in a mixing dish; then transfer them to your air fryer's basket.
2. Air-fry at 375F for 10 minutes. Serve warm.

Nutrition
- 122 Calories
- 9g Fat
- 10g Protein

257. Cornbread with Pulled Pancetta

Difficulty: Easy
Preparation Time: 24 minutes
Cooking Time: 19 minutes
Servings: 2
Ingredients
- 2½ cups pulled Pancetta (1 lean)
- 1 tsp. dried rosemary (1/4 green)
- 1/2 tsp. chili powder (1/4 condiment)
- 3 cloves garlic (1/4 condiment)
- 1/2 recipe cornbread (1 healthy fat)
- 1/2 tablespoon brown sugar (1/4 condiment)
- 1/3 cup scallions, thinly sliced (1/2 green)
- 1 tsp. sea salt (1/8 condiment)

Direction
1. Preheat a large non-stick pan over medium heat; now cook the shallots together with the garlic and the pulled bacon.
2. Next, add the sugar, chili powder, rosemary and salt. Cook, stirring regularly until thickened.
3. Preheat your air fryer to 335 ° F. Now, coat two mini loaf pans with cooking spray. Add the pulled bacon mixture and spread over the bottom with a spatula.
4. Spread the previously prepared cornbread batter over the spicy pulled bacon mixture.
5. Bake this cornbread in a preheated air fryer until a centered tester is clean, or for 18 minutes.

Nutrition
- 117 Calories
- 9.4g Fat
- 11g Protein

258. Bacon and Garlic Pizzas

Difficulty: Easy
Preparation Time: 10 minutes
Cooking Time: 10 minutes
Servings: 4
Ingredients:
- 4 dinner rolls, frozen
- 4 garlic cloves minced
- ½ tsp. oregano dried
- ½ tsp. garlic powder
- 1 cup ketchup
- 8 bacon slices, cooked and chopped
- 1 and ¼ cups cheddar cheese, grated

Directions:
1. Place the rolls on a work surface and press them to obtain 4 ovals.
2. Spray each oval with cooking spray, transfer them to the air fryer and cook at 370 ° F for 2 minutes.
3. Spread the ketchup on each oval, divide the garlic, sprinkle with oregano and garlic powder and garnish with bacon and cheese.
4. Return the pizzas to your hot air fryer and cook them at 370 ° F for another 8 minutes.
5. Serve hot for lunch.

Nutrition
- 104 Calories
- 9g Fat
- 8.5g Protein

259. Stuffed Meatballs

Difficulty: Average
Preparation Time: 10 minutes
Cooking Time: 10 minutes
Servings: 4
Ingredients:
- 1/3 cup bread crumbs (1 healthy fat)
- 3 tbsp. milk (1/2 condiment)
- 1 tablespoon ketchup (1/4 condiment)
- 1 egg (1 healthy fat)
- ½ tsp. marjoram, dried (1/4 condiment)
- Salt and black pepper to the taste (1/8 condiment)
- 1-pound lean beef, ground (1 lean)
- 20 cheddar cheese cubes (1/2 healthy fat)
- 1 tablespoon olive oil (1/8 condiment)

Direction
1. In a bowl, mix the breadcrumbs with ketchup, milk, marjoram, salt, pepper and egg and beat well.
2. Add the beef, mix and form 20 meatballs with this mixture.
3. Shape each meatball around a cube of cheese, sprinkle with oil and rub.
4. Place all the meatballs in your preheated air fryer and cook at 390 ° F for 10 minutes.
5. Serve them for lunch with a side of salad.

Nutrition
- 112 Calories
- 8.2g Fat
- 7.7g Protein

260. Steaks and Cabbage

Difficulty: Easy
Preparation Time: 10 minutes
Cooking Time: 10 minutes
Servings: 4
Ingredients:
- ½ pound sirloin steak, cut into strips (1 lean)
- 2 tsp. cornstarch (1/8 condiment)
- 1 tablespoon peanut oil (1/8 condiment)
- 2 cups green cabbage, chopped (1 green)
- 1 yellow bell pepper (1/2 green)
- 2 garlic cloves, minced (1/8 condiment)
- Salt and black pepper to the taste (1/8 condiment)

Directions:
1. In a bowl, mix the cabbage with salt, pepper and peanut oil, mix, transfer to air fryer basket, cook at 370 ° F for 4 minutes and transfer to the bowl.
2. Add the steak strips to the air fryer, also add bell pepper, garlic, salt and pepper, stir and cook for 5 minutes.
3. Add the cabbage on top, mix, divide into plates and serve for lunch. To enjoy!

Nutrition
- 111 Calories
- 7.2g Fat
- 8.7g Protein

261. Air Fryer Meat Loaf

Difficulty: Easy
Preparation Time: 11 minutes
Cooking Time: 20 minutes
Servings: 4
Ingredients:
- 1 pound 99% lean ground beef (1 lean)
- ½ teaspoon garlic powder (1/4 condiment)
- 3 egg whites, beaten (1 healthy fat)
- 1 cup grated kohlrabi (1 healthy fat)
- Salt and pepper to taste (1/4 condiment)

Directions:
1. Preheat the air fryer to 350F for five minutes.
2. In a bowl, mix all ingredients until well combined.
3. Pour the mixture into a greased loaf pan that will fit inside the air fryer. Cover with aluminum foil on top.
4. Place inside the preheated air fryer and cook for 35 to 45 minutes until the meat is cooked through.
5. Allow the meatloaf to cool before slicing.

Nutrition:
- 270 Calories
- 34g Protein
- 10g Fat

262. Air Fryer Roasted Beef

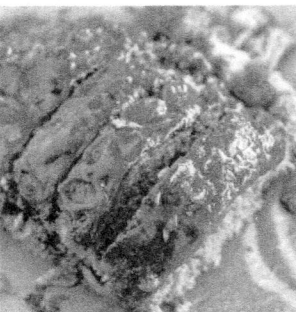

Difficulty: Average
Preparation Time: 8 minutes
Cooking Time: 60 minutes
Servings: 8
Ingredients:
- 4 pounds beef roast (1 lean)
- 2 teaspoons garlic powder (1/4 condiment)
- ½ teaspoon salt (1/8 condiment)
- ½ teaspoon pepper (1/8 condiment)
- 2 teaspoons thyme (1/4 green)
- 1 tablespoon olive oil (1/8 condiment)

Directions:
1. Preheat the air fryer to 350F for five minutes.
2. Pat dry the beef and place it on a working surface.
3. In a small bowl, combine the condiments and spices to form a dry rub.
4. Massage the beef with the dry rub all over the beef.
5. Place the seasoned beef inside the preheated air fryer and cook for 60 minutes.
6. Allow the beef to rest before slicing.

Nutrition:
- 434 Calories

- 61g Protein
- 12g Fat

263. Air Fried Burger Patties

Difficulty: Easy
Preparation Time: 8 minutes
Cooking Time: 15 minutes
Servings: 4
Ingredients:

- 1 teaspoon liquid smoke (1/8 condiment)
- ½ teaspoon garlic powder (1/8 condiment)
- ½ teaspoon salt (1/8 condiment)
- ½ teaspoon ground black pepper (1/8 condiment)
- 1 pound 99% lean ground beef (1 lean)
- 1 teaspoon parsley (1/2 green)

Directions:

1. Preheat the air fryer to 350F for five minutes.
2. Place all ingredients in a bowl.
3. Mix until well combined.
4. Form four burger patties from the mixture using your hands.
5. Place the patties inside the fridge to firm up.
6. After 2 hours, place the patties inside the air fryer basket.
7. Cook for 15 minutes.

Nutrition:

- 246 Calories
- 31g Protein
- 13g Fat

264. Air Fried Rib Eye Steak

Difficulty: Average
Preparation Time: 18 minutes
Cooking Time: 15 minutes
Servings: 1
Ingredients:

- ½ pound red eye steak, fat-trimmed
- ½ teaspoon salt
- ¾ teaspoon ground pepper
- ½ teaspoon garlic powder
- ¾ teaspoon steak seasoning

Directions:

1. Preheat the air fryer to 350F for five minutes.

2. Season the steak with the spices.
3. Situate in the air fryer and cook for 15 minutes.
4. Allow to rest before serving.

Nutrition:

- 540 Calories
- 44g Protein
- 28g Fat

265. Air Fryer Steak Bites and Mushrooms

Difficulty: Average
Preparation Time: 9 minutes
Cooking Time: 25 minutes
Servings: 4
Ingredients:

- 1 pound 99% lean steak (fat trimmed), cut into cubes (1 lean)
- 8 ounces mushrooms, sliced (1 healthy fat)
- 1 teaspoon melted butter (1/4 healthy fat)
- ½ teaspoon garlic powder (1/8 condiment)
- Salt and pepper to taste (1/8 condiment)

Directions:

1. Preheat the air fryer to 350F for five minutes.
2. Prep the bottom of the air fryer with foil.
3. Place all ingredients in a bowl. Toss to coat the beef and mushrooms with the seasoning.
4. Place the seasoned beef and mushrooms inside the foil-lined fryer basket.
5. Cook for 20 to 25 minutes.
6. Halfway through the cooking time, open the fryer basket and give a good shake for even cooking.

Nutrition:

- 299 Calories
- 14g Protein
- 5g Fat

266. Air Fried Lamb Chops

Difficulty: Difficult
Preparation Time: 12 minutes
Cooking Time: 25 minutes
Servings: 2
Ingredients:

- 5 cloves of garlic, sliced (1/8 condiment)

- 1 teaspoon garam masala (1/8 condiment)
- 1 teaspoon ground cinnamon (1/8 condiment)
- ½ teaspoon cayenne powder (1/8 condiment)
- ½ teaspoon salt (1/8 condiment)
- 1-pound lamb chops, fat trimmed (1 lean)

Directions:

1. Preheat the air fryer to 350F for five minutes.
2. Prep bottom of the air fryer with foil.
3. Place the garlic, garam masala, cinnamon, cayenne pepper, and salt. Mix to create the spice rub.
4. Massage the lamb chops with the spice rub.
5. Place inside the air fryer basket.
6. Cook for 20 to 25 minutes.

Nutrition:

- 338 Calories
- 46g Protein
- 12g Fat

267. Air Fried Roasted Lamb

Difficulty: Difficult
Preparation Time: 14 minutes
Cooking Time: 25 minutes
Servings: 1
Ingredients:

- 10 ounces butterflied lamb leg roast, fat trimmed (2 lean)
- 1 tablespoon olive oil (1/4 condiment)
- 1 teaspoon rosemary (1/4 green)
- 1 teaspoon thyme (1/4 green)
- ¼ teaspoon salt (1/8 condiment)
- ½ teaspoon black pepper (1/8 condiment)

Directions:

1. Preheat the air fryer to 360F for five minutes.
2. Prepare the bottom of the air fryer with foil.
3. Season the lamb leg roast with spices and condiments.
4. Place in the air fryer and cook for 15 to 20 minutes.

Nutrition:
- 181 Calories
- 18g Protein
- 3g Fat

268. Roast Lamb Rack

Difficulty: Difficult
Preparation Time: 12 minutes
Cooking Time: 30 minutes
Servings: 3
Ingredients:
- 1 ½ pounds rack of lamb (1 lean)
- Salt and pepper to taste (1/4 condiment)
- 1 teaspoon grated garlic (1/8 condiment)
- 1 teaspoon cumin seeds (1/4 healthy fat)
- 1 teaspoon olive oil (1/8 condiment)

Directions:
1. Preheat the air fryer to 350F for five minutes.
2. Coat the bottom of the air fryer with foil.
3. Season the rack of lamb with the spices.
4. Place in the air fryer and cook for 25 to 30 minutes.

Nutrition:
- 386 Calories
- 47.3g Protein
- 12g Fat

269. Air Fried Masala Chops

Difficulty: Easy
Preparation Time: 9 minutes
Cooking Time: 30 minutes
Servings: 1
Ingredients:
- ½ pound lamb chop, trimmed from fat (1 lean)
- 2 tablespoon ginger paste (1/4 condiment)
- ½ tablespoon red chili powder (1/4 condiment)
- 1 tablespoon garam masala (1/4 condiment)
- ½ teaspoon salt (1/4 condiment)

Directions:
1. Preheat the air fryer to 350F for five minutes.
2. Seal the bottom of the air fryer with foil.
3. Season the lamb chops with the spices.
4. Place inside the air fryer and cook for 25 to 30 minutes

Nutrition:
- 343 Calories
- 46g Protein
- 15g Fat

270. Mutton Chops

Difficulty: Average
Preparation Time: 11 minutes
Cooking Time: 25 minutes
Servings: 8
Ingredients:
- 8 mutton chops, trimmed from fat (2 lean)
- 1 tablespoon crushed garlic (1/4 condiment)
- Salt and pepper to taste (1/4 condiment)
- ½ teaspoon cumin (1/4 condiment)

Directions:
1. Preheat the air fryer to 350F for five minutes.
2. Seal the bottom of the air fryer with foil.
3. Season the mutton chops with spices.
4. Place in the air fryer basket and cook for 25 minutes.
5. Cook in batches if necessary.

Nutrition:
- 168 Calories
- 23g Protein
- 8g Fat

271. Rosemary Crusted Lamb Chops

Difficulty: Difficult
Preparation Time: 13 minutes
Cooking Time: 25 minutes
Servings: 2
Ingredients:
- 1-pound lamb chops, trimmed of fat (1 lean)
- 2 tablespoons fresh rosemary (1/4 green)
- ½ teaspoon salt (1/8 condiment)
- 1 teaspoon ground black pepper (1/8 condiment)
- 3 cloves garlic, minced (1/4 condiment)

Directions:
1. Preheat the air fryer to 350F for five minutes.
2. Seal the bottom of the air fryer with foil.
3. Season the lamb chops with the spices and condiments.
4. Place inside the air fryer basket.
5. Cook for 25 minutes until golden.

Nutrition:
- 335 Calories
- 45g Protein
- 15.7g Fat

272. Air Fryer Pork Chops

Difficulty: Average
Preparation Time: 6 minutes
Cooking Time: 25 minutes
Servings: 4
Ingredients:
- 1 tablespoon paprika (1/8 condiment)
- 1 ½ teaspoon salt (1/4 condiment)
- 1 teaspoon ground mustard (1/8 condiment)
- ¼ teaspoon garlic powder (1/8 condiment)
- 4 center cut bone-in pork chops, trimmed from fat (2 lean)

Directions:
1. Preheat the air fryer to 350F for five minutes.
2. Seal the bottom of the air fryer with foil.
3. Mix together the paprika, salt, mustard, and garlic powder to create a spice rub.
4. Massage the pork chops with the spice rub.
5. Place the seasoned pork chops inside the air fryer and cook for 20 to 25 minutes.

Nutrition:
- 234 Calories

- 40g Protein
- 7g Fat

273. Air Fryer Pork Tenderloin

Difficulty: Average
Preparation Time: 13 minutes
Cooking Time: 25 minutes
Servings: 4
Ingredients:

- ½ teaspoon black pepper (1/8 condiment)
- ¼ teaspoon garlic powder (1/8 condiment)
- ¼ teaspoon salt (1/8 condiment)
- 2 pounds pork tenderloin, trimmed from excess fat (1 lean)

Directions:

1. Preheat the air fryer to 350F for five minutes.
2. Seal the bottom of the air fryer with foil.
3. Mix together the black pepper, garlic powder, and salt to create a spice rub.
4. Massage the pork with the spice rub.
5. Place the seasoned pork tenderloin inside the air fryer and cook for 20 to 25 minutes.

Nutrition:

- 266 Calories
- 59g Protein
- 7g Fat

274. Mustard Pork Chops

Difficulty: Easy
Preparation Time: 11 minutes
Cooking Time: 20 minutes
Servings: 4
Ingredients:

- 4 tablespoons mustard (1/8 condiment)
- 2 tablespoons minced garlic (1/4 condiment)
- ½ teaspoon salt (1/8 condiment)
- 1 teaspoon ground black pepper (1/8 condiment)
- 4 pork chops, trimmed from fat (2 lean)

Directions:

1. Preheat the air fryer to 350F for five minutes.
2. Seal the bottom of the air fryer with foil.

3. Place the mustard, garlic, salt, and black pepper in a bowl. Mix until well combined.
4. Massage the pork chops with the spice rub.
5. Place seasoned pork chops inside the air fryer and cook for 20 minutes.

Nutrition:

- 346 Calories
- 41g Protein
- 17.9g Fat

275. Air Fryer Italian Pork Chops

Difficulty: Difficult
Preparation Time: 9 minutes
Cooking Time: 25 minutes
Servings: 2
Ingredients:

- 2 boneless pork loin chops, trimmed from fat (1 lean)
- ¼ teaspoon salt (1/8 condiment)
- 1 teaspoon Italian herb seasoning (1/8 condiment)

Directions:

1. Preheat the air fryer to 350F for five minutes.
2. Wrap the bottom of the air fryer with foil.
3. Season the pork loin chops with the spices and seasoning.
4. Place inside the air fryer basket and cook for 20 to 25 minutes.

Nutrition:

- 235 Calories
- 41g Protein
- 3g Fat

276. Air Fried Riblets

Difficulty: Easy
Preparation Time: 9 minutes
Cooking Time: 25 minutes
Servings: 2
Ingredients:

- 1-pound pork riblets (1 lean)
- 1 teaspoon salt (1/8 condiment)
- 6 cloves of garlic, minced (1/4 condiment)

Directions:

1. Preheat the air fryer to 350F for five minutes.
2. Wrap the bottom of the air fryer with foil.

3. Season the pork riblets with salt and garlic.
4. Place inside the air fryer and cook for 20 to 25 minutes.

Nutrition:

- 288 Calories
- 39g Protein
- 12g Fat

277. Pork Tenderloin with Fried Bell Peppers

Difficulty: Average
Preparation Time: 18 minutes
Cooking Time: 20 minutes
Servings: 4
Ingredients:

- 2 large bell peppers, seeded and julienned (1 green)
- 10 ounces Cremini mushrooms, diced (2 healthy fats)
- 1-pound pork tenderloin (1 lean)
- Salt and pepper to taste (1/8 condiment)

Directions:

1. Preheat the air fryer to 350F for five minutes.
2. Line the bottom of the air fryer with foil.
3. Place all ingredients in a bowl and toss to coat everything with the seasonings.
4. Place inside the air fryer basket and cook for 20 minutes.
5. Halfway through the cooking time, give the fryer basket a shake for even cooking.

Nutrition:

- 385 Calories
- 37g Protein
- 4.7g Fat

278. Air Fried Beef Jerky

Difficulty: Easy
Preparation Time: 11 minutes
Cooking Time: 15 minutes
Servings: 2
Ingredients:

- 12 ounces, sirloin beef, sliced (2 lean)
- 1 clove of garlic, minced (1/2 condiment)

- Salt and pepper to taste (1/2 condiment)

Directions:
1. Preheat the air fryer to 350F for five minutes.
2. Line the bottom of the air fryer with foil.
3. Place all ingredients in a bowl and toss to coat the beef slices with the seasoning.
4. Place beef slices in the air fryer and cook for 15 minutes.

Nutrition:
- 333 Calories
- 35g Protein
- 14g Fat

279. Air Fried Pot Roast

Difficulty: Average
Preparation Time: 12 minutes
Cooking Time: 60 minutes
Servings: 8
Ingredients:
- 4 pounds beef chuck roast (2 lean)
- Salt and pepper to taste (1/2 condiment)
- 5 cloves garlic, minced (1/2 condiment)
- 1 teaspoon thyme (1/2 green)

Directions:
1. Preheat the air fryer to 350F for five minutes.
2. Line the bottom of the air fryer with foil.
3. Score the beef using a knife.
4. Season the pot roast with the seasoning.
5. Place inside the air fryer basket and cook for 60 minutes.

Nutrition:
- 420 Calories
- 61g Protein
- 16g Fat

280. Air Fried Mongolian Beef

Difficulty: Average
Preparation Time: 9 minutes
Cooking Time: 20 minutes
Servings: 4
Ingredients:
- 2 cloves garlic, minced (1/4 condiment)

- 1 cup chopped scallions (1/2 green)
- ½ teaspoon minced ginger (1/4 condiment)
- 1 ½ pounds flank steak, thinly sliced (1 lean)
- 1 teaspoon sesame oil (1/4 condiment)
- Salt and pepper to taste (1/4 condiment)

Directions:
1. Preheat the air fryer to 350F for five minutes.
2. Line the bottom of the air fryer with foil.
3. Place all ingredients in a bowl. Toss to coat beef with the condiments.
4. Place inside the air fryer basket.
5. Cook for 15 to 20 minutes.

Nutrition:
- 258 Calories
- 37g Protein
- 9.7g Fat

Chapter 12. Air Fryer - Poultry Recipes

281. Air Fryer Chicken & Broccoli

Difficulty: Average
Preparation Time: 11 minutes
Cooking Time: 15 minutes
Servings: 4
Ingredients:

- Olive oil: 2 Tablespoons (1/8 condiment)
- Chicken breast: 4 cups, bone and skinless (cut into cubes) (2 lean)
- Low sodium soy sauce: 1 Tbsp. (1/8 condiment)
- Garlic powder: half teaspoon (1/8 condiment)
- Rice vinegar: 2 teaspoons (1/8 condiment)
- Broccoli: 1-2 cups, cut into florets (1 green)
- Hot sauce: 2 teaspoons (1/8 condiment)
- Fresh minced ginger: 1 Tbsp. (1/8 condiment)
- Sesame seed oil: 1 teaspoon (1/8 condiment)
- Salt & black pepper, to taste (1/8 condiment)

Directions:

1. In a bowl, add chicken breast, onion, and broccoli. Combine them well.
2. In another bowl, add ginger, oil, sesame oil, rice vinegar, hot sauce, garlic powder, and soy sauce mix it well. Then add the broccoli, chicken, and onions to marinade.
3. Coat well the chicken with sauces. Set aside in the refrigerator for 15 minutes
4. Place chicken mix in one even layer in air fryer basket and cook for 16-20 minutes, at 380 F. halfway through, toss the basket gently and cook the chicken evenly
5. Add five minutes more, if required.
6. Add salt and pepper if needed.
7. Serve warm with lemon wedges

Nutrition:

- 191 Calories
- 7g Fat
- 25g Protein

282. Mexican-Style Air Fryer Stuffed Chicken Breasts

Difficulty: Average
Preparation Time: 14 minutes
Cooking Time: 10 minutes
Servings: 2
Ingredients:

- Olive oil: 2 teaspoons (1/8 condiment)
- One chicken breast (skinless, boneless) (1 lean)
- Chili powder: 4 tsp., divided (1/8 condiment)
- Chipotle flakes: 2 tsp. (1/8 condiment)
- Half bell pepper, sliced (1/2 green)
- Mexican oregano: 2 tsp. (1/4 green)
- Salt and pepper, to taste (1/8 condiment)
- Ground cumin: 4 tsp., divided (1/8 condiment)
- Half juice of a lime (1/8 condiment)
- One jalapeno pepper, sliced (1/4 green)

Directions:

1. In a bowl, add two tsp of cumin and two tsp. of chili powder, mix well
2. Let the air fryer Preheat to 400 F
3. Pound the chicken breast until 1/4 inch of thickness remains.
4. In a bowl, mix remaining chili powder, chipotle flakes, salt, oregano, remaining cumin, and pepper. Rub this spice mix all over the chicken.
5. Put half the bell pepper, jalapeno, and onion in the breast half. Roll the chicken around it and secure it with large toothpicks.
6. Add olive oil on breast rolls and coat in the cumin-chili mixture.
7. Add chicken breast to air fryer and cook for six minutes.
8. Flip the breast rolls and cook for five minutes more until the chicken's temperature reaches 165 F.
9. Drizzle lime juice on top of breast rolls and serve hot.

Nutrition:

- 185.3 calories
- 14g protein
- 8.5g fat

283. Mixed Vegetables with Chicken

Difficulty: Easy
Preparation Time: 11 minutes
Cooking Time: 20 minutes
Servings: 2
Ingredients:

- Chicken breast: 4 cups, cubed pieces (1 lean)
- Half zucchini chopped (1/2 green)
- Italian seasoning: 1 tablespoon (1/4 condiment)
- Bell pepper chopped: 1/2 cup (1/2 green)
- Clove of garlic pressed (1/4 condiment)
- Broccoli florets: 1/2 cup (1/2 green)
- Olive oil: 2 tablespoons (1/4 condiment)
- Half teaspoon of chili powder, garlic powder,

pepper, salt, (1/4 condiment)

Directions:
1. Let the air fryer heat to 400 F and dice the vegetables
2. In a bowl, add the seasoning, oil and add vegetables, chicken and toss well
3. Place chicken and vegetables in the air fryer, and cook for ten minutes, toss halfway through, cook in batches.
4. Make sure the veggies are charred and the chicken is cooked through.
5. Serve hot.

Nutrition
- 230 Calories
- 26g Protein
- 10g Fat

284. Low Carb Parmesan Chicken Meatballs

Difficulty: Easy
Preparation Time: 19 minutes
Cooking Time: 12 minutes
Servings: 20
Ingredients:
- Pork rinds: 1/2 cup, ground (1 lean)
- Ground chicken: 4 cups (2 lean)
- Parmesan cheese: 1/2 cup grated (1/2 healthy fat)
- Kosher salt: 1 tsp. (1/8 condiment)
- Garlic powder: 1 tsp. (1/8 condiment)
- 1 egg beaten (1/2 healthy fat)
- Paprika: 1 tsp. (1/8 condiment)
- Pepper: 1/2 tsp. (1/8 condiment)
- Breading (1/4 condiment)
- Pork rinds: 1/2 cup ground (1/2 healthy fat)

Directions:
1. Let the Air Fryer pre-heat to 400°F.
2. Add cheese, chicken, egg, pepper, half cup of pork rinds, garlic, salt, and paprika in a big mixing ball. Mix well into a dough, make into 1and half-inch balls.

3. Coat the meatballs in pork rinds(ground).
4. Oil sprays the air fry basket and add meatballs in one even layer.
5. Let it cook for 12 minutes at 400°F, flipping once halfway through.
6. Serve with salad greens.

Nutrition
- 240 Calories
- 10g fat
- 20g protein

285. Sriracha-honey Chicken Wings

Difficulty: Easy
Preparation Time: 21 minutes
Cooking Time: 15 minutes
Servings: 2
Ingredients:
- Soy sauce: 1 and 1/2 tablespoons (1/4 condiment)
- Chicken wings: 4 cups (2 lean)
- Sriracha sauce: 2 tablespoons (1/4 condiment)
- Butter: 1 tablespoon (1/2 healthy fat)
- 1/2 cup honey (1/2 healthy fat)
- Juice of half lime (1/4 condiment)
- Scallion's cilantro, and chives for garnish (1/4 green)

Directions:
1. Let the air fryer pre-heat to 360 degrees F.
2. Put the chicken wings in an air fryer basket, cook for half an hour, flip the wings every seven minutes, and cook thoroughly.
3. Meanwhile, in a saucepan, add all the ingredients of the sauce and simmer for three minutes.
4. Take out the chicken wings and coat them in sauce well.
5. Garnish with scallions. Serve with a microgreen salad.

Nutrition:
- 207 Calories
- 22g Proteins
- 15g Fat

286. Orange Chicken Wings

Difficulty: Easy
Preparation Time: 19 minutes
Cooking Time: 14 minutes
Servings: 2
Ingredients:
- Honey: 1 tbsp. (1/2 healthy fat)
- Chicken Wings, Six pieces (3 lean)
- One orange zest and juice (1/2 healthy fat)
- Worcestershire Sauce: 1.5 tbsp. (1/4 condiment)
- Black pepper to taste (1/4 condiment)
- Herbs (sage, rosemary, oregano, parsley, basil, thyme, and mint) (1 green)

Directions:
1. Wash and pat dry the chicken wings
2. In a bowl, add chicken wings, pour zest and orange juice
3. Add the rest of the ingredients and rub on chicken wings. Let it marinate for at least half an hour.
4. Let the Air fryer preheat at 180°C
5. In an aluminum foil, wrap the marinated wings and put them in an air fryer and cook for 20 minutes at 180 C
6. After 20 minutes, remove aluminum foil and brush the sauce over the wings and cook for 15 minutes more. Then again, brush the sauce and cook for another ten minutes.
7. Take out from the air fryer and serve with salad greens.

Nutrition:
- 271 Calories
- 29g Proteins
- 15g Fat

287. Air Fryer Rotisserie Chicken

Difficulty: Average
Preparation Time: 11 minutes
Cooking Time: 60 minutes
Servings: 6

Ingredients:

- Paprika: 1 tsp. (1/4 condiment)
- One chicken (1 lean)
- Dried basil: 1 tsp. (1/4 green)
- Dried oregano: 1 tsp. (1/4 green)
- Pepper: 1/2 tsp. (1/4 condiment)
- Salt: 1 and 1/2 tsp. (1/4 condiment)
- Chopped cilantro and scallions (1/4 green)

Directions:

1. Let the air fryer preheat to 360F.
2. Incorporate all the spices and rub them all over the chicken.
3. Put the chicken in the air fryer and let it cook at 360F for half an hour or more, if required.
4. Serve with salad greens and top with scallions and cilantro.

Nutrition:

- 391 Calories
- 34g Protein
- 27g Fat

288. Teriyaki Chicken Drumsticks with Salad Greens

Difficulty: Easy
Preparation Time: 11 minutes
Cooking Time: 20 minutes
Servings: 6
Ingredients:

- 6 chicken drumsticks (3 lean)
- Teriyaki sauce: 1 cup (1 green)
- Salad greens: 1 cup (1/2 green)
- Sesame seeds and green onion, for garnish (1/2 green)

Directions:

1. Let the air-fryer preheat to 360F.
2. Pour teriyaki sauce in a big zip lock bag, add in chicken drumsticks.
3. Mix them so well coated. Let it marinate for half an hour.

4. Put drumsticks in a single layer in the air fryer basket, let it cook for 20 minutes.
5. Shake the basket multiple times for even cooking.
6. Top with green onions, sesame seeds, and serve with the side of salad greens.

Nutrition:

- 163 Calories
- 16g Protein
- 7g Fat

289. Air-fried Chicken Pie

Difficulty: Average
Preparation Time: 11 minutes
Cooking Time: 30 minutes
Servings: 2
Ingredients:

- Puff pastry: 2 sheets (1/2 healthy fat)
- Chicken thighs: 2 pieces, cut into cubes (1 lean)
- Small potatoes: 2, chopped (1/2 healthy fat)
- Mushrooms: 1/4 cup (1/2 healthy fat)
- Light soya sauce (1/4 condiment)
- 1 carrot, chopped (1 green)
- Black pepper to taste (1/4 condiment)
- Worcestershire sauce: to taste (1/4 condiment)
- Salt to taste (1/4 condiment)
- Italian mixed dried herbs (1/2 green)
- Garlic powder: a pinch (1/4 condiment)
- Plain flour: 2 tbsp. (1/4 healthy fat)
- Milk, as required (1/4 healthy fat)
- Melted butter (/8 healthy fat)

Directions:

1. Incorporate light soya sauce and pepper, add the chicken cubes and coat well.
2. In a pan over medium heat, sauté carrot, potatoes, and onion. Add some water, if required, to cook the vegetables.

3. Add the chicken cubes and mushrooms and cook them too.
4. Stir in black pepper, salt, Worcestershire sauce, garlic powder, and dried herbs.
5. When the chicken is cooked through, add some of the flour and mix well.
6. Add in the milk and let the vegetables simmer until tender.
7. Place one piece of puff pastry in the baking tray of the air fryer, poke holes with a fork.
8. Add on top the cooked chicken filling and eggs and puff pastry on top with holes. Cut the excess pastry off. Glaze with oil spray or melted butter
9. Air fry at 180 F for six minutes or until it becomes golden brown.
10. Serve with microgreens.

Nutrition:

- 224 calories
- 20g protein
- 18g fat

290. Air- Fried Grilled BBQ Chicken

Difficulty: Easy
Preparation Time: 19 minutes
Cooking Time: 12 minutes
Servings: 2

Ingredients:

- Chicken Steaks: 2 pieces (1 lean)
- Sea salt: 1 tsp. (1/4 condiment)
- 1 tsp. olive oil (1/4 condiment)
- Black Pepper 1/2 teaspoon (1/4 condiment)
- Blue Cheese & Butter (1/2 healthy fat)

Directions:

1. While making steak, the most important thing is to let the meat rest at room temperature for 30 minutes, for the minimum.
2. Start the recipe by letting the air fryer heat. For making any kind of steak, you should always preheat

the air fryer. Therefore, the meat would come out well, then turn the air fryer on at 400 F for 5 minutes.

3. Rub the steak with butter or herb-infused olive oil and sprinkle with sea salt and black pepper.
4. Place the stakes for 6 minutes in the air fryer, then turn over again for almost 6 minutes.
5. Yet again, rest the steak for the very least for 5 minutes, and then slice it.
6. The steaks will keep on cooking, even after it is done cooking.
7. Only combine the butter and the Blue Cheese in a small bowl to mix to make the cheese. You can serve the steak as you like.
8. Put the butter in a wrap and rolled it tightly, it would appear like a roll, keep it refrigerated, and cut off a few bits for each portion.

Nutrition:
- 200 Calories
- 20g Proteins
- 5g Fat

291. Crispy Parmesan Buttermilk Chicken Tenders

Difficulty: Average
Preparation Time: 13 minutes
Cooking Time: 18 minutes
Servings: 4
Ingredients:
- 1/2 cup of all-purpose flour (1/2 condiment)

- Buttermilk: 3/4 cup (1/2 healthy fat)
- Chicken breasts: 2, boneless, skinless (1 lean)
- Kosher salt: 3/4 teaspoon, divided (1/4 condiment)
- Grated Parmesan cheese: 1/4 cup (1/2 healthy fat)
- Black Pepper: 3/4 teaspoon, divided (1/4 condiment)
- Worcestershire sauce: 1 and 1/2 teaspoons, divided (1/4 condiment)
- Smoked paprika: half teaspoon, divided (1/4 condiment)
- Oil spray (1/4 condiment)
- Whole wheat breadcrumbs: 1 and 1/2 cups (1/2 healthy fat)
- One large egg (1/2 healthy fat)

Directions:
1. Cut the chicken into tenders.
2. In a bowl, add buttermilk and Worcestershire sauce (half of it), salt, and half of paprika and pepper. Add this mix in a zip lock bag with chicken tenders and let it marinate for six hours or more.
3. In a bowl, add melted butter and breadcrumbs, parmesan cheese and combine well
4. Whisk the egg with the remaining Worcestershire sauce.
5. In another bowl, add the smoked paprika, pepper, flour, and salt.
6. Coat the tenders in flour mixture, then in egg again, then in breadcrumbs mixture.
7. Let the air fryer preheat to 400 F. put the breaded tenders in the air fryer basket in one even layer.
8. Cook at 400 F for 13-15 minutes, flip the chicken after half time.
9. Serve with sauces and microgreen

Nutrition:
- 350 Calories
- 14g Fat
- 23g Protein

Difficulty: Easy
Preparation Time: 7 minutes
Cooking Time: 30 minutes
Servings: 4

Ingredients:
- Chicken wings: 4 cups (2 lean)
- Onion powder: 1 tsp (1/8 condiment)
- Corn starch: ¾ cup (1/8 condiment)
- Garlic powder: 1 tsp (1/8 condiment)
- Salt: ½ tsp (1/8 condiment)
- Korean Air Fried Chicken Sauce (1/8 condiment)
- Soy sauce: 1 Tbsp. (1/8 condiment)
- Korean chili paste: 2 Tbsp. (1/8 condiment)
- Honey: 3 Tbsp. (1 healthy fat)
- Ginger minced: 1 tsp (1/8 condiment)
- Garlic minced: 1 tsp (1/8 condiment)
- Brown sugar: 2 Tbsp. (1/2 healthy fat)
- 1/2 tsp. salts (1/8 condiment)

Directions:
1. Wash and pat dry the chicken wings, in a bowl, add ½ tsp of salt, onion powder, and garlic powder and then add chicken wings and coat them well
2. Then coat the wings in corn starch. And put them in the air fryer.
3. Let the wings cook at 390 F for half an hour. Rotate every ten minutes.
4. Korean Sauce
5. In a saucepan, over medium flame, add all ingredients and let it boil and simmer for five minutes. Turn the heat off
6. Add cooked wings to the sauce and coat well.
7. Serve with steamed vegetables.

Nutrition:

- 340 Calories
- 23g Protein
- 19g Fat

293. Air Fryer Grilled Chicken

Difficulty: Easy
Preparation Time: 11 minutes
Cooking Time: 20 minutes
Servings: 3
Ingredients:

- Chicken tenders: 4 cups (2 lean)

Marinade:

- Honey: 2 Tbsp. (1/8 condiment)
- Olive oil: 1/4 cup (1/8 condiment)
- White vinegar: 2 Tbsp. (1/8 condiment)
- Water: 2 Tbsp. (1/8 condiment)
- Half teaspoon salts (1/8 condiment)
- Garlic powder: 1 tsp. (1/8 condiment)
- Half teaspoon of paprika (1/8 condiment)
- Half teaspoon crushed red pepper (1/2 green)

Directions:

1. Incorporate all ingredients of the marinade and mix well.
2. Then add the chicken mix to coat. Cover with plastic wrap and marinate in the refrigerator for half an hour.
3. Put chicken tenders in the air fryer basket in one even layer.
4. Cook for 3 minutes at 390 F. flip the tenders over and cook for five minutes more or until chicken is completely cooked through.
5. Serve with the side of salad greens.

Nutrition:

- 230 calories
- 14g fat
- 20g protein

294. Smothered Chicken Thighs

Difficulty: Average
Preparation Time: 8 minutes
Cooking Time: 30 minutes
Servings: 4

Ingredients:

- 8-ounce of chicken thighs (3 lean)
- 1 tsp paprika (1/8 condiment)
- 1 pinch salt (1/8 condiment)
- Mushrooms: 1/2 cup (1/2 healthy fat)

Directions:

1. Let the air fryer preheat to 400F
2. Chicken thighs season with paprika, salt, and pepper on both sides.
3. Place the thighs in the air fryer and cook for 20 minutes.
4. Meanwhile, sauté the mushroom.
5. Take out the thighs from the air fryer serve with sautéed mushrooms and onions.
6. And serve with chopped scallions and on the side of salad greens

Nutrition:

- 466.3 Calories
- 32g Fat
- 41g Protein

295. Air Fryer Spicy Chicken & Vegetables

Difficulty: Average
Preparation Time: 8 minutes
Cooking Time: 20 minutes
Servings: 2
Ingredients:
Spiced Chicken

- Chicken breasts: 2 skinless, boneless (1 lean)
- Onion powder: 1/2 tsp. (1/8 condiment)
- Olive oil: 1/2 Tbsp. (1/8 condiment)
- Chili powder: 1 tsp. (1/8 condiment)
- Cumin: 1/4 tsp. (1/8 condiment)
- Paprika: 1/2 tsp. (1/8 condiment)
- Salt: 1/2 tsp. (1/8 condiment)
- Garlic powder: 1/2 tsp. (1/8 condiment)
- Pepper: 1/2 tsp. (1/8 condiment)

Vegetables

- Carrots: 2-3 large (1 green)
- Olive oil: 1/2 Tbsp. (1/8 condiment)
- Chopped scallions (1 green)
- Pinch of salt (1/8 condiment)

Directions:

1. Let the air fryer preheat to 325 F
2. In a big bowl, add all chicken spices and make a spice mix. Then add chicken breasts with half tbsp. of olive oil and coat well. Set it aside.
3. Cut the vegetables according to your preference. Cut onions in layers, and separate each layer, coat all the vegetables with half tbsp. of olive oil and salt
4. Lay vegetables in the air fryer first, then add chicken on top—Cook for almost 35 minutes or more. Flip the chicken halfway through and toss the vegetables.
5. Serve hot.

Nutrition:

- 344 Calories
- 28g Protein
- 11g Fat

296. Air Fryer Cornish Hen

Difficulty: Average
Preparation Time: 8 minutes
Cooking Time: 25 minutes
Servings: 3

Ingredients:

- One Cornish hen (1 lean)
- Salt & black pepper to taste (1/2 condiment)
- Olive oil spray (1/4 condiment)
- Paprika, ¼ tbsp. (1/4 condiment)

Directions:

1. Mix all spices and Rub the spices all over Cornish hen.

2. Coat the air fryer basket with olive oil.
3. Put Cornish hen in an Air fryer.
4. Cook for 25 minutes at 390 F. flip after half time.
5. Serve with a mixed green salad.

Nutrition:
- 300 Calories
- 25g Protein
- 21g Fat

297. Herb-Marinated Chicken Thighs

Difficulty: Average
Preparation Time: 9 minutes
Cooking Time: 10 minutes
Servings: 4
Ingredients:
- Chicken thighs: 8 skin-on, bone-in (4 lean)
- Lemon juice: 2 Tablespoon (1/8 condiment)
- Garlic powder: 2 teaspoons (1/8 condiment)
- Spike Seasoning: 1 teaspoon. (1/8 condiment)
- Olive oil: 1/4 cup (1/8 condiment)
- Dried basil: 1 teaspoon (1/2 green)
- Dried oregano: ½ teaspoon. (1/2 green)
- Black Pepper: 1/4 tsp. (1/8 condiment)

Directions:
1. In a bowl, add dried oregano, olive oil, lemon juice, dried sage, garlic powder, Spike Seasoning, onion powder, dried basil, black pepper.
2. In a zip lock bag, add the spice blend and the chicken and mix well.
3. Marinate the chicken in the refrigerator for at least six hours or more.
4. Preheat the air fryer to 360F.
5. Put the chicken in the air fryer basket, cook for six-eight minutes, flip the chicken, and cook for six minutes more.

6. Until the internal chicken temperature reaches 165F.
7. Take out from the air fryer and serve with microgreens.

Nutrition:
- 100 Calories
- 9g Fat
- 4g Protein

298. Air Fryer Nashville Hot Chicken with Spinach Salad

Difficulty: Average
Preparation Time: 11 minutes
Cooking Time: 25 minutes
Servings: 8
Ingredients:
- Buttermilk: 2 cups (1/2 healthy fat)
- Chicken thighs(bone-in): 8 (3 lean)
- Cayenne pepper: 1 tsp. (1/8 condiment)
- Hot sauce: 1/4 cup (1/8 condiment)
- Garlic powder: 2 Tbsp. (1/8 condiment)
- Salt: 1 tsp. (1/8 condiment)
- Low-fat butter: 1/2 cup (1/2 healthy fat)
- Flour: 2 cups (1/8 condiment)
- Black pepper: 1 tsp. (1/8 condiment)
- Old bay: 1 tsp. (1/2 green)
- Paprika: 1 tsp. (1/8 condiment)

Directions:
1. In a mixing bowl, add hot sauce and buttermilk, mix it well, then add chicken pieces.
2. Marinate in the refrigerator for 1 to 24 hours.
3. In a bowl, add garlic powder, flour, salt, black pepper, paprika, cayenne pepper, and old bay. Mix well.
4. Always cook the chicken in a single layer, in the air fryer
5. Take chicken out from buttermilk, coat in the flour mix. Situate the chicken rest on a cooling rack for 15 minutes before putting it in the air fryer.

6. Place the breaded chicken in the air fryer, leaving room between the pieces.
7. Cook for 25 minutes, at 390 F. after halftime, take the basket out and spray the chicken with olive oil
8. This step is optional. Mix two tbsp. Of hot sauce with melted butter. Brush the cooked crispy chicken with it.
9. Serve with the spinach salad.

Nutrition:
- 333 calories
- 20g Fat
- 26g protein

299. Lemon Pepper Chicken

Difficulty: Easy
Preparation Time: 9 minutes
Cooking Time: 16 minutes
Servings: 2

Ingredients:
- Two Lemons rind, juice, and zest (1/2 condiment)
- One Chicken Breast (1 lean)
- Minced Garlic: 1 Tsp (1/8 condiment)
- Black Peppercorns: 2 tbsp. (1/8 condiment)
- Chicken Seasoning: 1 Tbsp. (1/8 condiment)
- Salt & pepper to taste (1/8 condiment)

Directions:
1. Let the air fryer preheat to 180C. In a large aluminum foil, add all the seasonings along with lemon rind. Add salt and pepper to the chicken and rub the seasonings all over the chicken breast. Put the chicken in aluminum foil. And fold it tightly. Flatten the chicken inside foil with a rolling pin. Put it in the air fryer and cook at 180 C for 15 minutes. Serve hot.

Nutrition:
- 140 Calories

- 13g Protein
- 2g Fat

300. Air Fryer Low Carb Chicken Bites

Difficulty: Easy

Preparation Time: 14 minutes

Cooking Time: 10 minutes

Servings: 3

Ingredients:

- Chicken breast: 2 cups (1 lean)
- Kosher salt & pepper to taste (1/2 condiment)
- Smashed potatoes: 1 cup (1/3 healthy fat)
- Scallions: ¼ cup (1/2 green)
- One Egg beat (1/3 healthy fat)
- Whole wheat breadcrumbs: 1 cup (1/3 healthy fat)

Directions:

1. Boil the chicken until soft. Shred the chicken with the help of a fork. Add the smashed potatoes, scallions to the shredded chicken. Season with kosher salt and pepper. Coat with egg and then in bread crumbs. Put in the air fryer, and cook for 8 minutes at 380F. Or until golden brown. Serve warm.

Nutrition:

- 234 Calories
- 25g protein
- 9g fat

301. Shrimp Spring Rolls

Difficulty: Average
Preparation Time: 9 minutes
Cooking Time: 25 minutes
Servings: 4
Ingredients

- Deveined raw shrimp: half cup chopped(peeled) (1 lean)
- Olive oil: 2 and 1/2 tbsp. (1/8 condiment)
- Matchstick carrots: 1 cup (1/2 green)
- Slices of red bell pepper: 1 cup (1/2 green)
- Red pepper: 1/4 teaspoon(crushed) (1/4 green)
- Shredded cabbage: 2 cups (1 green)
- Lime juice: 1 tablespoon (1/8 condiment)
- Sweet chili sauce: half cup (1/8 condiment)
- Fish sauce: 2 teaspoons (1/8 condiment)
- Eight spring roll(wrappers) (1 healthy fat)

Direction

1. In a skillet, add one and a half tbsp. of olive, until smoking lightly. Stir in bell pepper, cabbage, carrots, and cook for two minutes. Turn off the heat, take out in a dish and cool for five minutes.
2. In a bowl, add shrimp, lime juice, cabbage mixture, crushed red pepper, and fish sauce. Mix well
3. Lay spring roll wrappers on a plate. Add 1/4 cup of filling in the middle of each wrapper. Fold tightly with

water. Brush the olive oil over folded rolls.
4. Put spring rolls in the air fryer basket and cook for 6 to 7 minutes at 390°F until light brown and crispy.
5. You may serve with sweet chili sauce.

Nutrition:

- 180 Calories
- 9g Fat
- 17g Protein

302. Air Fryer Scallops with Tomato Cream Sauce

Difficulty: Average
Preparation Time: 5 minutes
Cooking Time: 10 minutes
Servings: 2
Ingredients

- Sea scallops eight jumbo (4 lean)
- Tomato Paste: 1 tbsp. (1/4 condiment)
- Chopped fresh basil 1 tablespoon (1/2 green)
- 3/4 cup of low-fat Whipping Cream (1/2 healthy fat)
- Kosher salt half teaspoon (1/4 condiment)
- Ground Freshly black pepper half teaspoon (1/4 condiment)
- Minced garlic 1 teaspoon (1/4 condiment)
- Frozen Spinach, thawed half cup (1/2 green)

Direction

1. Take a seven-inch pan(heatproof) and add spinach in a single layer at the bottom
2. Rub olive oil on both sides of scallops, season with kosher salt and pepper.
3. on top of the spinach, place the seasoned scallops
4. Put the pan in the air fryer and cook for ten minutes at 350F, until scallops are cooked completely, and the internal temperature reaches 135F.
5. Serve immediately.

Nutrition:

- 259 Calories
- 19g Protein
- 13g Fat

303. Sriracha & Honey Tossed Calamari

Difficulty: Easy
Preparation Time: 9 minutes
Cooking Time: 20 minutes
Servings: 2
Ingredients

- Club soda: 1 cup (1/2 condiment)
- Sriracha: 1-2 Tbsp. (1/4 condiment)
- Calamari tubes: 2 cups (1 lean)
- Flour: 1 cup (1/2 healthy fat)
- Pinches of salt, freshly ground black pepper, red pepper flakes, and red pepper (1/4 condiment)
- Honey: 1/2 cup (1/2 healthy fat)

Direction

1. Cut the calamari tubes into rings. Submerge them with club soda. Let it rest for ten minutes.
2. In the meantime, in a bowl, add freshly ground black pepper, flour, red pepper, and kosher salt and mix well.
3. Drain the calamari and pat dry with a paper towel. Coat the calamari well in the flour mix and set aside.
4. Spray oil in the air fryer basket and put calamari in one single layer.
5. Cook at 375 for 11 minutes. Toss the rings twice while cooking. Meanwhile, to make sauce honey, red pepper flakes, and sriracha in a bowl, well.

6. Take calamari out from the basket, mix with sauce, cook for another two minutes more. Serve with salad green.

Nutrition
- 252 Calories
- 38g Fat
- 41g Protein

304. Air Fryer Southern Style Catfish with Green Beans

Difficulty: Average
Preparation Time: 8 minutes
Cooking Time: 23 minutes
Servings: 2
Ingredients
- Catfish fillets: 2 pieces (1 lean)
- Green beans: half cup, trimmed (1/2 green)
- Honey: 2 teaspoons (1/4 condiment)
- black pepper and salt, to taste (1/4 condiment)
- Crushed red pepper: half tsp. (1/2 green)
- Flour: 1/4 cup (1/4 condiment)
- One egg, lightly beaten (1/2 healthy fat)
- Dill pickle relish: 3/4 teaspoon (1/4 condiment)
- Apple cider vinegar: half tsp (1/4 condiment)
- 1/3 cup whole-wheat breadcrumbs (1/2 healthy fat)
- Mayonnaise: 2 tablespoons (1/4 condiment)
- Dill (1/2 green)
- Lemon wedges (1/4 condiment)

Direction
1. In a bowl, add green beans, spray them with cooking oil. Coat with crushed red pepper, 1/8 teaspoon of kosher salt, and half tsp. Of honey and cook in the air fryer at 400 F until soft and browned, for 12 minutes. Take out from fryer and cover with aluminum foil
2. In the meantime, coat catfish in flour. Then dip in egg to coat, then in breadcrumbs. Place fish in

an air fryer basket and spray with cooking oil.
3. Cook for 8 minutes, at 400F.
4. Sprinkle with pepper and salt. In the meantime, mix vinegar, dill, relish, mayonnaise, and honey in a bowl. Serve the sauce with fish and green beans.

Nutrition:
- 243 Calories
- 18g fat
- 33g Protein

305. Roasted Salmon with Fennel Salad

Difficulty: Easy
Preparation Time: 14 minutes
Cooking Time: 9 minutes
Servings: 4
Ingredients
- Skinless and center-cut: 4 salmon fillets (2 lean)
- Lemon juice: 1 teaspoon(fresh) (1/8 condiment)
- Parsley: 2 teaspoons(chopped) (1/4 green)
- Salt: 1 teaspoon, divided (1/8 condiment)
- Olive oil: 2 tablespoons (1/8 condiment)
- Chopped thyme: 1 teaspoon (1/4 green)
- Fennel heads: 4 cups (thinly sliced) (1/4 green)
- One clove of minced garlic (1/8 condiment)
- Fresh dill: 2 tablespoons, chopped (1/4 green)
- Orange juice: 2 tablespoons(fresh) (1/2 healthy fat)
- Greek yogurt: 2/3 cup(reduced-fat) (1/2 healthy fat)

Direction
1. In a bowl, add half teaspoon of salt, parsley, and thyme, mix well. Rub oil over salmon, and sprinkle with thyme mixture.
2. Put salmon fillets in the air fryer basket, cook for ten minutes at 350°F.

3. In the meantime, mix garlic, fennel, orange juice, yogurt, half tsp. of salt, dill, lemon juice in a bowl.
4. Serve with fennel salad.

Nutrition:
- 364 Calories
- 30g Fat
- 38g Protein

306. Air Fryer Catfish with Cajun Seasoning

Difficulty: Easy
Preparation Time: 5 minutes
Cooking Time: 27 minutes
Servings: 4
Ingredients
- Cajun seasoning: 3 teaspoons (1/2 condiment)
- Cornmeal: 3/4 cup (1/2 healthy fat)
- 4 catfish fillets (2 lean)

Direction
1. In a zip lock bag, add Cajun seasoning and cornmeal
2. Wash and pat dry the catfish fillets. Add them to the zip lock bag.
3. Coat well the fillets with seasoning
4. Put catfish fillets in the air fryer and cook for 15 minutes at 390 F, turn fillets halfway through. To get a golden color on the fillets, cook for five more minutes.
5. Serve with lemon wedges and spicy tartar sauce.

Nutrition
- 324 Calories
- 14g Fat
- 26.3g Protein

307. Air Fryer Sushi Roll

Difficulty: Difficult
Preparation Time: 91 minutes
Cooking Time: 9 minutes
Servings: 3
Ingredients
For the Kale Salad
- Rice vinegar: half teaspoon (1/8 condiment)
- Chopped kale: one and a 1/2 cups (1/2 green)
- Garlic powder:1/8 teaspoon (1/8 condiment)
- Sesame seeds: 1 tablespoon (1/4 healthy fat)
- Toasted sesame oil: 3/4 teaspoon (1/8 condiment)

- Ground ginger: 1/4 teaspoon (1/8 condiment)
- Soy sauce: 3/4 teaspoon (1/8 condiment)

Sushi Rolls
- Half avocado - sliced (1/2 healthy fat)
- Cooked Sushi Rice - cooled (1 healthy fat)
- Whole wheat breadcrumbs: half cup (1/2 healthy fat)
- Sushi: 3 sheets (1 lean)

Direction
Make the Kale Salad
1. In a bowl, add vinegar, garlic powder, kale, soy sauce, sesame oil, and ground ginger. With your hands, mix with sesame seeds and set them aside.

Sushi Rolls
2. Lay a sheet of sushi on a flat surface. With damp fingertips, add a tablespoon of rice, and spread it on the sheet. Cover the sheet with rice, leaving half-inch space at one end.
3. Add kale salad with avocado slices. Roll up the sushi, use water if needed.
4. Add the breadcrumbs in a bowl. Coat the sushi roll with Sriracha Mayo, then in breadcrumbs.
5. Add the rolls to the air fryer. Cook for ten minutes at 390 F, shake the basket halfway through.
6. Take out from the fryer, and let them cool, then cut with a sharp knife.
7. Serve with soy sauce.

Nutrition:
- 369 Calories
- 13.9g Fat
- 26g Protein

308. Air Fryer Garlic-Lime Shrimp Kebabs

Difficulty: Easy
Preparation Time: 5 minutes
Cooking Time: 19 minutes
Servings: 2

Ingredients
- 1 lime (1/4 condiment)
- Raw shrimp: 1 cup (1 lean)
- Salt: 1/8 teaspoon (1/4 condiment)
- 1 clove of garlic (1/4 condiment)
- Freshly ground black pepper (1/4 condiment)

Direction
1. In water, let wooden skewers soak for 20 minutes.
2. Let the Air fryer preheat to 350F.
3. In a bowl, mix shrimp, minced garlic, lime juice, kosher salt, and pepper
4. Add shrimp on skewers.
5. Place skewers in the air fryer, and cook for 8 minutes. Turn halfway over.
6. Top with cilantro and your favorite dip.

Nutrition:
- 76 Calories
- 13g Protein
- 9g fat

309. Fish Finger Sandwich

Difficulty: Average
Preparation Time: 10 minutes
Cooking Time: 9 minutes
Servings: 4
Ingredients
- Greek yogurt: 1 tbsp. (1/2 healthy fat)
- Cod fillets: 4, without skin (2 lean)
- Flour: 2 tbsp. (1/4 healthy fat)
- Whole-wheat breadcrumbs: 5 tbsp. (1/4 healthy fat)
- Kosher salt and pepper, to taste (1/4 condiment)
- Capers: 10–12 (1/2 healthy fat)
- Lemon juice (1/4 condiment)

Direction
1. Let the air fryer preheat.
2. Sprinkle kosher salt and pepper on the cod fillets, and coat in flour, then in breadcrumbs

3. Spray the fryer basket with oil. Put the cod fillets in the basket.
4. Cook for 15 minutes at 200 C.
5. In the meantime, blend with Greek yogurt, lemon juice, and capers until well combined.
6. On a bun, add cooked fish with pea puree. Add lettuce and tomato.

Nutrition:
- 240 Calories
- 12g Fat
- 20g Protein

310. Healthy Air Fryer Tuna Patties

Difficulty: Easy
Preparation Time: 15 minutes
Cooking Time: 11 minutes
Servings: 10

Ingredients
- Whole wheat breadcrumbs: half cup (1/4 healthy fat)
- Fresh tuna: 4 cups, diced (2 lean)
- Lemon zest (1/4 condiment)
- Lemon juice: 1 Tablespoon (1/4 condiment)
- 1 egg (1/4 healthy fat)
- Grated parmesan cheese: 3 Tablespoons (1/4 healthy fat)
- One chopped stalk celery (1 green)
- Garlic powder: half teaspoon (1/4 condiment)
- Dried herbs: half teaspoon (1/4 green)
- Salt to taste (1/8 condiment)
- Freshly ground black pepper (1/8 condiment)

Direction
1. In a bowl, add lemon zest, bread crumbs, salt, pepper, celery, eggs, dried herbs, lemon juice, garlic powder, parmesan cheese, and onion. Mix everything. Then add in tuna gently.

Shape into patties. If the mixture is too loose, cool in the refrigerator.
2. Add air fryer baking paper in the air fryer basket. Spray the baking paper with cooking spray.
3. Spray the patties with oil.
4. Cook for ten minutes at 360°F. Turn the patties halfway over.
5. Serve with lemon slices and microgreens.

Nutrition:
- 214 Calories
- 15g Fat
- 22g Protein

311.　Crab Cakes

Difficulty: Average
Preparation Time: 14 minutes
Cooking Time: 19 minutes
Servings: 6
Ingredients
- Crab meat: 4 cups (2 lean)
- 2 eggs (1 healthy fat)
- Whole wheat bread crumbs: ¼ cup (1/2 healthy fat)
- Mayonnaise: 2 tablespoons (1/2 healthy fat)
- Worcestershire sauce: 1 teaspoon (1/4 condiment)
- Old Bay seasoning: 1 and ½ teaspoon (1/4 condiment)
- Dijon mustard: 1 teaspoon (1/4 condiment)
- Black pepper to taste (1/4 condiment)
- Green onion: ¼ cup, chopped (1/4 green)

Direction
1. In a bowl, add Dijon mustard, Old Bay, eggs, Worcestershire, and mayonnaise mix it well. Then add in the chopped green onion and mix.
2. Fold in the crab meat to mayonnaise mix. Then add breadcrumbs, not to over mix.
3. Chill the mix in the refrigerator for at least 60 minutes. Then shape into patties.
4. Let the air-fryer preheat to 350F. Cook for 10 minutes.

Flip the patties halfway through.
5. Serve with lemon wedges.

Nutrition:
- 218 Calories
- 13g Fat
- 17g Protein

312.　Breaded Air Fried Shrimp with Bang-Bang Sauce

Difficulty: Difficult
Preparation Time: 9 minutes
Cooking Time: 22 minutes
Servings: 4
Ingredients
- Whole wheat bread crumbs: 3/4 cup (1/2 healthy fat)
- Raw shrimp: 4 cups, deveined, peeled (2 lean)
- Flour: half cup (1/8 condiment)
- Paprika: 1 tsp (1/8 condiment)
- Chicken Seasoning, to taste (1/8 condiment)
- 2 tbsp. of one egg white (1/2 healthy fat)
- Kosher salt and pepper to taste (1/8 condiment)

Bang-Bang Sauce
- Sweet chili sauce: 1/4 cup (1/8 condiment)
- Plain Greek yogurt: 1/3 cup (1/3 healthy fat)
- Sriracha: 2 tbsp. (1/8 condiment)

Direction
1. Let the Air Fryer preheat to 400 degrees.
2. Add the seasonings to shrimp and coat well.
3. In three separate bowls, add flour, bread crumbs, and egg whites.
4. First coat the shrimp in flour, dab lightly in egg whites, then in the bread crumbs.
5. With cooking oil, spray the shrimp.

6. Place the shrimps in an air fryer, cook for four minutes, turn the shrimp over, and cook for another four minutes. Serve with micro green and bang-bang sauce.

Bang-Bang Sauce
7. Incorporate all the ingredients and serve.

Nutrition:
- 229 calories
- 10g fat
- 22g protein

313.　Air Fryer Crispy Fish Sandwich

Difficulty: Easy
Preparation Time: 11 minutes
Cooking Time: 12 minutes
Servings: 2
Ingredients
- Cod :2 fillets (1 lean)
- All-purpose flour: 2 tablespoons (1/4 condiment)
- Pepper: 1/4 teaspoon (1/8 condiment)
- Lemon juice: 1 tablespoon (1/4 condiment)
- Salt: 1/4 teaspoon (1/8 condiment)
- Garlic powder: half teaspoon (1/8 condiment)
- One egg (1/2 healthy fat)
- Mayo: half tablespoon (1/4 healthy fat)
- Whole wheat bread crumbs: half cup (1/2 healthy fat)

Direction
1. In a bowl, add salt, flour, pepper, and garlic powder.
2. In a separate bowl, add lemon juice, mayo, and egg.
3. In another bowl, add the breadcrumbs.
4. Coat the fish in flour, then in egg, then in breadcrumbs.
5. With cooking oil, spray the basket and put the fish in the basket. Also, spray the fish with cooking oil.
6. Cook at 400 F for ten minutes. This fish is soft, be careful if you flip.

Nutrition:
- 218 Calories
- 12g Fat

- 22g Protein

314. Easy Shrimp Egg Rolls

Difficulty: Average
Preparation Time: 24 minutes
Cooking Time: 19 minutes
Servings: 6

Ingredients

- 2-3 cloves of minced garlic (1/2 condiment)
- 12-14 egg roll wrappers (1 healthy fat)
- Raw shrimp (roughly chopped): 4 cups, peeled and deveined (2 lean)
- Coleslaw mix: 3 cups (1 healthy fat)
- Sesame oil: 1 and 1/2 teaspoons (1/8 condiment)
- Soy sauce: 1 tablespoon (1/4 condiment)
- Fish sauce: 1 teaspoon (1/8 condiment)
- Salt, pepper to taste (1/8 condiment)
- Grated ginger: half tsp. (1/8 condiment)
- Two green onions chopped (1 green)
- Water: one cup (1/4 condiment)

Direction

1. In a skillet, add shrimp with garlic, kosher salt, and pepper, spray with cooking oil and sauté until shrimp is pink. Put off the heat and set it aside.
2. In a bowl, add coleslaw mix, cooked shrimp, green onions, fish sauce, soy sauce, sesame oil, and ginger. Mix well.
3. Add two tbsp. Of filling, in each wrapper, seal tightly with water.
4. With cooking oil, spray the air fryer basket. Situate egg rolls in a single layer in the basket. Spray with cooking oil.
5. Cook for 7 minutes at 400 degrees. Flip the rolls, then cook for five minutes more.

6. Serve with micro green salad.

Nutrition:

- 228 calories
- 11g fat
- 20g protein

315. Easy Shrimp PO' Boy

Difficulty: Easy
Preparation Time: 19 minutes
Cooking Time: 9 minutes
Servings: 4

Ingredients

- Iceberg lettuce: 2 cups shredded (1 green)
- Shrimp:4 cups, deveined (2 lean)
- Buttermilk: 1/4 cup (1/4 healthy fat)
- Fish Fry Coating: 1/2 cup (1/4 condiment)
- Creole Seasoning: 1 teaspoon (1/8 condiment)
- Eight slices of tomato (1/2 green)

Remoulade Sauce

- Creole Seasoning: half tsp. (1/8 condiment)
- Mayo: half cup(reduced-fat) (1/2 healthy fat)
- Half lemon's juice (1/8 condiment)
- Dijon mustard: 1 tsp (1/8 condiment)
- Worcestershire: 1 tsp (1/8 condiment)
- Minced garlic: one tsp. (1/8 condiment)
- One green onion chopped (1/4 condiment)
- Hot sauce: one tsp

Direction

Remoulade Sauce

1. Mix all ingredients in a bowl. Chill in Refrigerator.

Shrimp

2. In a zip lock bag, add buttermilk and Creole seasoning with shrimp and mix well, marinate for half an hour.
3. With cooking oil, spray the air fryer basket. Place the shrimp in the air fryer basket.
4. Spray the shrimp with olive oil.

5. Cook at 400 F for five minutes. Flip the shrimps over, and cook for extra five minutes.
6. Add the remoulade sauce on whole-wheat bread. Then add tomato slices and lettuce on top, then the shrimp. Enjoy

Nutrition:

- 247 Calories
- 19.3g fat
- 24.7g protein

316. Quick & Easy Air Fryer Salmon

Difficulty: Easy
Preparation Time: 6 minutes
Cooking Time: 13 minutes
Servings: 4

Ingredients

- Lemon pepper seasoning: 2 teaspoons (1/4 condiment)
- Salmon: 4 cups (2 lean)
- Olive oil: one tablespoon (1/4 condiment)
- Seafood seasoning: 2 teaspoons (1/4 condiment)
- Half lemon's juice (1/4 condiment)
- Garlic powder:1 teaspoon (1/8 condiment)
- Kosher salt to taste (1/8 condiment)

Direction

1. In a bowl, add one tbsp. of olive oil and half lemon juice.
2. Pour this mixture over salmon and rub. Leave the skin on salmon. It will come off when cooked.
3. Rub the salmon with kosher salt and spices.
4. Put parchment paper in the air fryer basket. Put the salmon in the air fryer.
5. Cook at 360 F for ten minutes. Cook until inner salmon temperature reaches 140 F.
6. Let the salmon rest five minutes before serving.
7. Serve with salad greens and lemon wedges.

Nutrition:

- 132 Calories
- 7.4g fat
- 22g protein

317. Air Fryer Parmesan Shrimp

Difficulty: Average
Preparation Time: 6 minutes
Cooking Time: 12 minutes
Servings: 4

Ingredients
- Olive oil: 2 tablespoons (1/2 condiment)
- Jumbo cooked shrimp: 8 cups, peeled, deveined (4 lean)
- Parmesan cheese: 2/3 cup(grated) (1/2 healthy fat)
- Pepper: 1 teaspoon (1/4 condiment)
- 4 cloves of minced garlic (1/2 condiment)
- Oregano: 1/2 teaspoon (1/4 green)
- Basil: 1 teaspoon (1/4 green)
- Lemon wedges (1/2 condiment)

Direction
1. Mix parmesan cheese, onion powder, oregano, olive oil, garlic, basil, and pepper in a bowl. Coat the shrimp in this mixture.
2. Spray oil on the air fryer basket, put shrimp in it.
3. Cook for ten minutes, at 350 F, or until browned.
4. Drizzle the lemon on shrimps before serving with a microgreen salad.

Nutrition:
- 198 Calories
- 13g Fat
- 12.7g Protein

318. Air Fryer Lemon Garlic Shrimp

Difficulty: Average
Preparation Time: 6 minutes
Cooking Time: 12 minutes
Servings: 2
Ingredients
- Olive oil: 1 Tbsp. (1/4 condiment)
- Small shrimp: 4 cups, peeled, tails removed (2 lean)
- One lemon juice and zest (1/4 condiment)
- Parsley: 1/4 cup sliced (1/4 green)
- Red pepper flakes(crushed): 1 pinch (1/4 condiment)
- Four cloves of grated garlic (1/8 condiment)
- Sea salt: 1/4 teaspoon (1/8 condiment)

Direction
1. Let air fryer heat to 400F
2. Mix olive oil, lemon zest, red pepper flakes, shrimp, kosher salt, and garlic in a bowl and coat the shrimp well.
3. Place shrimps in the air fryer basket, coat with oil spray.
4. Cook at 400 F for 8 minutes. Toss the shrimp halfway through
5. Serve with lemon slices and parsley.

Nutrition:
- 140 Calories
- 18g Fat
- 20g Protein

319. Air Fryer Shrimp Tacos

Difficulty: Average
Preparation Time: 16 minutes
Cooking Time: 16 minutes
Servings: 4
Ingredients
- Flour tortillas: 12 (2 healthy fat)
- Avocado sliced: 1 cup (1/4 healthy fat)
- Chipotle chili powder: 1 tsp (1/8 condiment)
- Raw jumbo shrimp: 24 pieces, deveined, peeled, without tail (4 lean)
- Smoked paprika: 1/2 tsp (1/8 condiment)
- Salt: 1/4 tsp (1/8 condiment)
- Olive oil: 1 tbsp. (1/8 condiment)
- Green salsa: ½ cup (1/4 healthy fat)

- Light brown sugar: 1 and 1/2 tsp (1/8 condiment)
- Garlic powder: 1/2 tsp (1/8 condiment)
- Low-fat sour cream: 1/2 cup (1/4 healthy fat)

Direction
1. Let the oven preheat to 400 F and spray the air fryer basket with oil spray.
2. In a bowl, mix chipotle chili powder, salt, brown sugar, smoked paprika, and garlic powder, mix well
3. Pat dry the shrimp, put shrimp in zip lock bag and add the seasonings and toss to coat well
4. Place shrimp in air fryer basket in one even layer, cook for four minutes and flip them overcook for four minutes more
5. For the sauce, mix sour cream and green salsa.
6. Put shrimp in a tortilla, top with sauce, shrimp, sliced avocado serves with lime wedges.

Nutrition:
- 228 Calories
- 18g Fat
- 20g Protein

320. Air Fryer Lemon Pepper Shrimp

Difficulty: Average
Preparation Time: 6 minutes
Cooking Time: 11 minutes
Servings: 2

Ingredients
- Raw shrimp: 1 and 1/2 cup peeled, deveined (1 lean)
- Olive oil: 1/2 tablespoon (1/4 condiment)
- Garlic powder: ¼ tsp (1/8 condiment)
- Lemon pepper: 1 tsp (1/4 condiment)
- Paprika: ¼ tsp (1/8 condiment)
- Juice of one lemon (1/4 condiment)

Direction
1. Let the air fryer preheat to 400 F

2. In a bowl, mix lemon pepper, olive oil, paprika, garlic powder, and lemon juice. Mix well. Add shrimps and coat well
3. Add shrimps in the air fryer, cook for 6 or 8 minutes and top with lemon slices and serve

Nutrition:
- 237 Calories
- 6g Fat
- 36g Protein

Chapter 14. Air Fryer - Vegetable Recipes

321. Healthy & Tasty Green Beans

Difficulty: Easy
Preparation Time: 10 minutes
Cooking Time: 10 minutes
Servings: 2

Ingredients:
- 2 cups green beans (1/2 green)
- 1/8 tsp ground allspice (1/8 condiment)
- 1/4 tsp ground cinnamon (1/8 condiment)
- 1/2 tsp dried oregano (1/4 green)
- 2 tbsp olive oil (1/8 condiment)
- 1/4 tsp ground coriander (1/8 condiment)
- 1/4 tsp ground cumin (1/8 condiment)
- 1/8 tsp cayenne pepper (1/8 condiment)
- 1/2 tsp salt (1/8 condiment)

Directions:
1. Add all ingredients into the bowl and toss well.
2. Add green beans into the air fryer basket and cook at 370 F for 10 minutes. Shake basket halfway through
3. Serve and enjoy.

Nutrition
- 158 Calories
- 14g Fat
- 2.1g Protein

322. Cheesy Brussels Sprouts

Difficulty: Easy
Preparation Time: 10 minutes
Cooking Time: 12 minutes
Servings: 4

Ingredients:
- 1 lb. Brussels sprouts, cut stems and halved (1/2 green)
- 1/4 cup parmesan cheese (1/2 healthy fat)
- 1 tbsp olive oil (1/4 condiment)
- 1/4 tsp garlic powder (1/4 condiment)
- Pepper (1/8 condiment)
- Salt (1/8 condiment)

Directions:
1. Preheat the air fryer to 350 F.
2. Toss Brussels sprouts, oil, garlic powder, pepper, and salt into the bowl.
3. Situate Brussels sprouts into the air fryer basket and cook for 12 minutes.
4. Top with cheese and serve.

Nutrition
- 132 Calories
- 7g Fat
- 7g Protein

323. Garlic Cauliflower Florets

Difficulty: Easy
Preparation Time: 10 minutes
Cooking Time: 20 minutes
Servings: 4

Ingredients:
- 4 cups cauliflower florets (1/2 green)
- 1/2 tsp cumin powder (1/8 condiment)
- 1/2 tsp coriander powder (1/8 condiment)
- 5 garlic cloves, chopped (1/8 condiment)
- 4 tablespoons olive oil (1/8 condiment)
- 1/2 tsp salt (1/8 condiment)

Directions:
1. Add all ingredients into the bowl and toss well.
2. Add cauliflower florets into the air fryer basket and cook at 400 F for 20 minutes. Shake halfway through.
3. Serve and enjoy.

Nutrition
- 153 Calories
- 14g Fat
- 2.3g Protein

324. Delicious Ratatouille

Difficulty: Difficult
Preparation Time: 10 minutes
Cooking Time: 15 minutes
Servings: 6

Ingredients:
- 1 eggplant, diced (1/2 green)
- 3 garlic cloves, chopped (1/4 condiment)
- 1 onion, diced (1/4 condiment)
- 3 tomatoes, diced (1/2 healthy fat)
- 2 bell peppers, diced (1/2 green)
- 1 tbsp vinegar (1/4 condiment)
- 1 1/2 tbsp olive oil (1/4 condiment)
- 2 tbsp herb de Provence (1/2 green)
- Pepper (1/8 condiment)
- Salt (1/8 condiment)

Directions:
1. Preheat the air fryer to 400 F.
2. Add all ingredients into the bowl and toss well.
3. Add vegetable mixture into the air fryer basket and cook for 15 minutes. Stir halfway through.
4. Serve and enjoy.

Nutrition
- 83 Calories
- 4g Fat
- 2g Protein

325. Simple Green Beans

Difficulty: Easy
Preparation Time: 10 minutes
Cooking Time: 10 minutes
Servings: 4
Ingredients:
- 2 cups green beans (1 green)

- 1 tsp olive oil (1/2 condiment)
- Pepper (1/4 condiment)
- Salt (1/4 condiment)

Directions:
1. In a bowl, toss green beans with oil. Season with pepper and salt.
2. Transfer green beans into the air fryer basket and cook at 390 F for 10 minutes.
3. Serve and enjoy.

Nutrition
- 27 Calories
- 1.2g Fat
- 1g Protein

326. Air Fryer Tofu

Difficulty: Easy
Preparation Time: 10 minutes
Cooking Time: 15 minutes
Servings: 4

Ingredients:
- 15 oz extra firm tofu, cut into bite-sized pieces (1 healthy fat)
- 1 tbsp olive oil (1/4 condiment)
- 2 tbsp soy sauce (1/4 condiment)
- 1 garlic clove, minced (1/4 condiment)
- Pepper (1/8 condiment)
- Salt (1/8 condiment)

Directions:
1. Add tofu, garlic, oil, soy sauce, pepper, and salt in a bowl and toss well. Set aside for 15 minutes.
2. Add tofu pieces into the air fryer basket and cook at 370 F for 15 minutes.
3. Serve and enjoy.

Nutrition
- 115 Calories
- 8g Fat
- 9.8g Protein

327. Healthy Zucchini Patties

Difficulty: Easy
Preparation Time: 10 minutes
Cooking Time: 30 minutes
Servings: 6

Ingredients:
- 1 cup zucchini, shredded and squeeze out all liquid (1/2 green)
- 1 egg, lightly beaten (1/4 healthy fat)
- 1/4 tsp red pepper flakes (1/4 condiment)
- 1/4 cup parmesan cheese, grated (1/4 healthy fat)
- 1/2 tbsp Dijon mustard (1/4 condiment)
- 1/2 tbsp mayonnaise (1/4 healthy fat)
- 1/2 cup breadcrumbs (1/2 healthy fat)
- Pepper (1/8 condiment)
- Salt (1/8 condiment)

Directions:
1. Mix all ingredients into the bowl until well combined.
2. Make patties from mixture and place them into the basket and cook at 375 F for 15 minutes.
3. Turn patties and cook for 15 minutes more.
4. Serve and enjoy.

Nutrition
- 80 Calories
- 3g Fat
- 4g Protein

328. Healthy Asparagus Spears

Difficulty: Easy
Preparation Time: 10 minutes
Cooking Time: 15 minutes
Servings: 4

Ingredients:
- 35 asparagus spears, cut the ends (2 green)
- 1/2 tsp garlic powder (1/4 condiment)
- 1 tbsp olive oil (1/4 condiment)
- Pepper (1/8 condiment)
- Salt (1/8 condiment)
- ¼ tsp. onion powder (1/4 condiment)

Directions:
1. Add asparagus into the large bowl. Drizzle with oil.
2. Sprinkle with onion powder, garlic powder, pepper, and salt. Toss well.
3. Arrange asparagus into the air fryer basket and cook at 375 F for 15 minutes.
4. Serve and enjoy.

Nutrition
- 75 Calories
- 4g Fat
- 4g Protein

329. Spicy Brussels Sprouts

Difficulty: Easy
Preparation Time: 10 minutes
Cooking Time: 14 minutes
Servings: 2

Ingredients:
- 1/2 lb. Brussels sprouts, trimmed and halved (1 lean)
- 1/2 tsp chili powder (1/4 condiment)
- 1/4 tsp cayenne (1/4 condiment)
- 1/2 tbsp olive oil (1/4 condiment)
- 1/4 tsp smoked paprika (1/4 condiment)

Directions:
1. Mix all ingredients into the large bowl and toss well.
2. Add Brussels sprouts into the air fryer basket and cook at 370 F for 14 minutes.
3. Serve and enjoy.

Nutrition
- 82 Calories
- 4g Fat
- 4g Protein

330. Cheese Broccoli Fritters

Difficulty: Average
Preparation Time: 10 minutes
Cooking Time: 30 minutes
Servings: 4

Ingredients:

- 2 eggs, lightly beaten (1/2 healthy fat)
- 3 cups broccoli florets, cook & mashed (1 lean)
- 2 cups cheddar cheese (1/2 healthy fat)
- 1/4 cup almond flour (1/4 condiment)
- 2 garlic cloves, minced (1/4 condiment)
- Pepper (1/4 condiment)
- Salt (1/4 condiment)

Directions:
1. Mix all ingredients into the bowl.
2. Make patties from mixture and place them into the basket and cook at 350 F for 15 minutes.
3. Turn patties and cook for 15 minutes more.
4. Serve and enjoy.

Nutrition
- 285 Calories
- 21g Fat
- 18g Protein

331. Air Fryer Bell Peppers

Difficulty: Easy
Preparation Time: 10 minutes
Cooking Time: 8 minutes
Servings: 3

Ingredients:
- ¼ tsp. onion powder (1/4 condiment)
- 3 cups bell peppers, cut into pieces (1 green)
- 1 tsp olive oil (1/2 condiment)
- 1/4 tsp garlic powder (1/4 condiment)

Directions:
1. Mix all ingredients into the large bowl and toss well.
2. Transfer bell peppers into the air fryer basket and cook at 360 F for 8 minutes. Stir halfway through.
3. Serve and enjoy.

Nutrition

- 52 Calories
- 2g Fat
- 1.2g Protein

332. Air Fried Tasty Eggplant

Difficulty: Easy
Preparation Time: 10 minutes
Cooking Time: 12 minutes
Servings: 2

Ingredients:
- 1 eggplant, cut into cubes (1 green)
- 1/4 tsp oregano (1/4 green)
- 1 tbsp olive oil (1/2 condiment)
- 1/2 tsp garlic powder (1/4 condiment)
- 1/4 tsp chili powder (1/4 condiment)

Directions:
1. Incorporate all ingredients into the huge bowl and toss well.
2. Transfer eggplant into the air fryer basket and cook at 390 F for 12 minutes. Stir halfway through.
3. Serve and enjoy.

Nutrition
- 120 Calories
- 7g Fat
- 2g Protein

333. Asian Green Beans

Difficulty: Average
Preparation Time: 10 minutes
Cooking Time: 10 minutes
Servings: 2

Ingredients:
- 8 oz green beans (1 green)
- 1 tbsp tamari (1/2 condiment)
- 1 tsp sesame oil (1/2 condiment)

Direction
1. Mix all ingredients into the big bowl and toss well.
2. Add green beans into the air fryer basket and cook at 400 F for 10 minutes.

3. Serve and enjoy.

Nutrition
- 60 Calories
- 2g Fat
- 3g Protein

334. Spicy Asian Brussels Sprouts

Difficulty: Average
Preparation Time: 10 minutes
Cooking Time: 15 minutes
Servings: 4
Ingredients:
- 1 lb. Brussels sprouts, cut in half (1 green)
- 1 tbsp gochujang (1/2 condiment)
- 1 1/2 tbsp olive oil (1/4 condiment)
- 1/2 tsp salt (1/4 condiment)

Directions:
1. In a bowl, mix olive oil, gochujang, and salt.
2. Add Brussels sprouts into the bowl and toss until well coated.
3. Add Brussels sprouts into the air fryer basket and cook at 360 F for 15 minutes.
4. Serve and enjoy.

Nutrition
- 94 Calories
- 5g Fat
- 4g Protein

335. Healthy Mushrooms

Difficulty: Easy
Preparation Time: 10 minutes
Cooking Time: 12 minutes
Servings: 2

Ingredients:

- 8 oz mushrooms, clean and cut into quarters (2 healthy fats)
- 1 tbsp fresh parsley, chopped (1/2 green)
- 1 tsp soy sauce (1/4 condiment)
- 1/2 tsp garlic powder (1/4 condiment)
- 1 tbsp olive oil (1/4 condiment)
- Pepper (1/8 condiment)
- Salt (1/8 condiment)

Directions:
1. Add mushrooms and remaining ingredients into the bowl and toss well.
2. Add mushrooms into the air fryer basket and cook at 380 F for 12 minutes. Stir halfway through.
3. Serve and enjoy.

Nutrition
- 90 Calories
- 7g Fat
- 4g Protein

336.   Cheese Stuff Peppers

Difficulty: Average
Preparation Time: 10 minutes
Cooking Time: 8 minutes
Servings: 4

Ingredients:
- 10 jalapeno peppers, halved, remove seeds and stem (4 lean)
- 1/2 cup cheddar cheese (1/4 healthy fat)
- 1/2 cup Monterey jack cheese, shredded (1/4 healthy fat)
- 8 oz cream cheese, softened (1/2 healthy fat)

Directions:
1. In a bowl, mix together Monterey jack cheese and cream cheese.
2. Stuff cheese mixture into jalapeno halved.
3. Place jalapeno pepper into the air fryer basket and cook at 370 F for 8 minutes.
4. Serve and enjoy.

Nutrition
- 365 Calories
- 33g Fat
- 13.2g Protein

337.   Cheesy Broccoli Cauliflower

Difficulty: Easy
Preparation Time: 10 minutes
Cooking Time: 20 minutes
Servings: 6

Ingredients:
- 4 cups cauliflower florets (1 green)
- 4 cups broccoli florets (1 green)
- 2/3 cup parmesan cheese, shredded (1 healthy fat)
- 5 garlic cloves, minced (1/2 condiment)
- 1/3 cup olive oil (1/4 condiment)
- Pepper (1/8 condiment)
- Salt (1/8 condiment)

Directions:
1. Add half cheese, broccoli, cauliflower, garlic, oil, pepper, and salt into the bowl and toss well.
2. Add broccoli and cauliflower to the air fryer basket and cook at 370 F for 20 minutes.
3. Add remaining cheese. Toss well.
4. Serve and enjoy.

Nutrition
- 165 Calories
- 13.6g Fat
- 6.4g Protein

338.   Air Fryer Broccoli & Brussels Sprouts

Difficulty: Average
Preparation Time: 10 minutes
Cooking Time: 30 minutes
Servings: 6

Ingredients:
- 1 lb. Brussels sprouts, cut ends (1 green)

- 1 lb. broccoli, cut into florets (1 green)
- 1 tsp paprika (1/4 condiment)
- 1 tsp garlic powder (1/4 condiment)
- 1/2 tsp pepper (1/4 condiment)
- 3 tbsp olive oil (1 healthy fat)
- 3/4 tsp salt (1/4 condiment)

Directions:
1. Add all ingredients into the bowl and toss well.
2. Add vegetable mixture into the air fryer basket and cook at 370 F for 30 minutes.
3. Serve and enjoy.

Nutrition
- 125 Calories
- 7.6g Fat
- 5g Protein

339.   Spicy Asparagus Spears

Difficulty: Easy
Preparation Time: 10 minutes
Cooking Time: 15 minutes
Servings: 4

Ingredients:
- 35 asparagus spears, cut the ends (2 green)
- 1/2 tsp chili powder (1/4 condiment)
- 1/4 tsp paprika (1/4 condiment)
- 1 tbsp olive oil (1/4 condiment)
- Pepper (1/8 condiment)
- Salt (1/8 condiment)

Directions:
1. Add asparagus into the large bowl. Drizzle with oil.
2. Sprinkle with paprika, chili powder, pepper, and salt. Toss well.
3. Add asparagus into the air fryer basket and cook at 400 F for 15 minutes.
4. Serve and enjoy.

Nutrition
- 75 Calories
- 3.8g Fat
- 4.7g Protein

340.   Stuffed Mushrooms

Difficulty: Average
Preparation Time: 10 minutes
Cooking Time: 8 minutes
Servings: 16

Ingredients:
- 16 mushrooms, clean and chop stems (3 healthy fats)
- 2 garlic cloves, minced (1/2 condiment)
- 1/2 tsp chili powder (1/4 condiment)
- 1/4 cup cheddar cheese, shredded (1/2 healthy fat)
- 2 oz crab meat, chopped (1 lean)
- 8 oz cream cheese, softened (1/2 healthy fat)
- 1/4 tsp pepper (1/4 condiment)

Directions:
1. In a bowl, mix cheese, mushroom stems, chili powder, pepper, crabmeat, cream cheese, and garlic until well combined.
2. Stuff mushrooms with cheese mixture and place them into the air fryer basket and cook at 370 F for 8 minutes.
3. Serve and enjoy.

Nutrition
- 65 Calories
- 5.3g Fat
- 2.6g Protein

341.   Almond Flour Battered 'n Crisped Onion Rings

Difficulty: Average
Preparation Time: 10 minutes
Cooking Time: 15 minutes
Servings: 3
Ingredients:

- ½ cup almond flour (1/4 healthy fat)
- ¾ cup coconut milk (1/4 healthy fat)
- 1 big white onion, sliced into rings (1 green)
- 1 egg, beaten (1/4 healthy fat)
- 1 tablespoon baking powder (1/4 condiment)
- 1 tablespoon smoked paprika (1/4 condiment)
- Salt and pepper to taste (1/8 condiment)

Directions:
1. Preheat the air fryer for 5 minutes.
2. In a mixing bowl, mix the almond flour, baking powder, smoked paprika, salt and pepper.
3. In another bowl, combine the eggs and coconut milk.
4. Soak the onion slices into the egg mixture.
5. Dredge the onion slices in the almond flour mixture.
6. Place in the air fryer basket.
7. Close and cook for 15 minutes at 3250F.
8. Halfway through the cooking time, shake the fryer basket for even cooking.

Nutrition:
- 217 Calories
- 5.3g Protein
- 18g Fat

342.   Tomato Bites with Creamy Parmesan Sauce

Difficulty: Easy
Preparation Time: 7 minutes
Cooking Time: 13 minutes
Servings: 4
Ingredients:
For the Sauce:

- 1/2 cup Parmigiano-Reggiano cheese, grated (1/4 healthy fat)
- 4 tablespoons pecans, chopped (1/2 healthy fat)
- 1 teaspoon garlic puree (1/8 condiment)
- 1/2 teaspoon fine sea salt (1/8 condiment)
- 1/3 cup extra-virgin olive oil (1/8 condiment)

For the Tomato Bites:
- 2 large-sized Roma tomatoes, cut into thin slices and pat them dry (1 green)
- 8 ounces Halloumi cheese, cut into thin slices (1 healthy fat)
- 1 teaspoon dried basil (1/2 green)
- 1/4 teaspoon red pepper flakes, crushed (1/8 condiment)
- 1/8 teaspoon sea salt (1/8 condiment)

Directions:
1. Start by preheating your Air Fryer to 385 degrees F.
2. Make the sauce by mixing all ingredients, except the extra-virgin olive oil, in your food processor.
3. While the machine is running, slowly and gradually pour in the olive oil; puree until everything is well - blended.
4. Now, spread 1 teaspoon of the sauce over the top of each tomato slice. Place a slice of Halloumi cheese on each tomato slice. Top with onion slices. Sprinkle with basil, red pepper, and sea salt.
5. Transfer the assembled bites to the Air Fryer. Spray with non-stick cooking spray and cook for about 13 minutes.
6. Arrange these bites on a nice serving platter, garnish with the remaining sauce, and serve at room temperature. Bon appétit!

Nutrition:
- 428 Calories
- 38g Fat

- 18g Protein

Difficulty: Easy
Preparation Time: 2 minutes
Cooking Time: 10 minutes
Servings: 4

Ingredients:
- 3/4-pound green beans, cleaned
- 1 tablespoon balsamic vinegar
- 1/4 teaspoon kosher salt
- 1/2 teaspoon mixed peppercorns, freshly cracked
- 1 tablespoon butter
- 2 tablespoons toasted sesame seeds to serve

Directions:
1. Set your Air Fryer to cook at 390 degrees F.
2. Mix the green beans with all of the above ingredients, apart from the sesame seeds. Set the timer for 10 minutes.
3. Meanwhile, toast the sesame seeds in a small-sized nonstick skillet; make sure to stir continuously.
4. Serve sautéed green beans on a nice serving platter sprinkled with toasted sesame seeds. Bon appétit!

Nutrition:
- 73 Calories
- 3g Fat
- 1.6g Protein

Difficulty: Average
Preparation Time: 4 minutes
Cooking Time: 16 minutes
Servings: 6

Ingredients:
- 1-pound cauliflower florets (1 green)
- 1-pound broccoli florets (1 green)

- 2 ½ tablespoons sesame oil (1/2 condiment)
- 1/2 teaspoon smoked cayenne pepper (1/4 condiment)
- 3/4 teaspoon sea salt flakes (1/4 condiment)
- 1 tablespoon lemon zest, grated (1/4 condiment)
- 1/2 cup Colby cheese, shredded (1/2 healthy fat)

Directions:
1. Prepare the cauliflower and broccoli using your favorite steaming method. Then, drain them well; add the sesame oil, cayenne pepper, and salt flakes.
2. Air-fry at 390 degrees F for approximately 16 minutes; make sure to check the vegetables halfway through the cooking time.
3. Afterward, stir in the lemon zest and Colby cheese; toss to coat well and serve immediately!

Nutrition:
- 133 Calories
- 9g Fat
- 6g Protein

Difficulty: Easy
Preparation Time: 3 minutes
Cooking Time: 12 minutes
Servings: 2
Ingredients:
- 2 tablespoons olive oil, melted (1/4 condiment)
- 4 eggs, whisked (1 healthy fat)
- 5 ounces' fresh spinach, chopped (1 green)
- 1 medium-sized tomato, chopped (1 green)
- 1 teaspoon fresh lemon juice (1/4 condiment)
- 1/2 teaspoon coarse salt (1/8 condiment)
- 1/2 teaspoon ground black pepper (1/8 condiment)
- 1/2 cup of fresh basil, roughly chopped (1/4 green)

Directions:
1. Add the olive oil to an Air Fryer baking pan. Make sure to tilt the pan to spread the oil evenly.
2. Simply combine the remaining ingredients, except for the basil leaves; whisk well until everything is well incorporated.
3. Cook in the preheated oven for 8 to 12 minutes at 280 degrees F. Garnish with fresh basil leaves. Serve.

Nutrition:
- 274 Calories
- 23g Fat
- 14g Protein

Difficulty: Average
Preparation Time: 5 minutes
Cooking Time: 15 minutes
Servings: 6

Ingredients:
For the Broccoli Bites:
- 1 medium-sized head broccoli, broken into florets (1 green)
- 1/2 teaspoon lemon zest, freshly grated (1/4 condiment)
- 1/3 teaspoon fine sea salt (1/8 condiment)
- 1/2 teaspoon hot paprika (1/8 condiment)
- 1 teaspoon shallot powder (1/8 condiment)
- 1 teaspoon porcini powder (1/8 condiment)
- 1/2 teaspoon granulated garlic (1/8 condiment)
- 1/3 teaspoon celery seeds (1/4 healthy fat)
- 1 ½ tablespoons olive oil (1/8 condiment)

For the Hot Sauce:
- 1/2 cup tomato sauce (1/2 healthy fat)
- 1 tablespoon balsamic vinegar (1/8 condiment)
- ½ teaspoon ground allspice (1/8 condiment)

Directions:

1. Toss all the ingredients for the broccoli bites in a mixing bowl, covering the broccoli florets on all sides.
2. Cook them in the preheated Air Fryer at 360 degrees for 13 to 15 minutes. In the meantime, mix all ingredients for the hot sauce.
3. Pause your Air Fryer, mix the broccoli with the prepared sauce and cook for a further 3 minutes. Bon appétit!

Nutrition:
- 70 Calories
- 4g Fat
- 2g Protein

347. Cheese Stuffed Mushrooms with Horseradish Sauce

Difficulty: Average
Preparation Time: 3 minutes
Cooking Time: 12 minutes
Servings: 5
Ingredients:
- 1/2 cup parmesan cheese, grated (1/4 healthy fat)
- 2 cloves garlic, pressed (1/4 condiment)
- 2 tablespoons fresh coriander, chopped (1/4 green)
- 1/3 teaspoon kosher salt (1/8 condiment)
- 1/2 teaspoon crushed red pepper flakes (1/8 condiment)
- 1 ½ tablespoons olive oil (1/4 condiment)
- 20 medium-sized mushrooms, cut off the stems (1 healthy fat)
- 1/2 cup Gorgonzola cheese, grated (1/2 healthy fat)
- 1/4 cup low-fat mayonnaise (1/4 healthy fat)
- 1 teaspoon prepared horseradish, well-drained (1/4 green)

- 1 tablespoon fresh parsley, finely chopped (1/4 green)

Directions:
1. Mix the parmesan cheese together with the garlic, coriander, salt, red pepper, and olive oil; mix to combine well.
2. Stuff the mushroom caps with the cheese filling. Top with grated Gorgonzola.
3. Place the mushrooms in the Air Fryer grill pan and slide them into the machine. Grill them at 380 degrees F for 8 to 12 minutes or until the stuffing is warmed through.
4. Meanwhile, prepare the horseradish sauce by mixing the mayonnaise, horseradish and parsley. Serve the horseradish sauce with the warm fried mushrooms. Enjoy!

Nutrition:
- 180 Calories
- 13.2g Fat
- 9g Protein

348. Broccoli with Herbs and Cheese

Difficulty: Average
Preparation Time: 8 minutes
Cooking Time: 17 minutes
Servings: 4
Ingredients:
- 1/3 cup grated yellow cheese (1/2 healthy fat)
- 1 large-sized head broccoli, stemmed and cut small florets (1 green)
- 2 1/2 tablespoons canola oil (1/8 condiment)
- 2 teaspoons dried rosemary (1/4 green)
- 2 teaspoons dried basil (1/4 green)
- Salt and ground black pepper to taste (1/8 condiment)

Directions:
1. Bring a medium pan filled with a lightly salted water to a boil. Then, boil the

broccoli florets for about 3 minutes.
2. Then, drain the broccoli florets well; toss them with canola oil, rosemary, basil, salt and black pepper.
3. Set your oven to 390 degrees F; arrange the seasoned broccoli in the cooking basket; set the timer for 17 minutes. Toss the broccoli halfway through the cooking process.
4. Serve warm topped with grated cheese and enjoy!

Nutrition:
- 111 Calories
- 2.1g Fat
- 8.9g Protein

349. Family Favorite Stuffed Mushrooms

Difficulty: Easy
Preparation Time: 4 minutes
Cooking Time: 12 minutes
Servings: 2

Ingredients:
- 2 teaspoons cumin powder (1/4 condiment)
- 4 garlic cloves, peeled and minced (1/4 condiment)
- 18 medium-sized white mushrooms (2 healthy fats)
- Fine sea salt and freshly ground black pepper to taste (1/8 condiment)
- A pinch ground allspice (1/8 condiment)
- 2 tablespoons olive oil (1/4 condiment)

Directions:
1. First, clean the mushrooms; remove the middle stalks from the mushrooms to prepare the "shells."
2. Grab a mixing dish and thoroughly combine the remaining items. Fill the mushrooms with the prepared mixture.
3. Cook the mushrooms at 345 degrees F heat for 12 minutes. Enjoy!

Nutrition:

- 179 Calories
- 15g Fat
- 6g Protein

350. Spanish-Style Eggs with Manchego Cheese

Difficulty: Difficult
Preparation Time: 10 minutes
Cooking Time: 38 minutes
Servings: 4
Ingredients:

- 1/3 cup grated Manchego cheese (1/2 healthy fat)
- 5 eggs (2 healthy fats)
- 2 green garlic stalks, peeled and finely minced (1 green)
- 1 ½ cups white mushrooms, chopped (1 healthy fat)
- 1 teaspoon dried basil (1/4 green)
- 1 ½ tablespoons olive oil (1/2 condiment)
- 3/4 teaspoon dried oregano (1/4 green)
- 1/2 teaspoon dried parsley flakes or 1 tablespoon fresh flat-leaf Italian parsley (1/4 green)
- 1 teaspoon porcini powder (1/8 condiment)
- Table salt and freshly ground black pepper to taste (1/8 condiment)

Directions:

1. Start by preheating your Air Fryer to 350 degrees F. Add the oil, mushrooms, and green garlic to the Air Fryer baking dish. Bake this mixture for 6 minutes or until it is tender.
2. Meanwhile, crack the eggs into a mixing bowl; beat the eggs until they're well whisked. Next, add the seasonings and mix again. Pause your Air Fryer and take the baking dish out of the basket.
3. Pour the whisked egg mixture into the baking dish with sautéed mixture. Top with the grated Manchego cheese.
4. Bake for about 32 minutes at 320 degrees F or until your frittata is set. Serve warm. Bon appétit!

Nutrition:

- 153 Calories
- 12g Fat
- 9g Protein

351. Famous Fried Pickles

Difficulty: Average
Preparation Time: 5 minutes
Cooking Time: 15 minutes
Servings: 6

Ingredients:

- 1/3 cup milk (1/2 healthy fat)
- 1 teaspoon garlic powder (1/8 condiment)
- 2 medium-sized eggs (1 healthy fat)
- 1 teaspoon fine sea salt (1/8 condiment)
- 1/3 teaspoon chili powder (1/4 condiment)
- 1/3 cup all-purpose flour (1/4 healthy fat)
- 1/2 teaspoon shallot powder (1/4 condiment)
- 2 jars sweet and sour pickle spears (1 healthy fat)

Directions:

1. Pat the pickle spears dry with a kitchen towel. Then take two mixing bowls.
2. Whisk the egg and milk in a bowl. In another bowl, combine all dry ingredients.
3. Firstly, dip the pickle spears into the dry mix; then coat each pickle with the egg/milk mixture; dredge them in the flour mixture again for additional coating.
4. Air fry battered pickles for 15 minutes at 385 degrees. Enjoy!

Nutrition:

- 58 Calories
- 2g Fat
- 3.2g Protein

352. Fried Squash Croquettes

Difficulty: Easy
Preparation Time: 5 minutes
Cooking Time: 17 minutes
Servings: 4

Ingredients:

- 1/3 cup all-purpose flour (1/4 condiment)
- 1/3 teaspoon freshly ground black pepper, or more to taste (1/4 condiment)
- 1/3 teaspoon dried sage (1/8 condiment)
- 4 cloves garlic, minced (1/4 condiment)
- 1 ½ tablespoons olive oil (1/4 condiment)
- 1/3 butternut squash, peeled and grated
- 2 eggs, well whisked (1 healthy fat)
- 1 teaspoon fine sea salt (1/8 condiment)
- A pinch of ground allspice (1/8 condiment)

Directions:

1. Thoroughly combine all ingredients in a mixing bowl.
2. Preheat your Air Fryer to 345 degrees and set the timer for 17 minutes; cook until your fritters are browned; serve right away.

Nutrition:

- 152 Calories
- 10g Fat
- 6g Protein

353. Tamarind Glazed Sweet Potatoes

Difficulty: Easy
Preparation Time: 2 minutes
Cooking Time: 22 minutes
Servings: 4

Ingredients:
- 1/3 teaspoon white pepper (1/8 condiment)
- 1 tablespoon butter, melted (1/4 healthy fat)
- 1/2 teaspoon turmeric powder (1/8 condiment)
- 5 garnet sweet potatoes, peeled and diced (2 healthy fat)
- A few drops liquid Stevia (1/8 condiment)
- 2 teaspoons tamarind paste (1/4 condiment)
- 1 1/2 tablespoons fresh lime juice (1/8 condiment)
- 1 1/2 teaspoon ground allspice (1/8 condiment)

Directions:
1. In a mixing bowl, toss all ingredients until sweet potatoes are well coated.
2. Air-fry them at 335 degrees F for 12 minutes.
3. Pause the Air Fryer and toss again. Increase the temperature to 390 degrees F and cook for an additional 10 minutes. Eat warm.

Nutrition:
- 103 Calories
- 9g Fat
- 1.9g Protein

354. Roasted Cauliflower with Pepper Jack Cheese

Difficulty: Average
Preparation Time: 4 minutes
Cooking Time: 21 minutes
Servings: 2

Ingredients:

- 1/3 teaspoon shallot powder (1/4 condiment)
- 1 teaspoon ground black pepper (1/8 condiment)
- 1 ½ large-sized heads of cauliflower, broken into florets (1 green)
- 1/4 teaspoon cumin powder (1/8 condiment)
- ½ teaspoon garlic salt (1/8 condiment)
- 1/4 cup Pepper Jack cheese, grated (1/4 healthy fat)
- 1 ½ tablespoons vegetable oil (1/8 condiment)
- 1/3 teaspoon paprika (1/8 condiment)

Directions:
1. Boil cauliflower in a large pan of salted water for approximately 5 minutes. After that, drain the cauliflower florets; now transfer them to a baking dish.
2. Toss the cauliflower florets with the rest of the above ingredients.
3. Roast at 395 degrees F for 16 minutes, turn them halfway through the process. Enjoy!

Nutrition:
- 271 Calories
- 23g Fat
- Protein

355. Asian Stir Fry

Difficulty: Easy
Preparation Time: 15 minutes
Cooking Time: 10 minutes
Servings: 4

Ingredients:
- 1 tsp. Olive oil (1/8 condiment)
- 1 Tsp. Low Soy Sodium Sauce (1/8 condiment)
- 1 Lime Wedge (1/8 Lime) (1/8 condiment)
- Split into strips 7 ounces of boneless, skinless chicken breast (2 lean)

- C 3/4 Broccoli blossoms (1 green)
- 1/2 C. Sliced Chestnuts (1/2 healthy fat)
- 1/4 hp. Red bell pepper split (1/4 green)
- 1/4 hp. Freshwater (1/8 condiment)
- New ground potatoes, to taste (1/4 condiment)

Directions:
1. Prepare meat and veggies.
2. Add oil, soy sauce and lime wedge juice in a medium to large skillet.
3. Put on medium heat, then add chicken. Cook chicken over regularly, tossing or stirring.
4. Remove the chicken from the saucepan and put it aside.
5. Add water to the saucepan and stir until the water gets warm.
6. Next, add the vegetables and mix well to ensure that they are all eaten.
7. Cover and let cook for 5-7 minutes until almost tender vegetables.
8. Remove the cover and add the chicken, cook over medium-high to high heat until the vegetables are cooked, and the liquid is evaporated completely

Nutrition:
13g Carbohydrates
4g Protein
8g Fat

356. Cauliflower Crust Pizza

Difficulty: Average
Preparation Time: 20 minutes
Cooking Time: 45 minutes
Servings: 4
Ingredients:
- 1 cauliflower (1 green)

- 1/4 grated parmesan cheese (1/2 healthy fat)
- 1 egg (1/4 healthy fat)
- 1Tsp Italian seasoning (1/8 condiment)
- 1/4 Tsp. kosher salt (1/8 condiment)
- 2 cups of freshly grated mozzarella (1/4 healthy fat)
- 1/4 cup of spicy pizza sauce (1/8 condiment)
- Basil leaves for garnishing (1/4 green)

Directions:
1. Begin by preheating your oven while using the parchment paper to rim the baking sheet.
2. Process the cauliflower into a fine powder, and then transfer to a bowl before putting it into the microwave.
3. Leave for about 5-6 minutes to get it soft.
4. Transfer the microwave cauliflower to a clean and dry kitchen towel.
5. Leave it to cool off.
6. When cold, use the kitchen towel to wrap the cauliflower and then get rid of all the moisture by wringing the towel.
7. Continue squeezing until the water is gone completely.
8. Put the cauliflower, Italian seasoning, Parmesan, egg, salt, and mozzarella (1 cup).
9. Stir very well until well combined.
10. Transfer the combined mixture to the baking sheet previously prepared, pressing it into a 10-inch round shape.
11. Bake for 10-15 minutes until it becomes golden in color.
12. Take the baked crust out of the oven and use the spicy pizza sauce and mozzarella (the leftover 1 cup) to top it.
13. Bake again for 10 more minutes until the cheese melts and looks bubbly.
14. Garnish using fresh basil leaves.

15. You can also enjoy this with salad.

Nutrition:
- 74 Calories
- 6g Protein
- 4g Fat

357. Thai Roasted Veggies

Difficulty: Easy
Preparation Time: 20 minutes
Cooking Time: 6 to 8 hours
Servings: 8

Ingredients:
- 4 large carrots, peeled and cut into chunks (2 green)
- 6 garlic cloves, peeled and sliced (1/4 condiment)
- 2 parsnips, peeled and sliced (1/2 green)
- 2 jalapeño peppers, minced (1/2 green)
- 1/2 cup Roasted Vegetable Broth (1 condiment)
- 1/3 cup canned coconut milk (1/2 healthy fat)
- 3 tablespoons lime juice (1/8 condiment)
- 2 tablespoons grated fresh ginger root (1/4 condiment)
- 2 teaspoons curry powder (1/8 condiment)

Directions:
1. In a 6-quart slow cooker, mix the carrots, garlic, parsnips, and jalapeño peppers.
2. In a small bowl, mix the vegetable broth, coconut milk, lime juice, ginger root, and curry powder until well blended. Pour this mixture into the slow cooker.
3. Cover and cook on low for 6 to 8 hours, do it until the vegetables are tender when pierced with a fork.

Nutrition:
- 69 Calories
- 3g Fat
- 1g Protein

358. Roasted Squash Puree

Difficulty: Easy
Preparation Time: 20 minutes
Cooking Time: 6 to 7 hours
Servings: 8

Ingredients:
- 1 (3-pound) butternut squash, peeled, seeded, and cut into 1-inch pieces (1 green)
- 3 (1-pound) acorn squash, peeled, seeded, and cut into 1-inch pieces (2 green)
- 3 garlic cloves, minced (1/4 condiment)
- 2 tablespoons olive oil (1/8 condiment)
- 1 teaspoon dried marjoram leaves (1/8 green)
- 1/2 teaspoon salt (1/8 condiment)
- 1/8 teaspoon freshly ground black pepper (1/8 condiment)

Directions:
1. In a 6-quart slow cooker, mix all of the ingredients.
2. Cover and cook on low for 6 to 7 hours, or until the squash is tender when pierced with a fork.
3. Use a potato masher to mash the squash right in the slow cooker.

Nutrition:
- 175 Calories
- 4g Fat
- 3g Protein

359. Creamy Spinach and Mushroom Lasagna

Difficulty: Easy
Preparation Time: 60 minutes
Cooking Time: 20 minutes
Servings: 6

Ingredients:
- 10 lasagna noodles (2 healthy fat)
- 1 package whole milk ricotta (1 healthy fat)
- 2 packages of frozen chopped spinach. (2 green)

- 4 cups mozzarella cheese (divided and shredded) (1 healthy fat)
- 3/4 cup grated fresh Parmesan (1/2 healthy fat)
- 3 tablespoons chopped fresh parsley leaves(optional) (1/4 green)

For the Sauce:
- 1/4 cup butter(unsalted) (1/4 healthy fat)
- 2 cloves garlic (1/8 condiment)
- 1 pound of thinly sliced cremini mushroom (1/4 healthy fat)
- 1 diced onion (1/8 condiment)
- 1/4 cup flour (1/4 condiment)
- 4 cups milk, kept at room temperature (1 healthy fat)
- 1 teaspoon basil(dried) (1/8 green)
- Pinch of nutmeg (1/8 condiment)

Directions:
1. Preheat oven to 352 degrees F.
2. To make the sauce, over a medium portion of heat, melt your butter, add garlic, mushrooms and onion. Cook and stir at intervals until it becomes tender at about 3-4 minutes.
3. Whisk in flour until lightly browned, it takes about 1 minute for it to become brown.
4. Next, whisk in the milk gradually, and cook, whisking always, about 2-3 minute till it becomes thickened. Stir in basil, oregano and nutmeg, season with salt and pepper for taste;
5. Then set aside.
6. In another pot of boiling salted water, cook lasagna noodles according to the package instructions.
7. Spread 1 cup mushroom sauce onto the bottom of a baking dish; top it with 4 lasagna noodles, 1/2 of the spinach, 1 cup mozzarella cheese and 1/4 cup Parmesan.
8. Repeat this process with remaining noodles, mushroom sauce, and cheeses.
9. Place into the oven and bake for 35-45 minutes, or until it starts bubbling. Then boil for 2-3 minutes until it becomes brown and translucent.
10. Let cool for 15 minutes.
11. Serve it with garnished parsley (Optional)

Nutrition:
- 488 Calories
- 19g Fats
- 25g Protein

360. Kale Slaw and Strawberry Salad + Poppyseed Dressing

Difficulty: Easy
Preparation Time: 10 minutes
Cooking Time: 20 minutes
Servings: 2

Ingredients:
- Chicken breast; 8 ounces; sliced and baked (2 lean)
- Kale; 1 cup; chopped (1/4 green)
- Slaw mix; 1 cup (cabbage, broccoli slaw, carrots mixed) (1 green)
- Slivered almonds; 1/4 cup (1/4 healthy fat)
- Strawberries; 1 cup; sliced (1/4 healthy fat)

For the dressing:
- Light mayonnaise; 1 tablespoon (1/8 healthy fat)
- Dijon mustard (1/8 condiment)
- Olive oil; 1 tablespoon (1/8 condiment)
- Apple cider vinegar; 1 tablespoon (1/8 condiment)
- Lemon juice; 1/2 teaspoon (1/8 condiment)
- 1 tablespoon of Honey (1/8 condiment)
- Onion powder; 1/4 teaspoon (1/8 condiment)
- Garlic powder; 1/4 teaspoon (1/8 condiment)
- Poppyseeds (1/8 healthy fat)

Directions:
1. Whisk the dressing ingredients together until well mixed, then leave to cool in the fridge.
2. Slice the chicken breasts.
3. Divide 2 bowls of spinach, slaw, and strawberries.
4. Cover with a sliced breast of chicken (4 oz. each), then scatter with almonds.
5. Divide the salad over the dressing and drizzle.

Nutrition:
- 340 Calories
- 14g Fats
- 6.2 g Protein

Chapter 15. Air Fryer - Salad Recipes

361.   Taste of Normandy Salad

Difficulty: Easy
Preparation Time: 25 minutes
Cooking Time: 5 minutes
Servings: 4 to 6

Ingredients:
For the walnuts

- 2 tablespoons butter (1/4 healthy fat)
- ¼ cup sugar or honey (1/8 condiment)
- 1 cup walnut pieces (1/4 healthy fat)
- ½ teaspoon kosher salt (1/8 condiment)

For the dressing

- 3 tablespoons extra-virgin olive oil (1/4 condiment)
- 1½ tablespoons champagne vinegar (1/8 condiment)
- 1½ tablespoons Dijon mustard (1/8 condiment)
- ¼ teaspoon kosher salt (1/8 condiment)

For the salad

- 1 head red leaf lettuce, shredded into pieces (1 green)
- 3 heads endive, ends trimmed and leaves separated (1 green)
- 2 apples, cored and divided into thin wedges (1/2 green)
- 1 (8-ounce) Camembert wheel, cut into thin wedges (1/2 green)

Direction
To make the walnuts

1. Dissolve the butter in a skillet over medium high heat. Stir in the sugar and cook until it dissolves. Add the walnuts and cook for about 5 minutes, stirring until toasty. Season with salt and transfer to a plate to cool.

To make the dressing

2. Whip the oil, vinegar, mustard, and salt in a large bowl until combined.

To make the salad

3. Add the lettuce and endive to the bowl with the dressing and toss to coat. Transfer to a serving platter.
4. Decoratively arrange the apple and Camembert wedges over the lettuce and scatter the walnuts on top. Serve immediately.

Meal Prep Tip: Prepare the walnuts in advance—in fact, double the quantities and use them throughout the week to add a healthy crunch to salads, oats, or simply to enjoy as a snack.

Nutrition:

- 699 Calories
- 52g fat
- 23g Protein

362.   Loaded Caesar Salad with Crunchy Chickpeas

Difficulty: Average
Preparation Time: 5 minutes
Cooking Time: 20 minutes
Servings: 6

Ingredients:
For the chickpeas

- 2 (15-ounce) cans chickpeas, drained and rinsed (1 healthy fat)
- 2 tablespoons extra-virgin olive oil (1/8 condiment)
- 1 teaspoon kosher salt (1/8 condiment)
- 1 teaspoon garlic powder (1/8 condiment)
- 1 teaspoon onion powder (1/8 condiment)
- 1 teaspoon dried oregano (1/8 green)

For the dressing

- ½ cup mayonnaise (1/8 healthy fat)
- 2 tablespoons grated Parmesan cheese (1/4 healthy fat)
- 2 tablespoons freshly squeezed lemon juice (1/8 condiment)
- 1 clove garlic, peeled and smashed (1/8 condiment)
- 1 teaspoon Dijon mustard (1/8 condiment)
- ½ tablespoon Worcestershire sauce (1/8 condiment)
- ½ tablespoon anchovy paste (1/2 healthy fat)

For the salad

- 3 heads romaine lettuce, cut into bite-size pieces (1 green)

Directions:
To make the chickpeas

1. Preheat the oven to 450°F. Line a baking sheet with parchment paper.
2. Add the chickpeas, oil, salt, garlic powder, onion powder, and oregano in a small container. Scatter the coated chickpeas on the prepared baking sheet.
3. Roast for about 20 minutes, tossing occasionally, until the chickpeas are golden and have a bit of crunch.

To make the dressing

4. In a small bowl, whisk the mayonnaise, Parmesan, lemon juice, garlic, mustard,

Worcestershire sauce, and anchovy paste until combined.

To make the salad

5. Combine the lettuce and dressing in a large container. Toss to coat. Top with the roasted chickpeas and serve.

Cooking Tip: Don't wash out that bowl you used for the chickpeas — the remaining oil adds a great punch of flavor to blanched green beans or another simply cooked vegetable.

Nutrition:
- 367 Calories
- 22g Total fat
- 12g Protein

363. Coleslaw Worth A Second Helping

Difficulty: Easy
Preparation Time: 20 minutes
Cooking Time: 10 minutes
Servings: 6

Ingredients:
- 5 cups shredded cabbage (2 green)
- 2 carrots, shredded (1 green)
- ½ cup mayonnaise (1/2 healthy fat)
- ½ cup sour cream (1/2 healthy fat)
- 3 tablespoons apple cider vinegar (1/2 condiment)
- 1 teaspoon kosher salt (1/4 condiment)
- ½ teaspoon celery seed (1/4 condiment)

Directions:
1. Add together the cabbage, carrots, and parsley in a large bowl.
2. Whisk together the mayonnaise, sour cream, vinegar, salt, and celery in a small bowl until smooth. Pour sauce over veggies and pour until covered. Transfer to a serving bowl and bake until ready to serve.

Nutrition:
- 192 Calories
- 18g Total fat

- 2g Protein

364. Romaine Lettuce and Radicchios Mix

Difficulty: Easy
Preparation Time: 6 minutes
Cooking Time: 0 minutes
Servings: 4

Ingredients:
- 2 tablespoons olive oil (1/4 condiment)
- A pinch of salt and black pepper (1/4 condiment)
- 2 spring onions, chopped (1 green)
- 3 tablespoons Dijon mustard (1/4 condiment)
- Juice of 1 lime (1/4 condiment)
- ½ cup basil, chopped (1/4 green)
- 4 cups romaine lettuce heads, chopped (2 green)
- 3 radicchios, sliced (1 healthy fat)

Directions:
1. In a salad bowl, blend the lettuce with the spring onions and the other ingredients, toss and serve.

Nutrition:
- 87 Calories
- 2g Fats
- 2g Protein

365. Greek Salad

Difficulty: Easy
Preparation Time: 15 minutes
Cooking Time: 15 minutes
Servings: 5
Ingredients:
For Dressing:
- ½ teaspoon black pepper (1/8 condiment)
- ¼ teaspoon salt (1/8 condiment)
- ½ teaspoon oregano (1/8 green)
- 1 tablespoon garlic powder (1/8 condiment)

- 2 tablespoons Balsamic (1/8 condiment)
- 1/3 cup olive oil (1/8 condiment)

For Salad:
- ½ cup sliced black olives (1/4 healthy fat)
- ½ cup chopped parsley, fresh (1/4 green)
- 1 small red onion, thin-sliced (1/4 healthy fat)
- 1 cup cherry tomatoes, sliced (1/4 healthy fat)
- 1 bell pepper, yellow, chunked (1/4 green)
- 1 cucumber, peeled, quarter and slice (1/4 green)
- 4 cups chopped romaine lettuce (1 green)
- ½ teaspoon salt (1/8 condiment)
- 2 tablespoons olive oil (1/8 condiment)

Directions:
1. In a small container, join all of the ingredients for the dressing and let this set in the freezer while you make the salad.
2. To assemble the salad, mix together all the ingredients in a large-sized bowl and toss the veggies gently but thoroughly to mix.
3. Serve the salad with the dressing in amounts as desired

Nutrition:
- 234 Calories:
- 16g Fat
- 5g Protein

366. Asparagus and Smoked Salmon Salad

Difficulty: Average
Preparation Time: 15 minutes
Cooking Time: 10 minutes
Servings: 8

Ingredients:

- 1 lb. fresh asparagus, shaped and cut into 1-inch pieces (1 green)
- 1/2 cup pecans, smashed into pieces (1/4 healthy fat)
- 2 heads red leaf lettuce, washed and split (1 green)
- 1/4 lb. smoked salmon, cut into 1-inch chunks (1 lean)
- 1/4 cup olive oil (1/4 condiment)
- 2 tablespoons. lemon juice (1/4 condiment)
- 1 teaspoon Dijon mustard (1/4 condiment)
- 1/2 teaspoon salt (1/4 condiment)
- 1/4 teaspoon pepper (1/4 condiment)

Directions:
1. Boil a pot of water. Stir in asparagus and cook for 5 minutes until tender. Let it drain; set aside.
2. In a skillet, cook the pecans over medium heat for 5 minutes, stirring constantly until lightly toasted.
3. Combine the asparagus, toasted pecans, salmon, and red leaf lettuce and toss in a large bowl.
4. In another bowl, combine lemon juice, pepper, Dijon mustard, salt, and olive oil. You can coat the salad with the dressing or serve it on its side.

Nutrition:
- 159 Calories
- 13g Fat
- 6g Protein

367.   Shrimp Cobb Salad
Difficulty: Easy
Preparation Time: 25 minutes
Cooking Time: 10 minutes
Servings: 2

Ingredients:

- 4 slices center-cut bacon (1 lean)
- 1 lb. large shrimp, peeled and deveined (1 lean)
- 1/2 teaspoon ground paprika (1/8 condiment)
- 1/4 teaspoon ground black pepper (1/8 condiment)
- 1/4 teaspoon salt, divided (1/8 condiment)
- 2 1/2 tablespoons. Fresh lemon juice (1/4 condiment)
- 1 1/2 tablespoons. Extra-virgin olive oil (1/4 condiment)
- 1/2 teaspoon whole grain Dijon mustard (1/4 condiment)
- 1 (10 oz.) package romaine lettuce hearts, chopped (2 green)
- 2 cups cherry tomatoes, quartered (1 green)
- 1 ripe avocado, cut into wedges (1 healthy fat)
- 1 cup shredded carrots (1 green)

Directions:
1. Cook the bacon for 4 minutes on each side in a large skillet over medium heat till crispy.
2. Take away from the skillet and place on paper towels; let cool for 5 minutes. Break the bacon into bits. Throw out most of the bacon fat, leaving behind only 1 tablespoon. in the skillet. Bring the skillet back to medium-high heat. Add black pepper and paprika to the shrimp for seasoning. Cook the shrimp for around 2 minutes on each side until it is opaque. Sprinkle with 1/8 teaspoon of salt for seasoning.
3. Combine the remaining 1/8 teaspoon of salt, mustard, olive oil and lemon juice together in a small bowl. Stir in the romaine hearts.
4. On each serving plate, place 1 and 1/2 cups of romaine lettuce. Add on top the same amounts of avocado,

carrots, tomatoes, shrimp and bacon.

Nutrition:
- 528 Calories
- 29g Fat
- 49g Protein

368.   Toast with Smoked Salmon, Herbed Cream Cheese, And Greens
Difficulty: Average
Preparation Time: 10 minutes
Cooking Time: 5 minutes
Servings: 2

Ingredients:
For the herbed cream cheese
- ¼ cup cream cheese, at room temperature (1/4 healthy fat)
- 2 tablespoons chopped fresh flat-leaf parsley (1/4 green)
- 2 tablespoons chopped fresh chives or sliced scallion (1/4 green)
- ½ teaspoon garlic powder (1/4 condiment)
- ¼ teaspoon kosher salt (1/4 condiment)

For the toast
- 2 slices bread (1 healthy fat)
- 4 ounces smoked salmon (2 lean)
- Small handful microgreens or sprouts (1 green)
- 1 tablespoon capers, drained and rinsed (1/4 green)
- ¼ small red onion, very thinly sliced (1/4 condiment)

Directions:
To make the herbed cream cheese
1. In a small container, put together the cream cheese, parsley, chives, garlic powder, and salt. Using a fork, mix until combined. Chill until ready to use.

To make the toast
2. Toast the bread until golden. Spread the herbed cream cheese over each piece of toast, then top with the smoked salmon.

Garnish with microgreens, capers, and red onion.

Nutrition:
- 325 calories
- 29g fat
- 17g protein

Difficulty: Easy

Preparation Time: 11 minutes

Cooking Time: 0 minutes

Servings: 2

Ingredients:

- 1 thin, cored, and chopped head iceberg lettuce (1 green)
- 8 ounces of boneless, skinless breast of chicken (2 lean)
- 2 hard-boiled, peeled, and chopped eggs (1 healthy fat)
- 2 tomatoes, cut (1 green)
- 1 avocado, peeled, sliced, and pitted (1/2 healthy fat)
- 1 cup of rallied carrots (1 green)
- ¼ cup shredded cheese with low fat, mild cheddar (1/2 healthy fat)
- Salad dressing, such as red wine vinaigrette or cucumber ranch dressing (1 condiment)

Directions:

1. Mix it all in a big bowl and throw. Break into different bowls and serve with your choice of dressing.

Nutrition:

- 410 calories
- 31g fat
- 16g protein

370.   Coconut-Crusted Chicken Salad

Difficulty: Average
Preparation Time: 9 minutes
Cooking Time: 15 minutes
Servings: 3
Ingredients
For the Vinaigrette:
- 1 tablespoon of extra virgin olive oil (1/4 condiment)
- 1 tablespoon of honey (1/4 condiment)
- A spoonful of white vinegar (1/4 condiment)
- 2 teaspoons Dijon mustard (1/8 condiment)

For the Chicken Salad:
- 6 tablespoons shredded coconut without sweetening (1 healthy fat)
- ¼ cup panko breadcrumbs (1/4 healthy fat)
- 2 tablespoons crushed cornflakes (1/4 healthy fat)
- Salt and black chili pepper, to taste (1/4 condiment)
- Egg whites, lightly beaten, or ½ cup liquid egg white replace (1/4 healthy fat)
- 1 (6-ounce) boneless, skinless breast of chicken, trimmed in fat (1 lean)
- 6 cups mixed greens for babies (2 green)
- ¾ cup scrambled carrots (1/4 green)
- 1 sliced cucumber (1/4 green)
- 1 sliced tomato (1/4 green)

Directions:
1. Preheat the oven to 375°F. Line a parchment-papered baking sheet. Whisk the oil, sugar, vinegar, and mustard together in a small cup. Mix the coconut, panko, cornflakes, salt, and pepper into a small, shallow bowl. Put egg whites in another bowl big enough to suit the chicken and beat them with a fork gently.
2. Season the chicken with salt and pepper. Tuck chicken in egg whites followed by a coconut-panko mixture, pressing coconut mixture on the chicken with your fingers if necessary. Place the chicken on the prepared baking sheet, coat lightly with spray, and bake for 15 minutes. Flip the chicken and bake until gently cooked, about some 10 to 15 minutes.
3. Add 3 cups of baby greens to each platter to serve. Top with onions, tomatoes, and cucumber. Slice the chicken diagonally and equally split between the salads. Drizzle and cover up.

Nutrition
- 491 calories
- 34g fat
- 21g protein

Difficulty: Average
Preparation Time: 11 minutes
Cooking Time: 16 minutes
Servings: 3

Ingredients
Toppings:
- ½ pound 93 percent lean ground turkey (1 lean)
- 1/2 cup dried, rinsed, and drained black beans (1/2 healthy fat)
- Seasoned jalapeño chili pepper (1/4 green)
- Beefsteak tomatoes, chopped (1/2 healthy fat)
- 1 Clove of garlic, minced and peeled (1/8 condiment)
- 3 tablespoons of chopped scallions (1/2 green)

- 2 tablespoons of fresh cilantro chopped, plus garnish (1/2 green)
- Salt and ground black pepper, sweet paprika to taste 1 ¼ teaspoon (1/8 condiment)

For the Avocado Dip:
- ¼ cup, 2% Greek yogurt (1/2 healthy fat)
- ¼ cup of water (1/2 condiment)
- 1 medium avocado, peeled, pitted, chopped, and split (1/2 healthy fat)
- 1 ½ spoonful of fresh cilantro (1/4 green)
- ½ tablespoon cayenne pepper (1/8 condiment)
- Salt and black chili pepper, to taste (1/8 condiment)

For the Salad:
- 5 cups shredded iceberg lettuce cup shredded (1 green)
- 1 Mexican cheese mixed beefsteak tomato, chopped (1/2 healthy fat)
- Tablespoons of fresh coriander (1/2 green)
- 2 spoons smashed tortilla chips (1/2 healthy fat)

Directions:
1. Heat a broad skillet over medium-high heat, without sticking. Use a wooden spoon to split the meat into small pieces and add the ground turkey to the skillet. Cook, stirring constantly, for 4 to 5 minutes until the meat is no longer pink.
2. Incorporate beans, jalapeño, onions, garlic, scallions, salt, pepper, and paprika. Reduce heat to low, cover, and cook for 15 minutes. Remove the lid from the skillet and cook for about 5 minutes until the liquid decreases.
3. In the meantime, make the avocado dip: add yogurt, sugar, half the avocado, cilantro, cayenne, salt, and pepper into a blender. Up to a smooth process; reserve.

4. Divide the lettuce into 4 slabs. Top with the mixture of beef, cheese, onions, cilantro, and chopped avocado left over. Add the avocado dip over the top and garnish the chips with crushed tortilla.

Nutrition
- 491 calories
- 28g fat
- 11g protein

372. Protein Salad with Buttermilk Dressing

Difficulty: Average
Preparation Time: 11 minutes
Cooking Time: 6 minutes
Servings: 3

Ingredients:
- 2 cups spring baby mix (1 green)
- 2 chopped scallions (1 green)
- 1 small, halved, sliced cucumber (1 green)
- 4 mushrooms with white buttons half-cut and sliced (2 healthy fat)
- ¼ medium avocado, chopped and peeled (1/2 healthy fat)
- ½ cup cottage cheese 2 percent (1/2 healthy fat)
- 1 hard-boiled egg, chopped and peeled (1/4 healthy fat)
- 3 tablespoons of low-fat buttermilk (1/4 healthy fat)
- 1 lemon juice (1/8 condiment)
- 1 clove of garlic, chopped (1/8 condiment)
- Salt and black chili pepper, to taste (1/8 condiment)

Direction
1. Put the spring mixture, scallions, cucumber, mushrooms, avocado, cottage cheese, and egg into a medium bowl.
2. Stir in buttermilk, lemon juice, garlic, salt, and pepper in a small bowl. Combine using a fork.

3. Drizzle over the salad, toss and serve.

Nutrition:
- 491 calories
- 38g fat
- 19g protein

373. Chicken Salad with Pineapple and Pecans

Difficulty: Average
Preparation Time: 13 minutes
Cooking Time: 9 minutes
Servings: 4

Ingredients
- 6-ounce boneless, skinless, cooked and cubed chicken breast (2 lean)
- Tablespoons of celery hacked (1/2 green)
- ¼ cup of cut pineapple (1/4 healthy fat)
- ¼ cup orange peeled segments (1/4 healthy fat)
- Tablespoon of pecans hacked (1/4 healthy fat)
- ¼ cup seedless grapes (1/4 healthy fat)
- Salt and black chili pepper, to taste (1/4 condiment)
- 3 Cups of cut romaine lettuce (1 green)

Directions:
1. Put chicken, celery, pineapple, grapes, pecans, and raisins in a medium dish. Kindly blend until mixed with a spoon, then season with salt and pepper.
2. Create a bed of lettuce on a plate. Cover with mixture of chicken and serve.

Nutrition
- 391 calories
- 37g fat
- 21g protein

374. Grilled Mediterranean Salad

Difficulty: Average
Preparation Time: 10 minutes

Cooking Time: 8 minutes
Servings: 3

Ingredients:

- ¼ cup balsamic vinegar (1/8 condiment)
- ½ teaspoon capers (1/8 condiment)
- ½ cup of coarse garlic (1/8 condiment)
- 2 tablespoons of dry-packed sun-dried tomatoes, roughly cut (1 healthy fat)
- 2 red bell peppers, sliced into large strips and seeded (1 healthy fat)
- 8 spikes of asparagus (2 green)
- Sliced zucchini (1 green)
- Teaspoons extra virgin olive oil (1/8 condiment)
- Salt and black chili pepper, to taste (1/8 condiment)
- 4 hard-boiled eggs, quartered and peeled (1 healthy fat)
- 2 tablespoons of Kalamata olives, finely chopped (1 healthy fat)
- ¼ cup crumbled feta cheese (1 healthy fat)
- Cut fresh basil to taste (1/8 green)

Directions:

1. Put the vinegar, capers, garlic, and sun-dried tomatoes into a food processor's cup. Method until well-knitted.
2. Combine the red peppers, asparagus, and zucchini in a large mixing bowl. Add extra virgin olive oil, salt, and pepper. Toss to merge.
3. Prepare a medium-high fire to barbecue. Cover the barbecue grills loosely with a cooking spray. Once the grill is hot, grill the vegetables until lightly charred, turning occasionally.
4. Add grilled veggies and vinaigrette in a bowl, and toss to combine. Divide the vegetables into four plates. Garnish with eggs, olives, feta, and basil.

Nutrition:

- 388 calories
- 34g fat
- 21g protein

375.   Super Green Salad

Difficulty: Easy
Preparation Time: 10 minutes
Cooking Time: 9 minutes
Servings: 3

Ingredients

- 4 cups of kale chopped (1 green)
- 4 cups of fresh spinach (1 green)
- 3 spoonful of extra virgin olive oil (1/4 condiment)
- 1 cup lemon juice (1/4 condiment)
- Salt and black chili pepper, to taste (1/8 condiment)
- 6 hard-boiled eggs, quartered and peeled (2 healthy fat)
- 2 big, peeled, pitted, and sliced avocado (1 healthy fat)
- 4 tablespoons of Parmesan cheese rubbed (1/2 healthy fat)

Directions:

1. Put the kale, spinach, olive oil, lemon juice, salt, and pepper into a large bowl. Toss the greens to mix, cover with dressing. Divide the salad into 4 slices.
2. Top with chicken and avocado on every bed of greens. Sprinkle with cheese on each salad and serve straight away.

Nutrition:

- 411 calories
- 27g fat
- 11g protein

376.   Avocado Lime Shrimp Salad

Difficulty: Easy
Preparation Time: 15 minutes

Cooking Time: 0 minutes
Servings: 2

Ingredients:

- 14 ounces of jumbo cooked shrimp, peeled and deveined; chopped (2 lean)
- 4 ½ ounces of avocado, diced (1 healthy fat)
- 1 ½ cup of tomato, diced (1/2 healthy fat)
- ¼ cup of chopped green onion (1/4 green)
- ¼ cup of jalapeno with the seeds removed, diced fine (1/4 green)
- 1 teaspoon of olive oil (1/8 condiment)
- 2 tablespoons of lime juice (1/4 condiment)
- 1/8 teaspoon of salt (1/8 condiment)
- 1 tablespoon of chopped cilantro (1/8 green)

Directions:

1. Get a small bowl and combine green onion, olive oil, lime juice, pepper, a pinch of salt. Wait for about 5 minutes for all of them to marinate and mellow the flavor of the onion.
2. Get a large bowl and combine chopped shrimp, tomato, avocado, jalapeno. Combine all of the ingredients, add cilantro, and gently toss.
3. Add pepper and salt as desired.

Nutrition:

- 314 Calories
- 26g Protein
- 9g Fiber

377.   Grilled Mahi-Mahi with Jicama Slaw

Difficulty: Average
Preparation Time: 20 minutes
Cooking Time: 10 minutes
Servings: 4
Ingredients:

- 1 teaspoon each for pepper and salt, divided (1/8 condiment)

- 1 tablespoon of lime juice, divided (1/8 condiment)
- 2 tablespoon + 2 teaspoons of extra virgin olive oil (1/4 condiment)
- 4 raw mahi-mahi fillets, which should be about 8 oz. each (2 lean)
- ½ cucumber (1/2 green)
- 1 jicama (1/4 condiment)
- 1 cup of alfalfa sprouts (1/2 green)
- 2 cups of coarsely chopped watercress (1/2 green)

Directions:
1. Combine ½ teaspoon of both pepper and salt, 1 teaspoon of lime juice, and 2 teaspoons of oil in a small bowl. Then brush the mahi-mahi fillets all through with the olive oil mixture.
2. Grill the mahi-mahi on medium-high heat until it becomes done in about 5 minutes, turn it to the other side, and let it be done for about 5 minutes. (You will have an internal temperature of about 145°F).
3. For the slaw, combine the watercress, cucumber, jicama, and alfalfa sprouts in a bowl. Now combine ½ teaspoon of both pepper and salt, 2 teaspoons of lime juice, and 2 tablespoons of extra virgin oil in a small bowl. Drizzle it over slaw and toss together to combine.

Nutrition:
- 320 Calories
- 44g Protein
- 11g Fat

378. Mozzarella Radish Salad

Difficulty: Easy
Preparation Time: 10 minutes
Cooking Time: 20 minutes
Servings: 2
Ingredients:
- 8 oz. radish (1 green)
- 4 oz. Mozzarella (1/2 healthy fat)

- 1 teaspoon balsamic vinegar (1/8 condiment)
- ½ teaspoon salt (1/8 condiment)
- 1 tablespoon olive oil (1/8 condiment)
- 1 teaspoon dried oregano (1/8 green)

Directions:
1. Wash the radish carefully and cut it into halves.
2. Preheat the air fryer to 360 F.
3. Put the radish halves in the air fryer basket.
4. Sprinkle the radish with salt and olive oil.
5. Cook the radish for 20 minutes.
6. Shake the radish after 10 minutes of cooking.
7. When the time is over – transfer the radish to the serving plate.
8. Chop Mozzarella roughly.
9. Sprinkle the radish with Mozzarella, balsamic vinegar, and dried oregano.
10. Stir it gently with the help of 2 forks.
11. Serve it immediately.

Nutrition:
- 241 Calories
- 17g Fat
- 17g Protein

379. Vegetables in Air Fryer

Difficulty: Easy
Preparation Time: 20 minutes
Cooking Time: 30 minutes
Servings: 2

Ingredients:
- 2 potatoes (1 healthy fat)
- 1 zucchini (1 green)
- 1 onion (1/4 green)
- 1 red pepper (1/4 green)
- 1 green pepper (1/4 green)

Directions:
1. Cut the potatoes into slices. Cut the onion into rings. Cut the zucchini slices. Cut the peppers into strips.
2. Put all the ingredients in the bowl and add a little salt,

ground pepper and some extra virgin olive oil. Mix well. Pass to the basket of the air fryer. Select 160°C (320°F), 30 minutes.
3. Check that the vegetables are to your liking.

Nutrition:
- 135 Calories
- 11g Fat
- 4g Protein

380. Tomato Salsa

Difficulty: Easy
Preparation Time: 5 minutes
Cooking Time: 0 minutes
Servings: 6

Ingredients:
- 1 garlic clove, minced (1/4 condiment)
- 4 tablespoons olive oil (1/4 condiment)
- 5 tomatoes, cubed (1 healthy fat)
- 1 tablespoon balsamic vinegar (1/8 condiment)
- ¼ cup basil, chopped (1/4 green)
- 1 tablespoon parsley, chopped (1/4 green)
- 1 tablespoon chives, chopped (1/4 green)
- Salt and black pepper to the taste (1/8 condiment)
- Pita chips for serving (1 healthy fat)

Directions:
1. Mix the tomatoes with the garlic in a bowl, and the rest of the ingredients except the pita chips, stir, divide into small cups and serve with the pita chips on the side.

Nutrition:
- 160 Calories
- 14g Fat
- 2.2g Protein

381. Blueberry Muffins

Difficulty: Average
Preparation Time: 15 minutes
Cooking Time: 35 minutes
Servings: 12

Ingredients:

- 2 eggs (2 lean)
- ½ cup fresh blueberries (1 healthy fat)
- 1 cup heavy cream (1 healthy fat)
- 2 cups almond flour (1/2 condiment)
- ¼ tsp. lemon zest (1/4 condiment)
- ½ tsp. lemon extract (1/4 condiment)
- 1 tsp. baking powder (1/8 condiment)
- 5 drops stevia (1/4 condiment)
- ¼ cup butter, melted (1/4 healthy fat)

Directions:

1. Heat the cooker to 350°F. Line muffin tin with cupcake liners and set aside.
2. Add eggs into the bowl and whisk until mixed.
3. Add remaining ingredients and mix to combine.
4. Pour mixture into the prepared muffin tin and bake for 25 minutes.
5. Serve and enjoy.

Nutrition:

- 190 Calories
- 17g Fats
- 10g Protein

382. Smooth Peanut Butter Cream

Difficulty: Average
Preparation Time: 10 minutes
Cooking Time: 0 minutes
Servings: 8

Ingredients:

- ¼ cup peanut butter (1/4 healthy fat)
- 4 overripe bananas, chopped (1 lean)
- 1/3 cup cocoa powder (1/2 condiment)
- 1/3 tsp. vanilla extract (1/2 condiment)
- 1/8 tsp. salt (1/8 condiment)

Directions:

1. In the blender, add all the listed ingredients and blend until smooth.
2. Serve immediately and enjoy.

Nutrition:

- 101 Calories
- 5g Fats
- 3g Protein

383. Chocolate Bars

Difficulty: Average
Preparation Time: 10 minutes
Cooking Time: 20 minutes
Servings: 16

Ingredients:

- 15 oz. cream cheese, softened (2 healthy fat)
- 15 oz. unsweetened dark chocolate (2 healthy fat)
- 1 tsp. vanilla (1 condiment)
- 10 drops liquid stevia (2 condiment)

Directions:

1. Grease an 8-inch square dish and set aside.
2. In a saucepan, dissolve chocolate over low heat.
3. Add stevia and vanilla and stir well.
4. Remove pan from heat and set aside.
5. Add cream cheese into the blender and blend until smooth.
6. Add melted chocolate mixture into the cream cheese and blend until just combined.
7. Transfer mixture into the prepared dish and spread evenly, and place in the refrigerator until firm.
8. Slice and serve.

Nutrition:

- 230 Calories
- 24g Fats
- 6g Protein

384. Avocado Pudding

Difficulty: Easy
Preparation Time: 20 minutes
Cooking Time: 0 minutes
Servings: 8

Ingredients:

- 2 ripe avocados, pitted and cut into pieces (2 lean)
- 1 tbsp. fresh lime juice (1/4 condiment)
- 14 oz. can coconut milk (1/2 healthy fat)
- 2 tsp. liquid stevia (1/4 condiment)
- 2 tsp. vanilla (1/4 condiment)

Directions:

1. Inside the blender, add all ingredients and blend until smooth.
2. Serve immediately and enjoy.

Nutrition:

- 317 Calories
- 30g Fats

- 3g Protein

385. Peanut Butter Coconut Popsicle

Difficulty: Average
Preparation Time: 15 minutes
Cooking Time: 0 minutes
Servings: 12

Ingredients:
- ½ cup peanut butter (1/2 healthy fat)
- 1 tsp. liquid stevia (1/4 condiment)
- 2 cans unsweetened coconut milk (2 healthy fat)

Directions:
1. In the blender, add all the listed ingredients and blend until smooth.
2. Pour mixture into the Popsicle molds and place in the freezer for 4 hours or until set.
3. Serve.

Nutrition:
- 155 Calories
- 15g Fats
- 3g Protein

386. Vanilla Avocado Popsicles

Difficulty: Easy
Preparation Time: 20 minutes
Cooking Time: 0 minutes
Servings: 6

Ingredients:
- 2 avocadoes (2 lean)
- 1 tsp. vanilla (1/4 condiment)
- 1 cup almond milk (1/2 healthy fat)
- 1 tsp. liquid stevia (1/4 condiment)
- ½ cup unsweetened cocoa powder (1/4 condiment)

Directions:
1. In the blender, add all the listed ingredients and blend smoothly.
2. Pour blended mixture into the Popsicle molds and place in the freezer until set.
3. Serve and enjoy.

Nutrition:
- 130 Calories
- 12g Fats
- 3g Protein

387. Chocolate Popsicle

Difficulty: Easy
Preparation Time: 20 minutes
Cooking Time: 10 minutes
Servings: 6

Ingredients:
- 4 oz. unsweetened chocolate, chopped (1 healthy fat)
- 6 drops liquid stevia (1/2 condiment)
- 1 ½ cups heavy cream (1/2 healthy fat)

Directions:
1. Add heavy cream into the microwave-safe bowl and microwave until it just begins boiling.
2. Add chocolate into the heavy cream and set aside for 5 minutes.
3. Add liquid stevia into the heavy cream mixture and stir until chocolate is melted.
4. Pour mixture into the Popsicle molds and place in freezer for 4 hours or until set.
5. Serve and enjoy.

Nutrition:
- 198 Calories
- 21g Fats
- 3g Protein

388. Raspberry Ice Cream

Difficulty: Easy
Preparation Time: 10 minutes
Cooking Time: 0 minutes
Servings: 2

Ingredients:
- 1 cup frozen raspberries (1 lean)
- ½ cup heavy cream (1/2 healthy fat)
- 1/8 tsp. stevia powder (1/8 condiment)

Directions:
1. Blend all the listed ingredients in a blender until smooth.
2. Serve immediately and enjoy.

Nutrition:
- 144 Calories
- 11g Fats
- 2g Protein

389. Chocolate Frosty

Difficulty: Easy
Preparation Time: 20 minutes
Cooking Time: 0 minutes
Servings: 4

Ingredients:
- 2 tbsp. unsweetened cocoa powder (1/2 condiment)
- 1 cup heavy whipping cream (1 healthy fat)
- 1 tbsp. almond butter (1 healthy fat)
- 5 drops liquid stevia (1/4 condiment)
- 1 tsp. vanilla (1/4 condiment)

Directions:
1. Add cream into the medium bowl and beat using the hand mixer for 5 minutes.
2. Add remaining ingredients and blend until thick cream form.
3. Pour in serving bowls and place them in the freezer for 30 minutes.
4. Serve and enjoy.

Nutrition:
- 137 Calories
- 13g Fats
- 2g Protein

390. Chocolate Almond Butter Brownie

Difficulty: Average
Preparation Time: 10 minutes
Cooking Time: 16 minutes
Servings: 4

Ingredients:
- 1 cup bananas, overripe (1 lean)
- ½ cup almond butter, melted (1/2 healthy fat)
- 1 scoop protein powder (1 healthy fat)
- 2 tbsp. unsweetened cocoa powder (1 condiment)

Directions:
1. Preheat the air fryer to 325°F. Grease air fryer baking pan and set aside.
2. Blend all ingredients in a blender until smooth.
3. Pour batter into the prepared pan, and place in the air fryer basket and cook for 16 minutes.
4. Serve and enjoy.

Nutrition:
- 82 Calories
- 2g Fats
- 7g Protein

391. Peanut Butter Fudge

Difficulty: Average
Preparation Time: 10 minutes
Cooking Time: 10 minutes
Servings: 20

Ingredients:
- ¼ cup almonds, toasted and chopped (1 healthy fat)
- 12 oz. smooth peanut butter (1/2 healthy fat)
- 15 drops liquid stevia (1/2 condiment)
- 3 tbsp. coconut oil (1/2 healthy fat)
- 4 tbsp. coconut cream (1/2 healthy fat)

Directions:
1. Line baking tray with parchment paper.
2. Melt coconut oil in a pan over low heat. Add peanut butter, coconut cream, stevia, and salt in a saucepan. Stir well.
3. Pour fudge mixture into the prepared baking tray and sprinkle chopped almonds on top.
4. Place the tray in the refrigerator for 1 hour or until set.
5. Slice and serve.

Nutrition:
- 131 Calories
- 12g Fats
- 5g Protein

392. Almond Butter Fudge

Difficulty: Average
Preparation Time: 10 minutes
Cooking Time: 10 minutes
Servings: 18

Ingredients:
- ¾ cup creamy almond butter (1 healthy fat)
- 1 ½ cups unsweetened chocolate chips (1 healthy fat)

Directions:
1. Line 8x4-inch pan with parchment paper and set aside.
2. Add chocolate chips and almond butter into the double boiler and cook over medium heat until the chocolate-butter mixture is melted. Stir well.
3. Place mixture into the prepared pan and place in the freezer until set.
4. Slice and serve.

Nutrition:
- 197 Calories
- 16g Fats
- 4g Protein

393. No Bake Optavia Fueling Peanut Butter Brownies

Difficulty: Average
Preparation Time: 5 minutes
Cooking Time: 30 minutes
Servings: 6

Ingredients:
- 3 tbsp. peanut butter (2 healthy fat)
- 1 cup water (1 condiment)
- 6 Optavia Double Chocolate Brownie Fueling packets (3 condiment)

Directions:
1. Put all ingredients in a bowl and mix until all elements are well incorporated.
2. Pour into silicone molds and place in the freezer.
3. Freeze for 30 minutes before eating.

Nutrition:
- 906 Calories
- 32g Fats
- 9g Protein

394. Peanut Butter Brownie and Ice Cream Sandwiches

Difficulty: Easy
Preparation Time: 2 minutes
Cooking Time: 2 minutes
Servings: 2

Ingredients:
- 1 Medifast Brownie Mix packet (1 condiment)
- 3 tbsp. water (1 condiment)
- 1 Peanut Butter Crunch Bar or any bar of your choice (1 healthy fat)
- 2 tbsp. peanut butter powder (2 healthy fat)

- 1 tbsp. water (1 condiment)
- 2 tbsp. cool whip (1 healthy fat)

Directions:
1. Melt the Brownie Mix with water.
2. Add in the Peanut Butter Crunch until a dough is formed.
3. Spoon 4 dough balls on a plate and flatten using the palm of your hands.
4. Make sure that the dough is ¼ inch thick.
5. Place in a microwave oven and cook for 2 minutes.
6. Meanwhile, mix the Peanut Butter Powder and water to form a paste.
7. Add cool whip. Set aside in the fridge to chill for at least 1 hour.
8. Take the cookies out from the microwave oven and allow them to cool.
9. Once cooled, spoon the Peanut Butter ice cream in between two cookies.
10. Serve immediately.

Nutrition:
- 410 Calories
- 13.2g Fat
- 8.3g Protein

395. Cranberry Salad

Difficulty: Easy
Preparation Time: 5 minutes
Cooking Time: 5 minutes
Servings: 2

Ingredients:
- 1 sugar-free cranberry Jell-O pack, ½ cup for snacks allowed (1/2 healthy fat)
- ½ cup celery chopped, (1 green)
- 7 Half Cut Walnut (1/2 healthy fat)

Directions:
1. Mix Jell-O according to the instructions of the box.
2. Add walnuts and celery.
3. Allow setting.
4. Shake until serving.

5. Distribute servings in 4 ½ cups.

Nutrition:
- 341 calories
- 11g Fats
- 4.1g Protein

396. Vanilla Bean Frappuccino

Difficulty: Easy
Preparation Time: 3 minutes
Cooking Time: 6 minutes
Servings: 4 servings

Ingredients:
- 3 cups unsweetened vanilla almond milk, chilled (1/2 healthy fat)
- 2 tsp. swerve (1/2 condiment)
- 1 ½ cups heavy cream, cold (1/2 healthy fat)
- 1 vanilla bean (1 lean)
- ¼ tsp. xanthan gum (1/2 condiment)

Directions:
1. Combine the almond milk, swerve, heavy cream, vanilla bean, and xanthan gum in the blender and process at high speed for 1 minute until smooth.
2. Pour into tall shake glasses, sprinkle with chocolate shavings, and serve immediately.

Nutrition:
- 193 Calories
- 14g Fats
- 15g Protein

397. Dark Chocolate Mochaccino Ice Bombs

Difficulty: Average
Preparation Time: 5 minutes
Cooking Time: 10 minutes
Servings: 4

Ingredients:
- ½ lb. cream cheese (1 healthy fat)

- 4 tbsp. powdered sweetener (1 condiment)
- 2 oz. strong coffee (1 condiment)
- 2 tbsp. cocoa powder, unsweetened (1 condiment)
- 1 oz. cocoa butter, melted (1/2 healthy fat)
- 2 ½ oz. dark chocolate, melted (1/2 healthy fat)

Directions:
1. Combine cream cheese, sweetener, coffee, and cocoa powder in a food processor.
2. Roll 2 tbsp. of the mixture and place on a lined tray.
3. Mix the melted cocoa butter and chocolate, and coat the bombs with it.
4. Freeze for 2 hours.

Nutrition:
- 127 Calories
- 13g Fats
- 1.9g Protein

398. Chocolate Bark with Almonds

Difficulty: Average
Preparation Time: 5 minutes
Cooking Time: 10 minutes
Servings: 12

Ingredients:
- ½ cup toasted almonds, chopped (1/2 healthy fat)
- ½ cup butter (1 healthy fat)
- 10 drops stevia (1 condiment)
- ¼ tsp. salt (1/2 condiment)
- ½ cup unsweetened coconut flakes (1/2 healthy fat)
- 4 oz. dark chocolate (1/2 healthy fat)

Directions:
1. Melt together the butter and chocolate in the microwave for 90 seconds.
2. Remove and stir in stevia.
3. Line a cookie sheet with waxed paper and spread the chocolate evenly.
4. Scatter the almonds and coconut flakes on top, and sprinkle with salt.
5. Refrigerate for one hour.

Nutrition:
- 161 Calories
- 15.3g Fats
- 1.9g Protein

399.   Optavia Mousse

Difficulty: Average
Preparation Time: 3 minutes
Cooking Time: 3 minutes
Servings: 2

Ingredients:
- 1 Medifast or Optavia hot cocoa packet (1 condiment)
- ½ cup sugar-free gelatin (1 condiment)
- 1 tbsp. light cream cheese (1/2 healthy fat)
- 2 tbsp. cold water (1/2 condiment)
- ¼ cup crushed ice (1/2 condiment)

Directions:
1. Place all ingredients in a blender.
2. Pulse until smooth.
3. Pour into glass and place in the fridge to set.
4. Serve chilled.

Nutrition:
- 156 Calories
- 3.7g Fat
- 5.7g Protein

400.   Coconut Coffee and Ghee

Difficulty: Easy
Preparation Time: 10 minutes
Cooking Time: 10 minutes
Servings: 5

Ingredients:
- ½ tbsp. coconut oil (1/2 condiment)
- ½ tbsp. ghee (1/2 condiment)
- 1 to 2 cups preferred coffee (or rooibos or black tea, if preferred) (1 healthy fat)
- 1 tbsp. coconut or almond milk (1/2 healthy fat)

Directions:
1. Place the almond (or coconut) milk, coconut oil, ghee, and coffee in a blender (or milk frothier).
2. Mix for around 10 seconds or until the coffee turns creamy and foamy.
3. Pour contents into a coffee cup.
4. Serve immediately and enjoy.

Nutrition:
- 150 Calories
- 15g Fats
- 0.1g Protein

A green lean and cleanse diet, or simply green lean diet, is a diet similar to the concept of a raw food vegan diet, but with less emphasis on raw foods and more emphasis on whole foods that are nonetheless prepared in a way to ensure minimum use of energy during preparation or preservation, for example through the practice of lactofermentation and cooking at low temperatures under 70 °C (158 °F).

The Lean and Green diet was a great diet to try. It can help you lose weight and eat healthy foods in the process. The diet practically makes the body burn fats much faster than carbohydrates; the foods you consume with this diet are quite rich in fats.

Carbs will be there, too but at far lower levels than before. Foods rich in carbohydrates are the body's primary fuel or the brain's food. (Our bodies turn carbs into glucose.) Because there are hardly any carbohydrates in this diet, the body will have to find a substitute source of energy to keep itself alive.

Once the body realizes that it does not have enough carbohydrates to cover the calories it burns, it turns to fat reserves to provide the required energy. Before that time, the body was using only 15% of its fat reserves for energy—the ratio changes once you start this diet. You will burn fats at a relatively faster rate than fat reserves, and after that, it will burn fat at a relatively faster rate than fat reserves. In this way, the body will find a way to get the required amount of energy from its fat stores keeping the carbs and calories under control.

If you did not change your way of living altogether and added good fats to your diet, it could take carbohydrates. In that case, you might be waiting for at least a year before you will start losing weight with this diet. For you, it is still worth doing this diet. Even if it is yearlong, you will see a great improvement in your overall health. Therefore, when you ingest fats, instead of your body storing them as fat, they are more likely to be converted into a source of energy.

As fat reserves continue to be burned, the body will tend not to gain weight. This is excellent news because fat reserves are not very easy to get rid of completely.

Many people who don't truly need to lose weight and are completely healthy still choose to follow the Optavia diet because it is a great way to keep their meals balanced. It is also the perfect way to cleanse the body of toxins, processed foods, sugars, and unnecessary carbs. The combination of these things is usually the main reason for heart failure, some cancers, diabetes, cholesterol, or obesity.

If you ask a nutritionist about this diet, they will recommend it without a doubt. So, if you feel like cleansing your body and starting a diet that will keep you healthy, well-fed, and slender, perhaps this diet should be your primary choice.

Engaging into lean and green diet is a good idea to improve not only our health, but also our environment. One should eat less meat products and consume more of fresh fruits and vegetables in order to lower the risk for heart disease and cancer. The latter are mostly linked with meat consumption because of the nitrates located in processed meats. Fruits and vegetables are very low-calorie foods, but they are high in fiber content and rich in vitamins. The vegetables and fruits that deserve to be consumed are the ones that are grown organically. It is very important to avoid processed foods since they contain a high percentage of fat. Green and lean diet is also linked with the environment preservation. By cutting down meat consumption by at least 50%, we save a lot from greenhouse gas emissions. Considering that meat production requires more energy, it causes more carbon dioxide emissions compared to vegetable production. Another advantage of green and lean diet is improved health care system and lower health problems cost.

Cooking in an air fryer is an awesome way to cook food. Wheat flour breaded fish can be easily prepared in an air fryer, which results in crispy crusts and juicy insides. People on a diet should opt for air frying as it prepares food without frying and reduces the oil content by half. Air frying vegetable strips away the vegetable's excess water, which makes the vegetable delicious and tasty. Using this with your Lean and green diet is a great help. To make the diet much easier, you will be glad to know that lean and green food can be used along with air frying to make the diet much easier.

The Lean and Green diet is a diet which claims to be the healthiest and environmentally sustainable. It is also a diet which has good weight loss and muscle building properties.

The Lean and Green Diet is based on these principles: A predominantly plant-based diet with an emphasis on vegetables, fruits, whole grains and beans. A high level of physical activity (at least 30 minutes of aerobic exercise 3 times a week). Adherence to the nutritional recommendations from governmental food agencies (WCRF/AICR). Lastly, increased consumption of fish, poultry, whole-grains and low-fat dairy products (in the case of vegetarians). These 4 principles present a total package which promises to allow for the identification, identification and implementation of an effective lifestyle change. However, as with many other diets, the Lean and Green Diet has not been rigorously tested and thus it is often difficult to find scientific evidence for the diet's effectiveness.

However, there is scientific evidence for one of the principles: an environmental approach to food. For example, the use of recycled packaging at supermarkets could reduce a consumer's carbon footprint by 5-10%, according to the University of British Columbia. This is in comparison to the use of environmentally unfriendly packaging. There can also be environmental gains from reduced packaging from suppliers. For example, Anheuser-Busch uses windmills to reduce its energy usage by 25% and reduce the amount of carbon dioxide released into the atmosphere by 9%.

In relation to this, a key principle of Lean and Green is that it must be environmentally sustainable. It is often suggested that consumers take advantage of their purchasing power and bring about a change in the food system.

At this moment of your journey, you must recognize that you've overcome the hardest task, i.e., the first dreadful step towards health and wellbeing. Please remember that this alone is a commendable feat and whoever survives the first step can survive the rest and come out at the other side thinner, stronger, wiser, happier, and overall better. Remember, the journey of a thousand miles still begins with just a single step indeed. So, stand tall, be confident, and just go ahead each day with your ideal vision of yourself in your mind, moving a bit closer to your goals every day.

The program has earned worldwide acclaim for its ability to deliver sustainable results without complicating people's meal program. It places very few food restrictions and inspires people to choose a healthier version of their daily food without compromising on taste and nutrition.

Made in the USA
Coppell, TX
26 March 2021